Tudor
Foreign
Policy

MODERN BRITISH FOREIGN POLICY

General Editor: MALCOLM ROBINSON
Head of the History Department, Radley College

Tudor Foreign Policy   P. S. CROWSON

In preparation
Stuart and Cromwellian Foreign Policy   G. M. D. HOWAT
The Eighteenth Century
The Nineteenth Century   P. M. HAYES
The Twentieth Century   P. M. HAYES

MODERN BRITISH FOREIGN POLICY

Tudor Foreign Policy

P. S. Crowson

ADAM & CHARLES BLACK
LONDON

First published 1973
A. & C. Black Ltd
4, 5 & 6 Soho Square, London W1V 6AD

ISBN 0 7136 1394 7 (cased)
    0 7136 1396 3 (paperback)

© 1973 Paul S. Crowson

Printed in Great Britain
by Billings & Sons Limited
Guildford and London

Contents

CHAPTER	PAGE
List of Maps	vii
List of Genealogies	viii
Bibliography and Abbreviations	ix
Preface	xiii

PART I. GRASS-ROOTS OF FOREIGN POLICY

1. Objectives of Tudor foreign policy—an introduction   3
2. Shakespeare's 'mutable rank-scented many'   10
3. Acknowledged initiators   18
4. Parliament   33
5. Personal interests, declared and undeclared   37

PART IIA
DYNASTY AND REALM—SECURITY AND ROLE

6. Henry VII: Dynastic defence—in danger from Burgundy and Ireland   47
7. Henry VII: Defence of the realm—in awe of France and Scotland   59
8. Henry VIII: Dynastic diplomacy—fulfilling one's role   67
9. Wolsey: Peace initiatives of a religious humanist   74
10. Henry VIII: Dynastic security—diplomatic pressure, 1525–32   92

11. Henry VIII: Sovereign independence—diplomatic defiance, 1530–34   102
12. Henry VIII: To underpin England's sovereign independence, 1534–40   111

PART IIB. BETWEEN TWO ERAS

A note on chapters 13 and 14   120
13. Towards a 'Unified kingdom of Great Britain', 1530–40   121
14. A new role or the old?—groping for national unity, identity and role, 1540–50   125

PART IIC
MONARCH AND PEOPLE—'OURSELVES ALONE'

15. Northumberland and Mary Tudor: Personal interest versus national identity   143
16. Elizabeth: Patriotic constraints on policy   158
17. Elizabeth: Succession, the prerogative of Time   162
18. Elizabeth: Defence of monarch and realm—in awe of France, 1558–1603   173
19. Elizabeth: Defence of monarch and realm from Rome and Spain, at low tension, 1568–73   188
20. Elizabeth: Defence of monarch and realm from Rome and Spain, at high tension, 1578–1603   199
21. Elizabeth: England and the North Netherlands, defence indivisible   214

PART III
ECONOMIC OBJECTIVES OF TUDOR FOREIGN POLICY

22. Wool, cloth and the Netherlands   237
23. Diversifying into other markets   245
24. Diversifying into other goods and services   255
25. Debt and policy, coinage and commerce   260

Index   267

Maps

		PAGE
1.	Bristol's Atlantic commerce	19
2.	Darien	25
3.	Burgundy in 1475	48
4.	Anglo-Irish clans	51
5.	The French Channel ports	60
6.	The Guienne expedition, 1512	70
7.	The Pale of Calais, 1513	72
8.	Languedoc, Provence and the duchy of Burgundy, 1525	89
9.	Annexation proposed in 1545	128
10.	Anglo-Scottish Warfare, 1542–49	137
11.	Metz, Toul and Verdun	148
12.	Ireland in the second half of the sixteenth century	156
13.	English garrison towns in 1594	186
14.	Spanish naval bases, 1585–1600	217
15.	The 'Low Countries' of north-west Europe	220
16.	Zeeland, Holland and Utrecht under pressure	226
17.	Spanish gains, 1584	228
18.	The Hanseatic League and the Baltic Sea	246

Genealogies

		PAGE
1.	Margaret of York and Burgundy	49
2.	Pretensions of the Pretenders	50
3.	Courtenay and de la Pole	56
4.	The claim of Joanna to Castile	63
5.	Regal aspirations of Edward of Stafford and Buckingham	68
6.	French law did not recognise descent through a woman	75
7.	John Stuart, Duke of Albany	76
8.	Contestants for the English throne, executed 1538–41	116
9.	James Hamilton, Earl of Arran and Chatelherault	131
10.	Before the Act of Succession, 1543	133
11.	Claims to the English throne	170
12.	Esmé Stuart and his cousin James VI	208

Bibliography and Abbreviations

This bibliography is also a key to the authors' surnames which are used in footnotes to refer to publications. The name following the title of a book is that of the publisher from whose latest edition of the work page references have been taken.

Andrews	K. R. Andrews: *Elizabethan Privateering*. Cambridge U.P.
Black	J. B. Black: *The Reign of Elizabeth*. Oxford U.P.
Bromley	J. S. Bromley: review of *Drake's Voyages* by K. R. Andrews in *Economic History Review*, 1968.
Challis	C. E. Challis: 'The debasement of the coinage' in *Economic History Review*, 1967.
Conway	Agnes Conway: *Henry VII's relations with Scotland and Ireland, 1485–1498*. Cambridge U.P.
Cruickshank	C. G. Cruickshank: *Elizabeth's Army*. Oxford U.P.
Curtis	E. Curtis: *A History of Ireland*. Methuen.
Davies	C. S. L. Davies: 'The Administration of the Royal Navy under Henry VIII' in *English Historical Review*, 1965.
Dickens	A. G. Dickens: *English Reformation*. Fontana.

Donaldson	Gordon Donaldson: 'Foundation of Anglo-Scottish Union' in *Elizabethan Government and Society: Essays presented to Sir John Neale*. Athlone Press.
Elton (a)	G. R. Elton: *The Tudor Constitution*. Cambridge U.P.
Elton (b)	G. R. Elton: 'Tudor revolution: a reply' in *Past and Present*, 1965.
Fisher	F. J. Fisher: 'Commercial trends and policy in sixteenth-century England' in *Economic History Review*, 1940.
Gould	J. R. Gould: 'The crisis in the export trade, 1586–1587' in *English Historical Review*, 1956.
Hale	J. R. Hale: 'Sixteenth-century explanations of war and violence' in *Past and Present*, 1971.
Henry	W. Henry: 'The Earl of Essex as a strategist and military organiser' in *English Historical Review*, 1953.
Hurstfield	J. Hurstfield: 'The Succession Struggle' in *Elizabethan Government and Society: Essays presented to Sir John Neale*. Athlone Press.
Jordan	W. K. Jordan: *Philanthropy in England, 1480–1660*. Allen & Unwin.
Laslett	Peter Laslett: *The World We Have Lost*. Methuen.
Lockyer	R. Lockyer: *Tudor and Stuart Britain*. Longmans.
Mattingly (a)	Garrett Mattingly: *The Defeat of the Spanish Armada*. Pelican.
Mattingly (b)	Garrett Mattingly: 'No peace beyond what line' in *Transactions of the Royal Historical Society*, 1962.
Merriman (a)	M. H. Merriman: 'The assured Scots: Scottish collaborators with England during the rough wooing' in *Scottish Historical Review*, 1968.

Bibliography and Abbreviations

Merriman (b)	R. B. Merriman: *Life and Letters of Thomas Cromwell*. Oxford U.P.
Neale (a)	J. E. Neale: *Elizabeth and her Parliaments, 1559–1581*. Jonathan Cape.
Neale (b)	J. E. Neale: *Elizabeth and her Parliaments, 1584–1601*. Jonathan Cape.
Neale (c)	J. E. Neale: *Essays in Elizabethan History*. Jonathan Cape.
Outhwaite	R. B. Outhwaite: 'Royal borrowing in the reign of Elizabeth I' in *English Historical Review*, 1971.
Pollard (a)	A. F. Pollard: *Cambridge Modern History*, volume II. Cambridge U.P.
Pollard (b)	A. F. Pollard: *Henry VIII*. Jonathan Cape.
Pollard (c)	A. F. Pollard: *Wolsey*. Longmans.
Prescott	H. F. M. Prescott: *Mary Tudor*. Eyre & Spottiswoode.
Price Zimmermann	T. C. Price Zimmermann: 'A note on Clement VII' in *English Historical Review*, 1967.
Rabb	Theodore K. Rabb: 'Investment in English overseas enterprise' in *Economic History Review*, 1966.
Rait	R. S. Rait: *Relations between England and Scotland*. Blackie.
Read (a)	Conyers Read: *Lord Burghley and Queen Elizabeth*. Jonathan Cape.
Read (b)	Conyers Read: *Mr Secretary Cecil and Queen Elizabeth*. Jonathan Cape.
Read (c)	Conyers Read: 'Profits of re-coinage' in *Economic History Review*, 1936.
Rowse	A. L. Rowse: *The England of Elizabeth*. Macmillan.
Scarisbrick	J. J. Scarisbrick: *Henry VIII*. Eyre & Spottiswoode.

Sutherland	N. M. Sutherland: 'Queen Elizabeth and the Conspiracy of Amboise' in *English Historical Review*, 1966.
Tawney & Power	R. Tawney & E. Power: *Tudor Economics Documents*. Longmans.
Thompson	I. A. A. Thompson: 'The Spanish council of war in the reign of Philip II' in *English Historical Review*, 1967.
Trevor-Roper	H. Trevor-Roper: 'Hugh Latimer and the English Commonwealth' in his *Collected Essays*. Macmillan.
Wernham (a)	R. B. Wernham: *Before the Armada*. Jonathan Cape.
Wernham (b)	R. B. Wernham: 'Elizabethan War Aims and Strategy' in *Elizabethan Government and Society: Essays presented to Sir John Neale*. Athlone Press.
Wiener:	Carol Z. Wiener: 'The beleaguered isle' in *Past and Present*, 1971.
Williamson (a)	J. A. Williamson: *Hawkins of Plymouth*. A. & C. Black.
Williamson (b)	J. A. Williamson: *The Ocean in English History*. Oxford U.P.

Also recommended:

J. D. Mackie: *The Early Tudors*. Oxford U.P. (Especially for Scottish affairs.)

Any articles on foreign affairs in the following journals: *English Historical Review, Transactions of the Royal Historical Society, Economic History Review, Past and Present, Scottish Historical Review*.

Preface

An invitation to write a history of Tudor foreign policy has been an opportunity to set down thoughts which are the result of thirty years of reading and teaching. Any sixteenth-century English history-book must owe an overwhelming debt to the giants of learning who dominate Tudor studies in Britain: J. B. Black, G. R. Elton, J. E. Neale, A. F. Pollard, Conyers Read, A. L. Rowse, J. J. Scarisbrick, R. B. Wernham, J. A. Williamson. In addition, I feel a personal debt to R. G. Collingwood whose inspiring ideas—as in his 'Autobiography' and in his essay on 'Human Nature and Human History'—enrich, for the ordinary reader, all subsequent experience of history.

ADDERBURY, OXON.   P. S. C.
1973

PART I

Grass-roots of
Foreign Policy

1 Objectives of Tudor foreign policy— an introduction

The overwhelming motive for foreign policy is national territorial defence. So permanent is man's territorial sentiment, so appalling to his spirit is the prospect of being over-run, that we identify, without anachronism, the relief of mind felt in September 1940 with that felt in August 1588. Nor does it suffice that great destruction shall be avoided, as by the Warsaw powers in Czecho-Slovakia, for even then the defeated feel that

> nothing is possible, but the shamed swoon
> of those consenting to the last humiliation.

For these reasons, a statesman who maintains efficient defence, that is to say successful and inexpensive defence against major danger, is in all ages a great statesman, who has served his people. Defence is the imperative object of foreign policy which a government and a people cannot evade when circumstances raise it. Happy is a country when circumstances do not raise this imperative; happy is the government which is free to have no foreign policy if it chooses, although, being free to choose, it may use its resources in the pursuit of economic advantage, ideological crusade, dynastic right, personal interest, or some conception of 'national glory'—in which pursuit it may of course experience success, disaster or disillusion. The governments of Tudor England were happy in this sense during the comparatively long span of thirty-five years from 1494 to 1529. During these years they were under no immediate compulsion to be active in foreign policy, but for the remainder of the century defence was a continuing and an agonising anxiety.

The threat came from two directions. The first and fundamental threat to England's territorial independence was presented by the expansive vigour of France, a vigour which received extra impulse from the mediaeval notion of 'empire', namely that Christendom ought to be a political entity. In face of this forceful idea England could anticipate no more than 'the courtesy of Polyphemus to Ulysses, namely to be the last devoured'. French aggression could be discounted only rarely between the emergence of France under Louis XI and her fall under the two Napoleons. The threat came from the skill of French rulers, from the population and wealth of France, from her proximity to England and from the character of the boundary between the two countries; for the sea, that looks on the map to be a barrier, is really nature's great highway—unless it is defended. Now sea-defence posed a difficult technical problem wherever sea-transport was by sail, since the invader's wind, for which the invader could wait, would necessarily blow the defenders back into their harbours. Since the danger of sea-borne invasion from France was paramount, except when her governments were occupied in Italy or with wars of religion, the rulers of England were always anxious to neutralise the Channel ports: Henry VII before Charles VIII turned his forces against Italy, Henry VIII when Francis redirected French aggression from Italy to the lower Rhine, and Elizabeth throughout her reign. Even when the danger from Spain hung over England, Elizabeth and her advisers saw clearly that Spain must not be overwhelmed but only weakened, for complete defeat would open the Netherlands to France who, feeble though she was in 1590, would again become the fundamental threat to England when her civil wars were over. 'The case will be hard with the Queen and with England, if ever the French possess, or the Spaniards tyrannise, the Netherlands', said the Earl of Sussex, even when the Armada was being built against his country.

The second threat to England was aroused somewhat gratuitously, one might think, by Henry VIII's breach with Rome. This danger, that Spain, France, and Scotland, singly or in a coalition, would invade as agents of the Pope, was a genuine preoccupation of Henry VIII from the time of his breach with Rome; it weighed with the dukes of Somerset and Northumberland, and of course

Objectives of Tudor foreign policy—an introduction

with Elizabeth. The conversion of Scotland to Protestantism greatly diminished the threat, though Mary Queen of Scots threatened to revive it as did her precocious son James VI until he finally chose his course in 1585. The Huguenot wars eliminated France and so this threat became for some years exclusively Spanish and, by this time, Charles V and Philip II had become the champions of the idea of 'empire'.

The fundamental threat from France, and the transient threat from Spain, were held back by luck and by judgement and application (by luck, for example, when Elizabeth survived smallpox in October 1562; by judgement and application, for example, when Hawkins rebuilt the navy in the years 1577 to 1588). All things considered this was done at a low cost. Taking the Tudor period as a whole the cost of defence was so low that surplus resources were often available for the pursuit of two supplementary objectives of foreign policy. The lesser of these two supplementary objectives of Tudor policy was the pursuit of economic advantage and that in a style that was new and highly extrovert, for, during this century, Tudor governments realised more and more that 'this island, which hath been but as the suburbs of the old world, hath become the bridge to the new'. Henry VII realised in a distant manner that England might possibly become a bridgehead. Then again, after 1540, Henry VII's vision was recovered and the surplus energies of nation and government were increasingly committed to trans-oceanic exploration, colonisation and aggression. Only in years of rare crisis like 1588 were all resources called back to the Channel for home defence.

Twentieth-century readers can sympathise with national defence as an object of foreign policy and even with this lesser supplementary objective, the pursuit of economic advantage. But we cannot easily understand the first supplementary objective of Tudor policy, an objective which possessed for them an importance second only to national defence itself. We cannot easily feel with men who battled so hard for dynastic claims, for national glory, or for a Crusader's victory on Europe's distant perimeter. In order to enter into the feelings of our ancestors, we have to sense their deep preoccupation with anarchy as one of the great threats to human welfare. Because order was sustained precariously, if at all, and then only by a ruling dynasty, men judged that public welfare and maintenance of the dynasty were closely allied. We cannot easily feel with Wolsey and the young Henry VIII who often saw England as a mere suburb of Christendom and were impelled by memories of Henry V to seek glory in the double conquest of Rome and Paris; for that is how they seemed to expend resources which were not to be needed for defence in the years 1511 to 1529. Yet that which seems gratuitous to us was not so to them. At least in respect of the 1520s we can soon perceive that, though Henry's foreign policy occasionally pursued the empty and the grandiose, it was chiefly concerned to preserve his dynasty, that is to say to preserve the security of succession which was synonymous with the freedom of the English community from anarchy and from invasion. This dynastic security was always a recognised aim of Tudor policy, but 'security' is too negative a word to do justice to the nature of the case. A ruling dynasty needed not only security, but also proof to itself of its worthiness to rule. Mediaeval government in Europe was created, in face of enormous difficulty, by a few exceptionally energetic families, often enough descended from Viking warriors who had once set out on plundering raids with the lusty object of proving their manhood. This Viking dynamic was harnessed by Christian influences into the crusades and into the pursuit of defined legal rights and the organisation of the great civilising institutions of Church and State. A self-conscious man of rank would wish to excel in some or all of these directions in order to prove to himself and to his fellows that he was worthy to occupy the rank to which he was born. Chaucer's Knight and Squire fulfilled themselves and the demand of those centuries by making 'a kind of military grand tour . . . campaigning with the Teutonic knights in Prussia . . . thence to Rhodes and Cyprus and finally to Granada'.[1] They were the counterpart of our 'Freedom Fighters' in Spain in 1936, of our VSO workers in 1960 and perhaps of various protest marchers in 1970. Henry's personal need to fight as a crusader and to pursue his dynastic rights in France was a genuine psychological hunger, not only in the man himself, but in the minds of his subjects on their

[1] Alfred W. Pollard: Notes to *Canterbury Tales*, Macmillan.

Objectives of Tudor foreign policy—an introduction

monarch's behalf. Crusading still seemed an urgent matter in the century of Lepanto and so also was insistence on dynastic right at a time when it could bring about the union of Aragon and Castile, of Scotland and England. The unbelievable panache with which Henry dominated the nation, secured his dynasty and held anarchy at bay cannot be dissociated from his passionate zeal to do all that was expected of regal manhood.

In the middle part of the Tudor century the crusading zeal of Christians against Moslems changed quite suddenly into ideological warfare *between* Christians; this was a novel and perturbing form of conflict, 'wars . . . fought in the name of religion within Christendom itself'.[1] But the new crusades on behalf of the creeds of Catholic or Protestant, at least as much as the old crusades against the Moslem, became identified with dynastic ambition. Philip II, when he sought to invade England, and the Duke of Somerset when he invaded Scotland with supplies of Protestant Bibles as well as a more traditional armament, were, for all the world, like a Chinese Communist Army entering Tibet with an armament of tanks and the thoughts of Chairman Mao. A people—like a dynasty—seems to prove its right to be what it is by crusading for a world in which it can be what it is. The health of a nation, once it has secured its defence, depends on its vision of a role in world affairs: 'England has lost her Empire, but has not discovered her role', men said in 1950; 'Western Germany has achieved prosperity, but cannot now discover a role—nor can Japan', men have been heard to say more recently. Perhaps in 1970 we can sympathise, better than was possible in 1940 or 1950, with the hunger that sends a nation out on a crusade.

The great aim of Tudor foreign policy, as of all foreign policy, was defence against invasion. The major supplementary aim was the maintenance of the dynasty, an aim which was sometimes tantamount to national defence and was sometimes a showing forth of dynastic worth in terms of family vigour or of ideological warfare. The lesser supplementary aim of Tudor foreign policy was a search for economic opportunity, especially along the new sea routes. These were the three aims of the governing councils of Tudor

[1] Hale. For abbreviations used in footnotes, see pp. ix–xii.

England, but over against the government's own policy, there sometimes stood the personal ambitions of individual members of the government—the personal interest of Wolsey, of Leicester or of Essex—and these private interests may have initiated or influenced policy. Again, special relations with foreign governments were sometimes initiated by private people acting in a private capacity, that is by merchants, by religious volunteers, by rioting apprentices, just as in other centuries policy has been initiated or influenced or disturbed by the East India Company, by combatant volunteers in Spain, by demo groups outside foreign embassies.

The intention of this book is, first, to illustrate the ways in which Tudor relations with foreign governments were influenced by these private groups and by the private interests of individual members of Tudor governments; secondly and against that background to display the grand policies of national defence and dynastic continuity, together with the ideological underswell that continually rose and ebbed away; finally to consider that pursuit of economic advantage to which Tudor governments applied the residue of their resources.

And here one must plainly confess how gravely the 'medium' is bound to falsify the 'message', for the foreign policy of this little country was like the navigating of a sailing dinghy across an Atlantic. The reader of this abbreviated account knows in advance that the crossing was achieved; he is to be pardoned for supposing that a safe crossing was assured unless some gross error of navigation were perpetrated. The reader wishes therefore to understand what were the main navigational decisions and whether there was any likelihood of gross error. Now the man in the dinghy knows that his overall navigation must be correct; yet primarily he is concerned to circumvent the next mountainous wave, to ride out the force-twelve gust in the force-nine gale, to repair the frayed halyard before it snaps. In a multitude of detailed decisions, one unlucky error can sink man and boat without trace, however correct his overall navigation. This is the incessant anxiety of small-state foreign policy. When little states have lost their independence—Burgundy in 1516, Poland in 1795, Czecho-Slovakia in 1968—we allow ourselves to assume that forces beyond all human evasion made such results inevitable. When little states have survived in defiance of probability—Piedmont in

Objectives of Tudor foreign policy—an introduction

1713, Turkey in 1920, Britain in 1940—we allow ourselves to assume that it could not have been otherwise, for that is the message conveyed by the summary generalisations of any readable volume. But the men who have directed the foreign policies of small states have known that they were more likely to be swamped because of some error in detail than of a major error in general direction. The concern for daily details of policy reduced William Cecil to 'such a torment . . . with the Queen's Majesty as an ague hath not in five fits'. William Thomas, clerk to the Council of Edward VI, knew that England's affairs required deft manipulation: 'neither is our force so ordered that we may trust thereby to win our time, nor our treasure such as we may purchase it, therefore our extremist shift is to work by policy'.[1] 'To work by policy' is ever 'the extremist shift' of all little states. Elizabeth and Cecil found it easy enough to agree on the major objective of foreign policy; it was disagreement about detail that kept them in daily friction with each other, in a fever of anxiety within themselves—'Is she right, or am I?'—together with the knowledge that an unlucky error could set up reverberations which would swamp everything.

The central importance of detail in the foreign policy of little states, the fevered anxiety of every move when a little state is gambling for its survival, this is the truth about foreign policy which most books are bound to conceal. But the reader can find this fever in R. B. Wernham's pages on the later years of Henry VII and in Conyers Read's biography of William Cecil (as he can find it also in, say, the twentieth-century story of the decision to invest Britain's limited resources in radar).

[1] Wernham (a), p. 195.

2 Shakespeare's 'mutable rank-scented many'

The English population of two and a half million in 1500 must have been a nation of about one million adults, outnumbered two to one by Spaniards and three or four to one by Frenchmen. Even though the vast and anonymous majority of this million was not preoccupied with political affairs, yet large sections could feel and act in political matters—in none more vehemently than in matters that involved foreigners. This fact of popular feeling against foreigners could sometimes be wielded by government as a major force in foreign policy; it could always become a limiting factor in foreign policy. When it was not taken into account the anonymous public might express itself abruptly with direct action, as in the Steelyard riots of October 1494, so carefully recorded by Edward Hall, a dedicated lover of London:

'King Henry of England . . . not only banished all Flemish wares and merchandise out of his realm and dominions but also restrained all English merchants from their repair and traffic into any of the lands and territories of the king of Romans or the Archduke his son. . . . The restraint made by the king sore grieved and hindered the [English] merchants being adventurers: For they, by force of this commandment, had no occupying to bear their charges and support their countenance and credit. And yet one thing sore nipped their hearts, for the Easterlings which were at liberty brought into the realm such wares as they were wont and accustomed to do and so served their customers throughout the whole realm. By reason whereof the [English] masters being destitute of sale and commutation neither retained so many covenant-servants and apprentices as they before were accustomed and in especial Mercers, Haberdashers and Clothe workers, nor yet gave to their servants so great stipend and salary as before that restraint they used to do. For which cause the said servants intending to work their malice on the Easterlings, the Tuesday before St Edward's day came to the Steelyard in London and began to rifle and spoil such chambers and warehouses as they could get into. So that the Easterlings had much ado to withstand and repulse them out of their gates. And when the gates were firmed and closed, the multitude rushed and beat at the gates with clubs and levers to have entered, but the Easterlings by the help of Carpenters and Smiths which came to their aid by water out of the borough of Southwark had so strongly shored and fortified themselves that they could not prevail. The Mayor of London hearing of this riot, assembled the magistrates and officers of the city together and so, being furnished both with men and weapon, set forward toward the Steelyard. As soon as the coming of the Mayor was intimate and known to the riotous persons, they fled away like a flock of sheep; howbeit he apprehended diverse malefactors and committed them to several prisons. And upon inquiry before the king's commissioners, there were found guilty above eighty servants and apprentices (and not one householder) which were confederate together to make this attempt and sworn in no wise to discover or reveal the same: Whereof some, that were the chieftains and beginners of this mischievous riot, were sent to the Tower and there long continued. But in conclusion, because none of their masters were found culpable of this naughty act, the king of his goodness remitted their offence and restored them to their liberty.'

Again, in 1517, increased imports once more competed with the products of English craftsmen. Londoners felt a seething hostility to foreign traders who lived among them, the more so as these foreigners seemed to be favoured and privileged by king and court. 'Then suddenly was a common secret rumour and no man could tell how it began, that on May day next the city would rebel and slay all the aliens.' A moderate effort by the mayor to forestall this outbreak had the effect of setting it off. Two or three crowds, each three or four hundred strong, looted the houses of aliens (but apparently without killing anyone). The reaction of king and court against the Londoners was fairly savage: 'thirteen found guilty of high treason and adjudged to be hanged, drawn and quartered.... Then were the prisoners that were judged brought to the places of execution and executed in most rigorous manner, for the Lord Edmund Howard, son to the Duke of Norfolk and Knight Marshal, showed no mercy, but extreme cruelty to the younglings in their execution.' But the rest of the 'poor younglings and old false knaves to the number of 400 men and 11 women' were pardoned. This was the Evil May Day of 1517.[1]

If monarch, mayor and aldermen had any foreign policy behind this rigour, perhaps it is stated by Antonio, the Merchant of Venice:

> 'Since that the trade and profit of the city
> Consisteth of all nations ...
> The Duke cannot deny the course of Law ...'

wherever it exists to protect aliens.

In each of these cases chronic xenophobia was triggered by a particular economic intrusion. But popular feeling against foreigners was equally to be fired by religious sentiment and by a defensive cultural patriotism.

Thus patriotic anti-clericalism turned some parts of the English populace against the Italian and Romish characteristics of their Church; similarly, in 1549, there was xenophobic opposition to protestant innovations, for these too seemed to be an alien intrusion. Above all popular resentment was powerful against foreigners when economic and religious detonators worked together. Specifically, popular opinion could not, in mid-century, accept obedience to a Pope in Spanish hands when Spain was holding back England's Atlantic enterprise; thus support for a breach with Rome was a long-term reaction to the Papal treaty of Tordesillas, which had divided the world between Spain and Portugal and so helped to create 'a pattern which continually set English nationalism at loggerheads with English catholicism ...; this pattern consisted of a powerful Spain, seeking not only to curb the Atlantic enterprises of the north-European peoples but to control the Mediterranean,

[1] The quotations are from Edmund Hall's Chronicle, 1806 edition.

the Italian Peninsula and with them a reluctant but often rather powerless Papacy'.[1]

The association of Roman doctrine with commercial exclusion was a very bitter fact for ordinary folk as well as for the learned and the politically active: 'William Collins, of Oxford, age 40, seaman, ten years in the galleys; John Farenton, of Windsor, 49, gunner, six years in the galleys; John Burton, of Bar Abbey, 22, seaman, two hundred lashes and six years in the galleys; Paul de Leon, of Rotterdam, 22, seaman, two hundred lashes and six years in the galleys; William Griffin, of Bristol, 24, seaman, two hundred lashes and eight years in the galleys; George Ribley, of Gravesend, 30, seaman, burnt at the stake, but first strangled; John Moon, of Looe, 26, seaman, two hundred lashes and six years in the galleys; John Lee, of "Sebria" in England, 20, seaman or gunner, two hundred lashes and eight years in the galleys; William Brown, of London, 25, steward, two hundred lashes and six years in the galleys; John Gilbert, of London, 29, seaman, three hundred lashes and ten years in the galleys; Roger Armar, of Gueldres (Netherland), 24, armourer, two hundred lashes and six years in the galleys; Michael Morgan, of Cardiff, 40, seaman, two hundred lashes and eight years in the galleys; John Brown, of Ireland, 28, seaman, two hundred lashes and eight years in the galleys; John Williams, of Cornwall, 28, two hundred lashes and eight years in the galleys; Robert Plinton, of Plymouth, 30, two hundred lashes and eight years in the galleys; John Grey, Englishman, 22, gunner, two hundred lashes and eight years in the galleys; George Dee or Day, Englishman, 30, seaman, three hundred lashes and eight years in the galleys.'[2] The recognisable offence in each of these men was that he had, under John Hawkins, broken into Spain's Caribbean monopoly, but his punishment was by the Inquisition for heresy. In the minds of men on both sides, the maintenance of Spanish monopoly was associated with Roman Catholicism, its breach with protestantism. Roman Catholicism stood for a limitation on England's Oceanic enterprise. Popular enthusiasm for this enterprise made Francis Drake 'a folk-hero in his day, "Robin Hood M.P.", the godly and eloquent answer to

[1] Dickens, pp. 155–6.
[2] Williamson (a), p. 154.

chronic unemployment',[1] a hero over whom the popular mind could happily exult: 'the sun himself cannot forget his fellow-traveller'. Thousands of unknown men crowded aboard England's privateers to swell the ranks of the boarding parties; they were after their 33% share of the prize-money, for that, with their victuals, was all the pay they got.[2] These men—this great anonymous human effort—helped to cripple Spain, to give power and effect to Elizabethan foreign policy.

In the end, England's official foreign policy did detach itself from the activities of these unknown Englishmen and made peace with Spain in 1604, but the popular will pursued its own policy in the Caribbean without interruption. 'There never has been beyond the line . . . any kind of peace . . . but whoever proves the stronger shall be taken for lord.'[3]

Nearer home the association of protestantism with patriotism and with economic expansion gave Flemish refugees a welcome very different from that accorded to aliens in 1517. 'You would never believe,' wrote Clais van Wervekin to his wife, 'how friendly the people are together and the English are the same and quite loving to our nation. . . . Send my money and the three children. Come at once and do not be anxious.'[4] This was from Norwich in 1567. Protestant patriotism was likewise the force that created England's military intervention in the Dutch wars when in May 1572, the first three hundred men, paid for by public subscription, left London to help the sea-beggars, newly established in Flushing.

A belief that English prosperity depended on foreigners could, then, be almost as powerful as the belief that aliens were intruders who drove Englishmen to poverty or unemployment. Thus, in January 1528, textile workers rioted in Somerset, Wiltshire and East Anglia, when Wolsey declared war against Charles V, a war which interrupted our sales in the Netherlands and Spain; trade was resumed in March. Opposition to the annulment of Henry's marriage with Catherine (evinced by the London congregation

[1] Bromley.
[2] Andrews, p. 39.
[3] Marie de Medici: to James I, quoted in Mattingly (b).
[4] Tawney & Power, p. 299.

which walked out of Church when prayer was offered for Anne Boleyn), could come from fear that trade with Antwerp would be lost; indeed short-cloth exports from London, which had been 75,000 in 1529, and were to be 83,000 in 1535, fell to 66,000 at the height of this marriage crisis.

A sense of common interest with foreigners was not only economic. At a spiritual level some large groups of anonymous folk felt that their experience of life only made sense in association with the beliefs of a single Christendom, and not otherwise. Many who marched with the Pilgrimage of Grace and many, though perhaps fewer, who marched in 1569 with the Northern Earls must have felt this. 'But certainly by the time the Queen died, no good Englishman could have defined his national identity without some mention of his distaste for Rome',[1] and for every anonymous Englishman who went abroad to train as a Catholic priest many others went to fight for the Dutch rebels against Philip's inquisition.

Popular feeling in respect of foreigners was usually fired by particular economic or religious changes. But apart from these vagaries of feeling, England's foreign policy could be inhibited by simple resentment at taxation and conscription, as when efforts to collect the 'Amicable Grant' in 1525 stirred overwhelming opposition and royal councillors were jostled by irate crowds who denounced war with France as a waste of money, likely to conquer 'not one foot'. Foreign policy could be limited by the simple inability of villages to stand more than a small amount of conscription if they were to get in the harvest, as in the 1590s, or by direct public opposition to the government's policies in home affairs, as when, in 1549, England's foreign policy was crippled by the need to control domestic rebellions in Cornwall and Norfolk.

In foreign countries, as much as in England, powerful movements of popular feeling at the grass roots have influenced foreign relations. English foreign policy in the sixteenth century was advanced by opportunities, and impeded by obstacles, which were generated by popular feeling in neighbouring countries. The Calvinism of France and the popular patriotism of the Netherlands added something to England's resources. Above all in Scotland and in Ireland, popular

[1] Weiner.

feeling was of paramount importance to England. The Scottish alliance of 1560 was made possible by movements of public opinion which defied official Scottish policy and official English folly. Scottish public opinion in the sixteenth century began to think of poverty as the consequence of alliance with France whereas trade would follow upon friendship with England: 'For the love of France the realm of Scotland suffers great pain as daily appears. . . . If we would keep amity with the realm of England we were out of all these dangers.'[1] Similarly more and more Scotsmen after 1530 adopted protestant beliefs and looked to England as their example and place of refuge; and, as the Scots did not develop a religious literature in their own Gaelic, they looked to England for their Bibles and service books. Protestantism made English to be the chief language of the Scottish people and Scottish governments were unable to turn their people wholly against the English even after the terrible English invasions of the 1540s: 'the caus that Inglis men is fawvorit and the authorite nocht obeyit . . . [is that] . . . part of the legis has tayn new opinions of the scriptour.'[2] The Scots wanted, above all, 'other good English books of Tyndale's and Frith's translations'.[3] When the English garrisons withdrew in 1550, as many as one hundred and fifty lesser noblemen were executed by the new rulers of Scotland because of their previous collaboration with the English occupying armies.

In Ireland, popular beliefs had the reverse effect. A heroic tradition was kept alive by Gaelic bards who idealised the vendetta with its associated glories of clan warfare and tribal rivalry. Alliance or collaboration was not possible between such a society and the legalised administration of Tudor England. But during the Wars of the Roses some clans had acquired the habit of allying with English factions or with England's continental enemies. Tudor administrators were thus faced with Irish clans who could assist the enemies of England's settled government but could not come to terms with it. This was a desperate deadlock, burdensome, even murderous, to both peoples.

[1] Quoted in Donaldson, p. 284.
[2] Quoted in Donaldson, p. 286.
[3] Quoted in Donaldson, p. 286.

The changing mood of the 'manie' was powerful enough in its season to prevent, to limit, or even to generate foreign policy. Governments did well to appreciate this force—if possible to harness the generous energy of popular initiative because they could not in any case disperse it.

3 Acknowledged initiators

Nearer to the government than the very grass roots of public feeling, and consciously concerned to shape foreign policy, were the self-appointed pressure groups and publicists who have existed in all ages but who multiplied their influence in Tudor England by means of the printing press. Group spokesmen and lone writers invented new policies and thus widened the government's field of choice; such men became influential in rousing public feeling in support of one policy or in opposition to another. Moreover the private enterprise of these groups devised and manufactured the weapons of government policy—for example, galleons newly devised by ocean-going merchants, cannonry forged in new metallurgical industries, gunpowder ground in new powder mills.

Most of these citizens who, without being members of the government, tried to urge foreign policy upon it, were traders; that is to say, men whose daily business depended on direct or indirect contact with foreigners. Traders had inclined to the Yorkist party rather than to the Lancastrian. They blamed the house of Lancaster for an irresponsible act of piracy in 1449—the seizure of a fleet of 110 vessels Flemish, Dutch and Hanseatic—and consequently for an endless aftermath of reprisals against English merchants. London citizens admitted the Yorkists in 1460, even though Lancastrians held the Tower; London excluded Queen Margaret after her victory at St Albans (1461), but they proclaimed Edward IV as their king. Edward in 1471 made his return to England in a ship of the Hanse; he restored trading relations between England and the Hanse and established their warehouses in London, Boston and

Acknowledged initiators

King's Lynn. Influential London citizens could not be ignored by the Tudor successors of Edward IV and Richard III. London merchants consistently urged and supported the efforts of Henry VII to improve trade with the Netherlands—the Merchant Adventurers advancing with the export of cloth as the Merchant Staplers declined with their export of wool. Merchants hoped also for some trade in the Baltic in spite of the overwhelming power of the Hanse. West of England traders sought greater trade in Bordeaux and Seville. It was in Bristol that there first emerged a wholly new attitude to world-wide geography, an attitude which in the end captured the

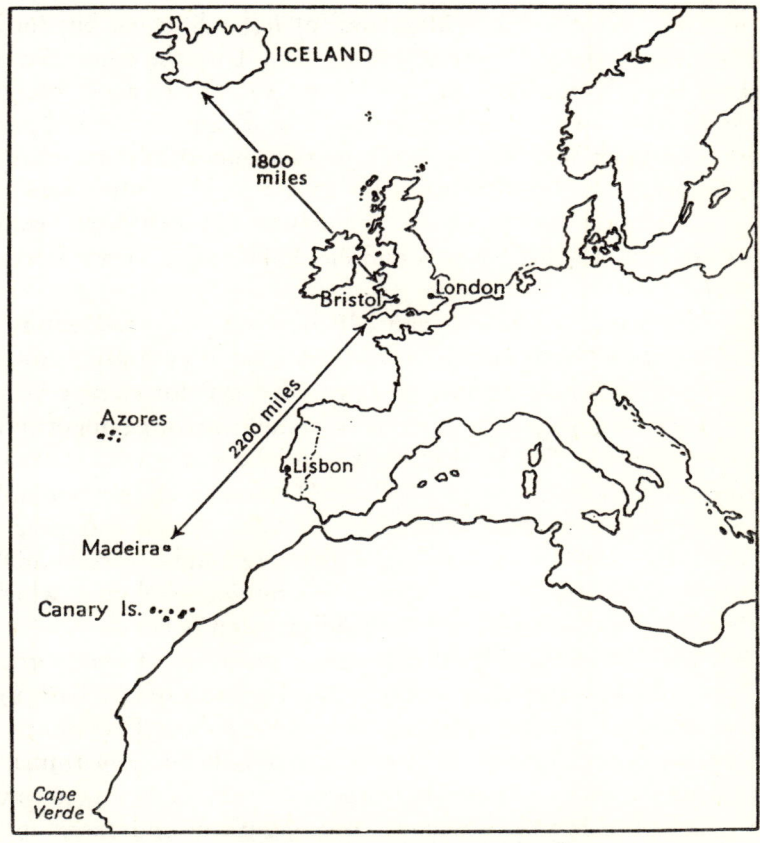

Map 1. Bristol: her Atlantic commerce in the late fifteenth century

mind of the nation, dominated our governments and swung the focus of foreign policy away from Europe to the western and eastern shores of the Atlantic and Indian oceans. Trading with Iceland and also with Madeira, Bristol merchants knew traditional stories of lands beyond the Atlantic. In 1480 John Jay sent an eighty-ton ship to 'traverse the seas' to the west of Ireland in quest of the Island of Brazil. A Spanish official reported in 1498 that 'for the last seven years the people of Bristol have sent out every year two, three or four caravels in search of the Island of Brazil and the Seven Cities'.[1] Doubtless for these reasons, John Cabot came to Bristol in 1490 and brought to the city the Renaissance idea of searching, not for Brazil or for the 'Wineland and Markland' of Icelandic saga, but for a short route to the rich products of Cathay. Thus the enterprise of Bristol brought to the mind of Henry VII the idea of foreign endeavour in a wholly new direction. The disappearance and presumed death of John Cabot came in 1498 but Bristol merchants had gained enough information by 1501 to add another item to England's armoury of hypotheses: namely that his new-found lands were not Asia and that a way round should be sought via the northwest.

The activities of Sebastian Cabot's 'Bristol company of adventurers into New found lands' occupied the years 1500 to 1510. By then the zeal of the Bristol merchants was expended and for twenty years merchant traders were more concerned to exploit existing opportunities for trade with Europe than to imagine and search out new ones further off. But in the 1530s William Hawkins and his Plymouth associates began to send expeditions to West Africa and Brazil; from that decade new ideas of England's interest and new techniques of seamanship and warfare began a continuous evolution which within fifty years transformed England's foreign policy.

But before the opening of this second great era of commercial influence on foreign policy, religion also began to offer a basis for an assertion of private influence on public policy. If commerce gave private men the knowledge and need to influence government, religion gave them courage and urgency to do so. By 1530 new ideas were making their impact on government and these, in a

[1] Williamson (b), p. 13.

few years, would tear apart England's existing relationship with Rome and thereafter would distort her relationship with all the other countries of Europe. 'Henry's mind was on the move, but who', it has been asked, 'was moving it?'[1] *Obedience of the Christian Man* was written by William Tyndale and was brought to Henry's notice by Anne Boleyn; it maintained that a monarch ought to be pope in his own land. *A supplication for the Beggars* by Simon Fish, although chiefly concerned to attack the avarice of clergymen, left Henry with the thought that he must break with Rome before he could deal effectively with his own clergy. At about this time an unknown Fellow of Jesus College, Cambridge, working privately at Waltham, suggested to Henry the diplomatic gambit of referring his divorce petition to the universities of Europe. Thus Thomas Cranmer, this very private citizen, started up two years of complicated diplomatic manoeuvre, wholly futile in its outcome, but nevertheless a testimony to the manner in which private suggestion could initiate public policy. Meanwhile, on the outer circumference of the government stood Thomas Cromwell, personal secretary to Thomas Wolsey, brooding the Erastian notions of Marsiglio of Padua that Christ and his Church were subject to the Emperor.

These ideas, under stress of the actual breach with Rome, quickly became the commonplaces of public policy and of national feeling. Experience of the breach with Rome, of isolation from Europe, of withstanding the French invasion fleet (two hundred strong) in 1545, bred in all parts of the English community a secular religion, a new and intense nationalism, with the courage and urgency to protest its beliefs. This was the force behind the protest of Courtenay and Wyatt (that is of both Catholic and Protestant Englishmen) against Mary Tudor's marriage with Philip of Spain. It was the force behind thousands who applauded the protest of John Stubbe against Elizabeth's projected marriage to a Frenchman; Stubbe's publication of *Discovery of a Gaping Gulf whereunto England is like to be swallowed by another French marriage if the Lord forbid not the banns* (1579) was punished with the loss of his right hand, but he raised his bloody stump as he gave his patriotic shout 'God save the Queen'—and the queen, for all her anger, seems to have given more attention to

[1] Scarisbrick, p. 247.

such protest than James I gave to parliament's opposition to Spanish or French marriages.

In the same way, inward religious conviction and patriotism moved Thomas Morgan to lead the first three hundred volunteers whose private enterprise began England's intervention in the Netherlands in 1572. This self-effacing and splendid commander served in the Netherlands for most of the next fifteen years as 'the old warrior'; he first arrived in June 1572, just in the nick of time to save Flushing from the Spaniards and thus, if our Armada story is correct, to save England from invasion in 1588. He was followed, and superseded, by other leaders of varying temperament and skill; they too were always moved by some degree of personal conviction: John Norris, Francis de Vere, Peregrine Bertie, alias Lord Willoughby ('Peregrine' because he was born of pious parents exiled abroad by the Marian persecution).

So complete was the acceptance by government and people of the general policy of national self-determination, that any counter-policy of a return by England to the Roman Catholic community was advocated only by rare and isolated individuals: by Cardinal Allen who advocated the total subjugation of England's secular interests to Spain, and so to Rome; by Jesuits who risked and suffered martyrdom with the same single object; by such laymen as William Stanley, commanding the defence of Deventer, and Rowland Yorke, commanding the fortress of Zutphen, both of whom went over to the enemy and so gave Parma the crossings of the river Ijsel and access into the Dutch heartland (1587).[1] Known to be Catholics, they had been appointed to these commands, in spite of Dutch protests, by Leicester who staked 'his life on the loyalty of his officers', but they betrayed the generosity or stupidity of their commander 'in the service of the Almighty and of the greatest and justest monarch in all the world [Philip] and under a general so peerless [Parma] . . . to reduce our people to the obedience of Christ's Church and deliver our Catholic friends and brethren from the damnable and intolerable yoke of heresy'.[2] In the service of the

[1] See map 16 on p. 226.
[2] Cardinal William Allen and Father Robert Parsons on the surrender of Deventer, quoted in Mattingly (a), p. 83.

Acknowledged initiators

same cause, Father Parsons developed in the 1590s his intricate diplomatic scheme to secure succession to the English throne for Isabella, daughter of Philip II and wife of the Archduke Albert.

As religious belief and quasi-religious national feeling prompted private Englishmen, on one side or the other, to urge their private ideas of England's proper foreign policy, so religion fused with commerce and became a single dominant source of unofficial influence on official policy. The traders whose influence was paramount originated in Plymouth as much as in London and more frequently than in Bristol. From 1540 these men had a policy towards foreign powers which, in its objects and methods, was their own, sometimes pursued without reference to the English government, sometimes collaborating with the government and at last absorbed by it. One can doubt whether the British government of the 1940s would have had any foreign policy but for radar and the British aircraft industry; so one can doubt whether Elizabeth's government would have been able to maintain any foreign policy but for the ideas and enterprise that came from Plymouth. William Hawkins senior (*c.* 1490–1554) with his associates was by 1540 already importing salt, wine, sugar, pepper, soap from western France, Portugal, Spain and the Canaries against tin and cloth from England's south-western counties. He had already traded experimentally with West Africa and Brazil. In the year 1540 he exported twenty-four pounds worth of goods to those areas in order to import goods which sold for £615. Thus he was acquiring for himself, and ultimately for the government, the experience of long-range navigation which would make possible long-range warfare and the sort of foreign policy that depends on long-range influence.

William Hawkins, sometime Mayor, sometime MP for Plymouth, was well known to Thomas Cromwell and to the Privy Council; consequently, when war with France came in 1544, he and others were commissioned by the government to waylay French ships that entered the Channel from the west, an operation which he performed with such excess of zeal that he captured a French ship after the peace treaty had been signed in 1546, and was finally imprisoned (to pacify Charles V) for capturing a Netherland ship with an allegedly French cargo.

In the activities of 'Old Master William Hawkins' we can detect the tenuous beginnings of two lines of policy: that Englishmen ought to push their trade into the new worlds notwithstanding the monopolies asserted by Spain and Portugal; and that whenever the enemy came he was best encountered at the western entrance of the Channel. Thomas Wyndham of Norfolk and London collaborated with 'Old Master William' and with William Hawkins II (1519-89). Roused by the collapse of the Antwerp cloth market (1551), Wyndham adopted the first of these lines of policy and sent expeditions to Morocco in 1548 and to the Gold Coast (further along the West Africa coast than Hawkins had ever ventured) in 1553 and in later years, notwithstanding the prohibition of Philip and Mary.

Meanwhile John Hawkins (1532-95), leaving his elder brother William to manage the family's affairs in Plymouth, took to London the knowledge which he had gained as a trader in the Canary Islands; in particular he had learnt many of the secrets of Spain's export of Negro slaves from West Africa to the Caribbean. Moreover, in 1559 Hawkins married Catherine Gonson, daughter of Benjamin Gonson, Treasurer of the Navy; this brought him to the edge of government and he was able to form a syndicate that included Admiral Sir William Wynter for the promotion of a precise, albeit a private, foreign policy: Spain was to be persuaded of the advantageous and peaceful character of direct English trade with her American colonies. Then, in exchange for permission to trade, Spain was to be offered private English help against French interlopers and privateers. The second syndicate of 1564 included three eminent Privy Councillors and sailed with the Queen's commission. Both syndicates were financially successful but failed to achieve their general purpose. The third, of 1567-68, sailed after the queen had refused a Spanish request to ban Caribbean voyages and Hawkins had fired on Spanish ships which entered Plymouth with the apparent purpose of preventing his voyage. This expedition was almost totally destroyed by the Spaniards in violation of a promise of safe-conduct. This was the disaster of San Juan de Uloa, which ended the attempts to win an entry into the Caribbean for peaceful traders. But the general policy was bequeathed to later generations and they

Acknowledged initiators

acquired such an empire there as could, in the eighteenth century, be named 'the brightest jewel in His Majesty's crown'.

Private policy in the Caribbean became openly aggressive after 1568. The aggression may have been promoted and financed by a syndicate of west of England men resident in London: John Hawkins, Humphrey Gilbert, Richard Grenville and William Wynter, while William Hawkins remained in Plymouth to direct all the practical preparations on behalf of the syndicate. On their behalf, Drake raided and robbed Nombre de Dios in 1573. John Oxenham, in 1576–77, tried to create a permanent fastness on the southern stretch of the Panama isthmus—the first of many attempts to set up a base

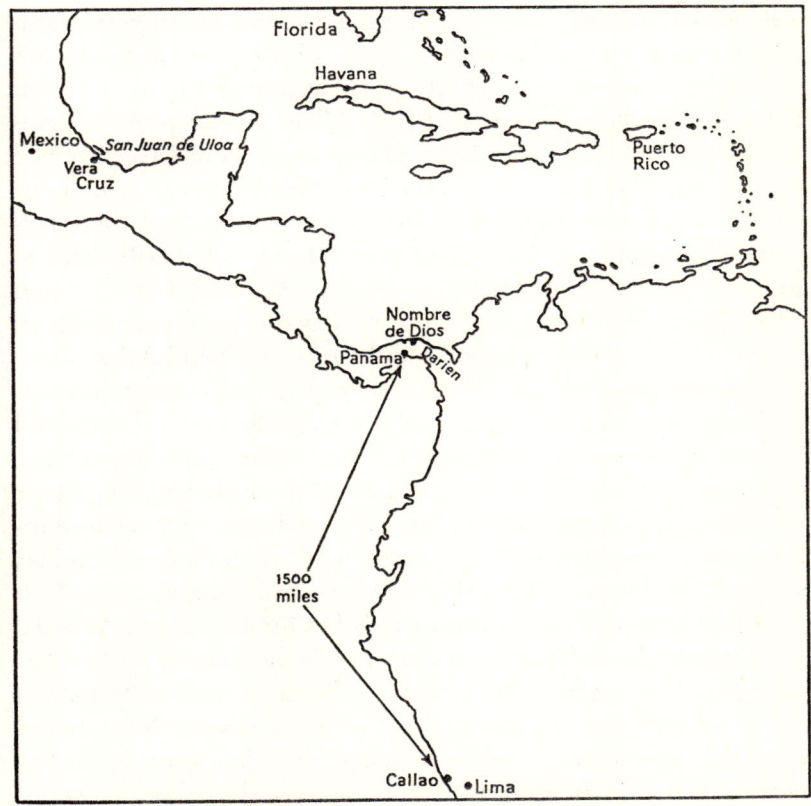

Map 2. Darien: between the Pacific and the Caribbean

in the far west from which English sea-power could dominate Spanish shipping. Drake sailed again in 1577, perhaps to join hands with Oxenham, and not merely to effect a single brilliant raid. In any case, experience of this privateering gave to these privateers (and hence to the English government) the notion of the 'silver blockade', blockading the flow of bullion from Central America to Spain by capturing the bullion ships in the Caribbean or off the Azores. Though the blockade was never well enough established to bring Spain to her knees, yet its temporary imposition was sufficient to postpone her expeditions and to disrupt her policies.

In some ways this 'silver blockade' can be regarded as a logical extension of the second line of policy to be detected in the career of 'Old Master William', the idea of going to meet the enemy far out to sea and at least at the western approaches to the Channel. This second line of policy was effectively rehearsed in the months that followed the disaster at San Juan de Uloa. These were the crisis months of 1568 and 1569: Mary Queen of Scots had recently fled to England; Alva had occupied the Netherlands with an army large enough to menace England as soon as he had subdued the rebels there; the defeat and death of Condé at Jarnac left La Rochelle as the heart and centre of Huguenot resistance. But, under the direction of Admiral de Coligny, a force of fifty privateers (thirty of them English, three or four belonging to the Hawkins family) devastated Spanish shipping in the Channel, virtually cut her communications with the Netherlands, added vastly to the difficulties of Alva and permitted the Dutch revolt to gather momentum; the whole result is described by James A. Williamson as 'one of the more recondite effects of sea-power'. This operation, encouraged and applauded by the English government, was nevertheless the work of private men in idea and in execution; it contained within itself many suggestions which would find expression in government policy for meeting the Armada.

These private traders did not only initiate the strategy with which foreign policy would meet the enemy; they also evolved the tactical weapon which this strategy needed. Queen Elizabeth's Navy Board consisted, until 1580, of able men whose experience was limited to home waters. Their ships were too large, too broad in the beam, and too heavily manned for ocean service. Their navy was reasonably efficient for defence in home waters, 'for petty campaigns that were short of serious war; and the queen and her people paid about twice as much as they should have done for the service rendered'.[1] John Hawkins, through his father-in-law, Benjamin Gonson, may have exerted argument within earshot of the Navy Board since 1559. From 1564 he was in personal contact with William Cecil and the queen. Thus government circles must have become aware of the argument for less majestic ships, which would not shake loose at the joints in Atlantic gales, would carry smaller crews and would cost less. The influence of the argument appeared in 1570 with the new naval ship *Foresight* and again in 1575 with the *Revenge*, still in 1591 one of the world's most efficient fighting ships. Above all it appeared with the appointment, in November 1577, of John Hawkins to be Joint Treasurer of the Navy. This appointment was the decision of the Lord Treasurer Burghley, in itself therefore an act of government rather than of private initiative; furthermore John Hawkins was sustained in office by Elizabeth and Burghley in spite of all the attacks of his critics. For the remaining eighteen years of his life, then, he was a member of the government and his actions were strictly actions of government, yet so deeply were they rooted in private experience and so keenly criticised in official circles (by none more vehemently than by Admiral Sir William Wynter, senior officer in the Navy Board), that one can fairly ascribe to private enterprise the great influence which these actions had on England's relations with her foreign neighbours. In the ten years before the fight with the Armada, all of the main fighting ships of the navy were reconditioned: large amounts of decaying timber were replaced, superstructures were removed, ships were lengthened by being cut in two and having an extra section added amidships. Then, in 1586, began the expansion of the fleet by new additional ship-building as distinct from replacements.

While he altered the design of royal ships Hawkins also altered the arrangements for manning them; in particular, he reduced manpower from one man for every $1\frac{1}{2}$ tons of shipping to one man for every two tons of shipping, so that more food could be carried and a fleet could endure at sea for five months. The fighting tech-

[1] Williamson (a), p. 245.

niques which Drake had perfected could be matched by the ships and by the thinking of the Navy Board; the Lord Admiral Howard could appoint Francis Drake, the great merchant seaman, as his Vice-Admiral and the ships of the Royal Naval could work with, and indeed lead, the fighting merchant-men.

Hawkins supervised a reconstruction of the fleet and also a reconstruction of the terms on which the government paid for this rebuilding. By means of two bargains which he entered upon with the government, the first in 1579 and the second in 1585, he saved the government about £4,000 a year in comparison with the amounts previously spent for the provision of a less efficient fleet.

When one considers that the English fleet was able, only by a narrow margin of superiority, to edge the Armada up the Channel and out of the Calais anchorage; that the English government was able, only by a narrow margin, to pay for the minimal defences that it maintained in 1588; that Hawkins put through his reforms in face of harassing opposition which included a Privy Council inquiry into his alleged corruption; that, in the ultimate weeks of battle 'not one [ship] had fallen out for sea-damage or the enemy's shot'— then one recognises the great contribution of the ideas, attitudes and traditions of the Plymouth traders among whom the Hawkins family was foremost.

But the defeat of the Armada was not an isolated, self-contained event. During the two previous years, English privateers preyed continually on shipping in Spanish coastal waters. For fifteen years afterwards, these same men persistently destroyed or captured home-bound merchant ships and thus drained away Spain's enormous powers of naval recuperation. The two years of effort before 1588 did something to weaken the Armada; the fifteen years of effort afterwards weakened and finally exhausted Spain's attacks on England. The ship-owners who were primarily responsible for this long offensive were the least war-like of all English shipping interests. They were the traders of Chester, Bristol and also London, whose trade was with Spain or with Spain's European dependencies. They were, of course, desperately anxious to keep peace between Spain and England, because continuance of trade depended on this; they were utterly opposed to Drake's aggressive raids in 1572 and

1577. But, in May 1585, Philip suddenly seized all English ships in Spanish ports. The English group which had been most favourable to Spain suffered the greatest loss and, almost overnight, became fighting leaders against her. In July 1585, the Lord Admiral Charles Howard began to issue 'letters of reprisal' to any merchant who could prove his losses. By these letters, the merchant was authorised to find compensation as best he could, that is by capturing Spanish ships, and he was protected against any charge of piracy in English law-courts. John Watts was an experienced trader in Spanish merchandise—for many years he had been an export factor in Cadiz; he, or perhaps his syndicate, lost five ships in 1585. He became, and remained for many years, a leading organiser of raiding expeditions. The captured ships and their cargoes brought him greater profit than he would have gained in peaceful trade. Thomas Myddelton had been an export factor in Flushing until 1578. After he had settled down in London, he became involved in trade with Spain. For almost twenty years after 1585 he was busy organising, and investing in, raiding expeditions. James Lancaster had been an export factor in Seville until 1581. In 1587 he was one of the privateer captains in Drake's Cadiz expedition. For this expedition was in principle a private joint-stock enterprise, a large syndicate of merchants, all supported with 'letters of reprisal', employing Drake as their managing director; the queen invested six ships in the enterprise. Their capture of the *San Felipe*, with its cargo worth £100,000, gave the enterprise its dividend. All the famous expeditions after 1589, as well as hundreds of unknown sorties, were organised on this basis. Myddelton was treasurer of expeditions in 1591, 1592 and 1596, and also of the final Drake-Hawkins expedition of 1595. The effect of this incessant pressure on Spain was twofold. Immediately, she was forced to concentrate her naval power for the protection of her vital bullion fleet. This left the rest of her commerce largely unprotected; her ordinary shipping was at the mercy of privateers who could number their prizes by the hundred: 'the merchants of Seville and Portugal who used to venture to the Indies are broken by losses of goods and ships since the wars' (1597).[1] This was the exhaustion which undermined Spain's ability

[1] Quoted in Andrews, p. 226.

to make war. One can add that Raleigh in 1585, and the London Company in 1606, were able to colonise Virginia without interference only because Spanish naval power had to limit its range to the Caribbean.

The policy of Tudor governments towards foreigners could, then, be influenced by ideas and by methods of action which were derived from religious writers or from trading families. There was also a third group by which Tudor governments might be influenced. This third group consisted of writers in the field of speculative geography. They shared with men of religion an academic approach to problems, but they made it their business also to converse with traders and explorers who knew their geography from first-hand experience. Sir Thomas More and his friends thought speculatively about the new worlds; his brother-in-law, John Rastell, sailed in 1517 to seek lands for colonisation, but his crew would not go further than Waterford. Brilliant ideas emerged and perhaps found no support; such was the notion of Robert Thorne of Seville (*c.* 1525) that the best way to the Pacific was by direct navigation from England over the North Pole. Much more important was John Dee, tutor to the children of the Duke of Northumberland, a mathematician and inventor of aids to navigation. His mind was active on all the possible approaches to the seas of the far east; he favoured the north-eastern passage, because he believed that the ports and markets of northern Asia would provide a marvellous 'vent' for English cloth, but he was vividly interested also in the passage to the north-west and in the Straits of Magellan. His ideas influenced the active mind of Northumberland; they influenced the explorations of the Muscovy Company, Frobisher's search for a north-west passage and Grenville's project to acquire the hypothetical continent of Terra Australis Incognita. Such a man generated his range of fertile ideas by amassing and meditating upon every geographical idea from every writer, Greek or Roman, mediaeval or contemporary. He was able to influence ministers of the crown, sea-captains and Elizabeth herself.

Richard Hakluyt was famous in his own day, and has since remained so, for maintaining intense public interest in the 'Voyages and Discoveries of the English Nation, made by Sea or over Land to the most remote and farthest distant Quarters of the earth', but his special contribution was that, like Sir Humphrey Gilbert, he gave publicity to the new idea of colonising some part of North America. Two other writers, Christopher Carlisle and George Peckham, supported the argument of Hakluyt and of Gilbert that such a colony could serve three purposes: it could be a base from which attacks could be made on Spanish shipping in the Caribbean; it could be a base from which expeditions could search for the north-west passage; above all it could help to solve England's acute social problem of a rising population without a sufficient increase in jobs to provide work for all. Gilbert's *Discourse for a Discovery for a new Passage to Cataia* (1576) urged that we should settle in America 'such needy people of our country, which now trouble the commonwealth and through want here at home are enforced to commit outrageous offences, whereby they are daily consumed with the gallows'. English settlers in North America and the natives of that continent could in any case be expected to provide a 'vent' for England's woollen cloth. In 1583 Gilbert was drowned as he returned from an unsuccessful attempt to establish a colony in Newfoundland, but the work was continued by Sir Walter Raleigh, his half-brother, and, though these attempts were likewise unsuccessful, a new line of policy had won a permanent place in the deliberations of Englishmen and of English governments. If English settlements in North America have not opened up a navigable north-west passage, they have certainly provided bases for operations against Spanish America, but above all they have provided tremendous markets for the products of the mother country.

Writers, London merchants and expert navigators combined in the last twelve years of the reign to send expeditions to India. The early expeditions, led by George Raymond and James Lancaster in 1591, and by Benjamin Wood in 1596, were lost in the disasters which were the natural consequence of long and difficult voyages, destroying crews by the mere pressure of disease. Yet the Londoners were convinced of the profitability of Portuguese trade, and ventured £68,000 in 1601; the East India Company was formed and chartered, and future English governments were given a basis for influence in a wholly new part of the world, the basis also for a new sort of influence on their European neighbours.

On these many oceanic ventures of Elizabethan Englishmen, England's future foreign policy was largely to depend. In this reign a mere five hundred persons constituted the small group whose enterprise and money gave England the means to follow a policy that was becoming world-wide.[1] These were the people who 'put their means in supposition' with argosies 'bound to Tripolis'; others 'to the Indies', others yet 'at Mexico' and others for Venice. 'But ships were but boards, sailors but men; there were land-rats and water-rats, water thieves and land thieves, that is pirates: and then there were the perils of waters, winds and rocks.' Many a ship 'dock'd in sand, vailing her high top lower than her ribs to kiss her burial'.[2]

[1] See Rabb.
[2] All the quotations in the paragraph are from *The Merchant of Venice*.

4 Parliament

Tudor parliaments were an important means of communication between Tudor governments and the politically active part of the nation. One might suppose that these parliaments would have been an important channel of influence as between citizens who had urgent ideas about foreign policy and the government which they needed to impress. In fact, the importance of Tudor parliaments, in this respect, seems to have been negligible: parliaments did serve an important purpose in great diplomatic contests, but not often, perhaps not ever, as the means whereby the government's range of ideas was enriched by its citizens. New ideas reached privy councillors and the monarch by way of informal private suggestion long before they became the subject of parliamentary debate.

I shall hazard a suggestion of two occasions on which parliament enlightened the government. The first occasion was in 1515 when the depth and vigour of parliament's anti-clericalism came as a revelation to Henry VIII and stirred the evolution in his mind of the whole range of ideas which began with an assertion of lay authority over the Catholic clergy of the realm and culminated in an assertion of royal authority to the exclusion of the Pope of Rome.

The second occasion was the speech of Thomas Cromwell to the parliament of 1523. This may have been a very remarkable instance of private initiative in foreign affairs; on the other hand it may not have been a parliamentary occasion at all, for the speech which was drafted may not have been delivered.[1] The speech, at its face value, rejected England's traditional foreign policy of involvement in

[1] See Merriman (b), p. 30.

Europe. Instead of conquering an empire in France while we passively guarded our Scottish frontier—in the manner of Edward III and Henry V—we ought, said Cromwell, to aim primarily at the conquest and annexation of Scotland. Cromwell spoke as follows of difficulties attendant on any attempt to conquer France: 'there never was nation more marvellously lynkyd together than they be amongst themselves'; the Frenchman 'knoweth that in arms our nation is invicible, so knoweth he our impatience to continue in war many years and in especial in winter for we desire nought else but to try it with our hands at once and the marvellous charge ... that we must needs be continually at for victuals and other necessaries is so great that at length we must needs weary ourselves as often as we assemble to fight. I can see nothing but manifest danger on every side to be towards [an English army in France], how they should be victualled, for though we made here never so good diligence to prepare victuals for them in due time, yet stood both we and they in danger of the wind. The harm which we ourselves should sustain in sowldying [i.e. victualling] of so great an army ... were able ere three summers were expired to exhaust and utterly consume all the coin and bullion within this realm.' Turning to the alternative policy, he spoke with optimistic enthusiasm: 'if it would please his [Henry's] maganimous courage to convert first and chief his whole intent and purpose not only to the over-running and subduing of Scotland but also to join the same realm unto his, so that both they and we might live under one Bessaunce [i.e. imperial bounty], Law and Polity for ever. . . . He should thereby wyn the highest honour that ever did any noble progenitors. . . . His strength should be of no small part increased.'

This speech may have been the brilliant vision of a private citizen, acutely experienced by long residence abroad in the possibilities and problems of Europe, sowing in the mind of Henry VIII the idea of a 'Greater Britain' which the king may have attempted in 1540. Unfortunately we do not know whether Henry ever did adopt a policy of 'Greater Britain'; we do not know whether Cromwell ever delivered his speech; we cannot know, supposing that he did deliver it, whether he was making the speech of a private member of parliament or was speaking as the mouthpiece of Cardinal Wolsey, thus

Parliament

playing a minor part in a conflict between king and cardinal, one the champion of a traditional foreign policy, the other favouring a different one. In either case we are bound to marvel at the prophetic accuracy of this speech as we reflect on the actual circumstance in which the old alliance between Scotland and France became, in 1560, the new alliance of Scotland with England, and Admiral Wynter's fleet blockaded Leith against French reinforcements. Almost to the very words uttered by Cromwell in 1523, the French king 'left the said Scots his ancient allies... at this time undefended by reason of our sovereign navy... nor never dare send them succour so long as he shall know the narrow seas substantially to be kept'.

Parliaments, under suitable circumstances, might have had an important positive influence on Tudor foreign policy, but it would appear that they did not exercise any such influence in fact. Even the tense parliamentary opposition to Mary Tudor's marriage with Philip, opposition inspired by fear that England would decline to the status of Milan, had no effect on her decision. The actual influence of the parliament of 1515 and the possible influence of Thomas Cromwell in the parliament of 1523 were rare occasions. Tudor Parliaments were not important as the means of communication by which citizens brought positive ideas to the knowledge of the government. As between the government and parliament, the initiation of foreign policy belonged to the government. Parliament was, of course, vastly important in enabling the government to assess the strength of national feeling. Foreign policy in the early 1520s failed dismally because it out-ran public support; the government had taken insufficient care to use parliament as the sounding board whereby it might assess public feeling. Henry VIII in all the critical diplomacy of the 1530s was very careful to use parliament for this purpose.

Again governments could use parliament, that great assembly of the nations' senior Justices of the Peace, to mobilise the enthusiasm of the great body of local administrators in support of the chosen policy of the government. Every crisis in Elizabeth's relations with Scotland, France and Spain was the proper occasion for a parliament in which the government could rally the political part of the nation to meet the crisis.

Finally, the government could use the clamorous pressures of Parliament in order to justify its actions in the eyes of foreign diplomats. Espcially was this so in 1587, when Elizabeth made a great parade of her abhorrence of the execution of Mary Queen of Scots and directed the attention of diplomats (especially Scottish ones) to the irresistible pressure of parliament.

But such a useful weapon was, as is so often the case with useful weapons, sometimes an embarrassment to the government in the pursuit of its chosen policy, either because parliament was seeking to push the government further than it wished to go, as in the Elizabethan persecution of Roman Catholics and in the defence of England against Mary Stuart's succession to the English throne, or because parliament was seeking to push the Crown in a direction which seemed actively disadvantageous to the Crown, as when the parliament of Mary Tudor's reign consistently and successfully resisted the inclination of Philip and Mary to order the execution of Elizabeth (surely a vital move if Roman Catholicism was to be maintained). Similarly, the parliament of 1559 pressed for protestant religious changes, which Elizabeth and Cecil thought would be fatal to our diplomatic interests at the peace negotiations at Cateau-Cambrésis, because there we depended entirely on Philip for the defence of our interests. Again parliament's frequent demand that Elizabeth should provide, or at least name, her successor was in complete conflict with her policy of securing the friendly behaviour of Scottish rulers by holding out the distant prospect of an English throne as James's ultimate reward for good behaviour. Finally, parliament pressed Elizabeth to accept the sovereignty of the Netherlands long after she had wisely decided that any such responsibility would desperately burden this country.

Parliament was an institution which, usually but not always, enabled Tudor governments to pursue their own foreign policies more efficiently than would have been possible without it. Occasionally it resisted or embarrassed governments as they pursued their chosen policies. Parliament was not, however, the soil in which wholly new policies grew to be an influence in the councils of state. It lacked the generative influence of mercantile groups or of doctrinaire religious minorities.

5 Personal interests, declared and undeclared

Nowadays a member of parliament, of a county council, or of any governing committee, who finds that an item on the agenda impinges on his private business or his private enthusiasms, will 'declare his interest', so that everyone can make allowance for the prejudice which this may cause him to bring to the discussion. We have to ask ourselves whether, in Tudor times, the private and perhaps undeclared ambitions of members of the governing council may have given government foreign policy a novel bias or objective which was contrary to the declared interest of monarch and nation.

For the reign of Henry VII the question hardly arises for the king was such a political giant that his advisers could scarcely contemplate any ambition beyond that of serving his policies. But, during the years of Wolsey's eminence, the question arises so acutely that A. F. Pollard explained the diplomacy of Wolsey chiefly in terms of his ambition to use the resources of England in order to win and retain his power as cardinal and *legate a latere* and then to secure his own election as Pope. This is an explanation which has held the field among historians for fifty years but has been satisfactorily demolished by Professor Scarisbrick. Wolsey's preference (and this was public enough to be known to Henry) was for European peace, in line with the thinking of such international humanists as Erasmus.

Wolsey was, however, faced with a personal dilemma during his last years of power. Henry wanted a nullification of his marriage with Catherine of Aragon and Wolsey had to get this or lose his influence and position. But Anne Boleyn whom Henry would marry was niece of the third Duke of Norfolk, Wolsey's most bitter enemy. A marriage between Anne and Henry could hardly fail to increase the power of Norfolk and reduce that of Wolsey. Consequently Wolsey will have had a powerful motive for moving slowly towards annulment of Henry's first marriage in the hope that time would allow the king to fall out of love with Anne before he was free to marry her. Furthermore, Wolsey had a suitable candidate for Henry's hand in the person of Renée, a daughter of the late Louis XII of France, and this marriage would itself be a natural outcome of the Anglo-French alliance which Wolsey established in 1527 as the necessary and only way of emancipating the Pope from Charles V and securing the marriage annulment. One can then suspect Wolsey of adopting delaying tactics in order to preserve his own supreme power within the government; Anne Boleyn and Henry probably did suspect Wolsey of just this sort of deceitful purpose. Yet, when one comes to scrutinise the events of 1526 to 1529, one can acquit Wolsey of any such evasion.[1]

Thomas More, who followed Wolsey as Chancellor, had a sectional interst, but he declared it very plainly when he was invited to become Lord Chancellor and Henry VIII agreed not to 'molest his conscience'. In effect, Thomas More was a follower of Erasmus, a religious humanist who saw the prosperity of Europe and the fulfilment of human nature in an international catholicism, reformed in the light of contemporary criticism and classical scholarship, guided by the Pope and giving peace to Europe. Three ideas were central to his vision: that the ultimate guide and co-ordinator would be the Pope, that the ultimate community would be international, and that the driving force would be human intellect, emancipated and active to interpret the Christian revelation. But the real Pope Clement of 1530 was a strictly national potentate whose decisions were dictated by the diplomatic needs of a particular state in central Italy, and the papacy was soon to repudiate the emancipation of active thinking by putting on the Index the books of Erasmus (and by implication the beliefs of More). In face of papal nationalism and the counter-reformation, More's policy towards the papacy

[1] See Chapter 10.

Personal interests, declared and undeclared

was bankrupt; had More survived he would have shared with Cardinal Reginald Pole the full hostility of the papacy; religious humanism had to find such future as it was to enjoy within the context of nation-states (within, for example, the Church of the England of Elizabeth, Burghley, Jewel and Hooker). More's vision of policy was exasperating because it combined such high-minded purpose with complete indifference to the developing facts of his day.

As for Thomas Cromwell, one is bound, in the light of all that Professor A. G. Dickens has said in *English Reformation*, to believe that he was a deep and genuine Protestant, anxious to promote protestant habits in his own country even to the extent of investing his private money in order to circulate the best possible translation of the Bible, and anxious also to promote diplomatic alliance with the protestant princes of Germany. In a sense this was an interest which Cromwell was careful to keep undeclared for he knew very well that Henry's religious beliefs were catholic and conservative. But, if Cromwell's private hopes for England were not openly declared, they were sufficiently evident for Henry to be aware of them, to exaggerate them grossly when the time came to execute his faithful servant, and to guard against their influence on England's diplomacy whenever he wished.

Edward Seymour, Duke of Somerset and Protector from February 1547, also had a deep interest in the spread of protestantism. Luckily, perhaps, there was no monarch to inhibit his zeal, because the wagon-loads of Bibles which his invading army distributed in Scotland in 1547 did something towards the conversion of Scotsmen to protestantism; this in turn did much more than the battle of Pinkie to bring them to an ultimate belief that England was a better ally than France.

Unfortunately there was likewise no monarch to protect the nation's diplomacy from the private interests of John Dudley, Duke of Northumberland and dominant personality in the Privy Council from October 1549 until July 1553. This able member of an upstart family had, like Charles II a century later, a keen notion of the diplomatic interests of this country and did in some ways promote those interests, but he was governed by a corrupt greed to enrich himself and his political associates, to retain the utmost political power for himself, and ultimately to promote his son and daughter-in-law to the throne of England to the exclusion of Mary Tudor. The corruption of his government divided the country and therefore weakened the government in all negotiations. The plan to exclude Mary Tudor from the succession ended all possibility of friendship with the Hapsburgs—of playing off the friendship of France and of Spain against each other. Consequently, he accepted a peace treaty with France, 'the most ignominious treaty signed by England during the century'.[1] He gave his help to the general growth of French power in the 1550s, with the minor consequence that England lost Calais, and the major consequence that French garrisons were established in Scotland and would have been infinitely prejudicial to England's interests, but for the breakdown of French power in the Huguenot wars.

Sir William Paget was, in these middle years of the century, an interesting individualist among privy councillors. An intense nationalist, he could (like de Gaulle) appreciate the nationalism of others. 'Let the Scots be Scots' was his slogan in 1547, but it had no effect on public policy. Under Mary Tudor, his nationalism caused him to favour an alliance with Spain which should be an alliance as between equals and should exclude all subservience to Spain and to Rome. Again, the opinions of this interesting *politique* had no influence on policy, but he did contribute to the rejection of Spanish demands for the execution of Princess Elizabeth by emphasising the effect of such an action on national feeling. He almost managed to baulk Mary Tudor's desire to fight France in the Spanish interest in January 1557.

The intense ambition of Northumberland, but not his ability, dominated the politics of his third son, Robert Dudley, from 1564 Earl of Leicester. Many well-informed men, including William Cecil, expected that Dudley's desire to marry Queen Elizabeth would induce him to kill his wife, Amy Robsart; in September 1560 she did break her neck when she fell down stairs. Robert Dudley was strong in his support of Roman Catholics in the early years of the reign, hoping at one time to marry Mary Queen of Scots, at another (1569) urging the Duke of Norfolk to the same

[1] Pollard (a), p. 499.

course; in the later years, he was as ardent as Walsingham to promote 'the spiritual fruit' of protestantism. Always he was an advocate of energetic military action, in 1562 and 1567 in aid of the Huguenots and for the recovery of Calais, in 1571 and thereafter on behalf of the Dutch. In spite of his personal dominance over the heart of the Queen, in spite of his energy, ambition and arrogance, he was always, except once, kept under the firm control of the Queen and her Council, who used his undoubted panache to rouse the valour of her subjects to fight in the Netherlands or, if the need had arisen, against a Spanish landing in 1588.

The single occasion on which he kicked over the traces and went some way to diverting foreign policy from the line chosen by the queen was when, in January 1586, he accepted from the states-general of the northern provinces of the Netherlands the office of governor-general, an office which belonged to the King of Spain's deputy in the Netherlands. If Elizabeth's representative could claim to be a species of viceroy in the Netherlands, then he was asserting that Elizabeth was sovereign there. This was a position which she repeatedly rejected in her dealings with the Dutch and in her dealings with Spain. Leicester's independent action embarrassed Elizabeth, but she did not allow her policy to be diverted.

One may fairly say that Leicester proved to be an unsatisfactory commander in the Netherlands, but, for all his influence and cynical private ambition, he never managed to divert foreign policy to serve his private purposes. The same can be said of Robert Devereux, second Earl of Essex, another man of overwhelming ambition, but one whose ambition and whose hunger for military glory were so warmly and so frankly proclaimed as to be almost lovable. A brief offensive he could direct brilliantly. In the 1590s he organised and paid for his own channels of diplomatic intelligence, but, though the queen was old by this time, Essex never managed to deflect her policy and give it a bias of his own choosing. When he failed to carry out her policy in Ireland but returned to London at his own decision (September 1599), he found that he had returned to disgrace; when he reacted treasonously to this disgrace his brilliance did not save him from execution.

An honourable councillor like Sir Francis Walsingham, who

at all times proclaimed his private enthusiasm for the protestant religion in whatever country it might be—such a man presented no problem for Elizabeth. His interest was declared, his advice would be heard, his administration in the queen's interest would be impeccable.

Many Tudor councillors, including some whose interests have already been considered, had an undeclared class interest because they belonged to the duelling aristocracy, in contrast to councillors like Thomas Wolsey, William Cecil and Nicholas Bacon whose training was literary and legal. This duelling aristocracy 'was coming to share, both for profit and intellectual delight, the educational norms of the progressive bourgeoisie and sought means for differentiating its status from theirs.... it needed firm central government . . . but had not yet been emotionally integrated into it'.[1] These men found a means of differentiation partly in the law of honour and the duel 'that existed for the man who saw himself as exceptional'[2] and also in active warfare in which they could outshine their despised colleagues, the mere desk-borne councillors. This strongly-developed personal impulse towards military honour was an ever-present factor in Tudor councils. Thus the council of Mary Tudor resisted, on the best possible grounds, her demand for a declaration of war against France, but (says R. B. Wernham): 'The French attack upon Douai and the resulting declaration of war between Spain and France in January 1557, did a little to weaken the resolution of the more soldierly knights and nobles of Paget's faction, who began to scent opportunities for personal gain and glory.'

We have asked whether the private ambitions of Tudor statesmen were the directing force behind any important lines of Tudor foreign policy and we find that the answer is that such private ambitions were not influential, simply because Tudor monarchs were sufficiently active to keep policy under their own vigilant control. All Tudor monarchs, except Edward VI, controlled their ministers as Henry VIII once claimed that he controlled Stephen Gardiner: 'Marry, I myself could use him and rule him to all manner of pur-

[1] Hale.
[2] Hale.

Personal interests, declared and undeclared

poses, as seemed good to me.' Northumberland was the exceptional minister over whom no monarch exerted direction. Wolsey, in the years of Henry's indolence, might have been a second exception, but was not.

* * *

A government's foreign policy may derive impetus from sources which are external to the collective will of the government itself. These last four chapters have surveyed such external sources. We conclude that the private enthusiasms or selfish interests of members of the government were not an important influence, that parliament as an assembled institution was not important, and that the large anonymous multitude was not important either. On the other hand, men of exceptional learning, or exceptional religious enthusiasm, could occasionally give a new impetus to foreign policy and so also could the writings of academic geographers, but most important of all was the influence of the new generation of ocean-going traders. Yet when one has given all possible regard to the importance of these external sources of impetus, it becomes evident that foreign policy was pre-eminently a matter for the government itself, for the inner circle of ruling councillors and above all for the monarch.

In foreign policy as in all other aspects of Tudor government and life, those institutions which ostensibly performed particular functions in the life of the nation are found, upon enquiry, to be actually performing those functions. This is perhaps the very definition of a healthy society—and such was the health of Tudor England. By contrast, during the middle years of the fifteenth century, England's official institutions of government had given only an empty performance of an empty ritual: parliaments had met and cases had been tried in courts of law, but these had, in the fifteenth century, been empty proceedings; the real decisions were made, irresponsibly, elsewhere according to a system which has become known, aptly indeed, as 'bastard feudalism'. Tudor foreign policy, like all Tudor government, was rooted in the national background, and that background we have considered, but enterprise and decision belonged to the monarch and his central advisers (apart from the few exceptions which have been mentioned). It is the enterprise of these men that we must consider now.

PART IIA
Dynasty and Realm—
Security and Role

6 Henry VII: Dynastic defence—in danger from Burgundy and Ireland

In the ninety years, 1399 to 1489, England suffered five changes of dynasty; each change involved warfare—the military defeat and dispossession of the reigning monarch. Henry VII's personal wish to give permanence to his dynasty was in line with the first need of the people of England. After too much royal instability and too little public order, they needed a secure dynasty, energetically imposing the king's peace as the first condition of material prosperity and of progress in 'godly living' and 'new learning'. The civil wars in England were fought, in the first instance, between rival English families. But by 1470 the Lancastrians came to be associated with France and the Yorkists with Burgundy; hence one may fairly ask whether the wars in England did not become an epiphenomenon or reflection of the more important struggle of French against Burgundian. Burgundy was at its most extensive in 1468, at which time Charles the Bold married Margaret of York and became brother-in-law of the Yorkist King of England. Thereafter, the Yorkists were likely to keep the English crown, so long as the Burgundians continued to prosper. If Charles the Bold had won three solid victories in 1476 and 1477, the French monarch would have been too desperately engaged to support Henry Tudor, Duke of Richmond.

The Lancastrians had linked their fortunes with a branch of the French royal house when Henry VI married Margaret of Anjou in 1445; in the event, it was the French monarchy of Louis XI which outmanoeuvred Charles the Bold of Burgundy. The beginning of Louis' offensive against Burgundy was associated with the suc-

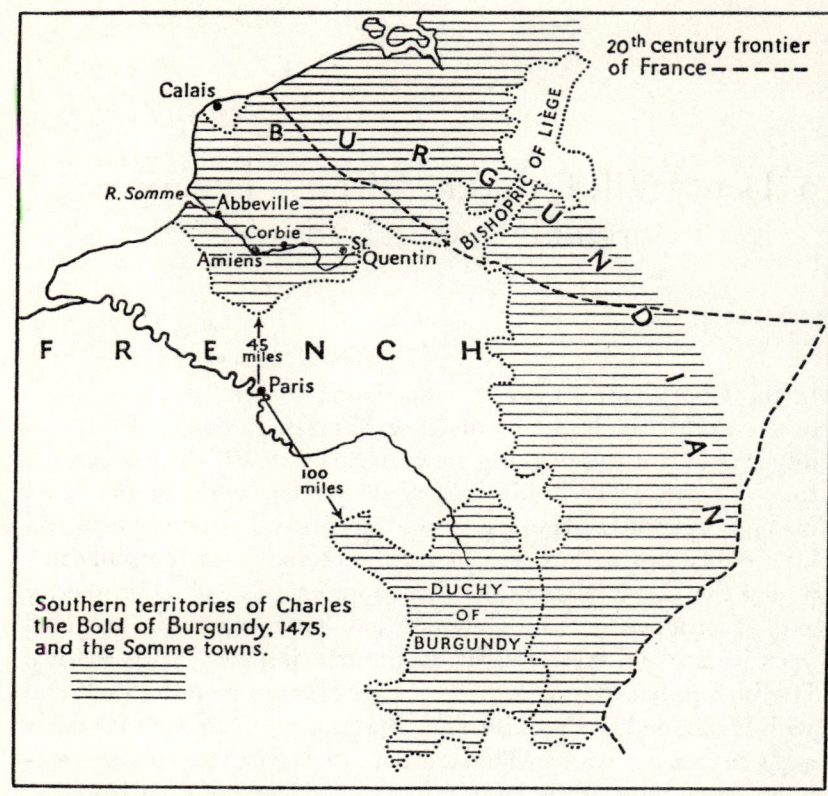

Map. 3. Burgundy in 1475. The southern territories of Charles the Bold, and the Somme towns

cessful Lancastrian rising of 1470 which Louis helped to promote. By the rising, Edward IV was deposed for two years. But this success was premature and the Yorkist Edward IV, who had taken refuge with his sister Margaret in Brussels, was re-equipped and shipped back to England, to recover his throne by the battles of Barnet and Tewkesbury. Charles of Burgundy then planned a great Anglo-Burgundian offensive against France. But Louis bought off Edward at the treaty of Picquigny (1475) for an immediate payment of 75,000 crowns with a pension of 75,000 a year and some commercial concessions. Edward may have been shrewd

Dynastic defence—in danger from Burgundy and Ireland

to accept these terms for the immediate interest of England, but the treaty contributed to the rapid decline of Burgundy. When Edward's dynasty reached its next phase of weakness (1485) and again needed Burgundian help, no such help was to be had. For Charles the Bold was defeated and killed by the Swiss at Nancy (1477); Louis XI gained Picardy and the Somme towns after all, together with the duchy of Burgundy. Thereafter Louis' successor, the regent Anne of Beaujeu, financed the 1485 campaign of Henry Tudor because it was a natural episode in the continuing struggle of France with Burgundy; the Yorkist dowager-duchess, Margaret

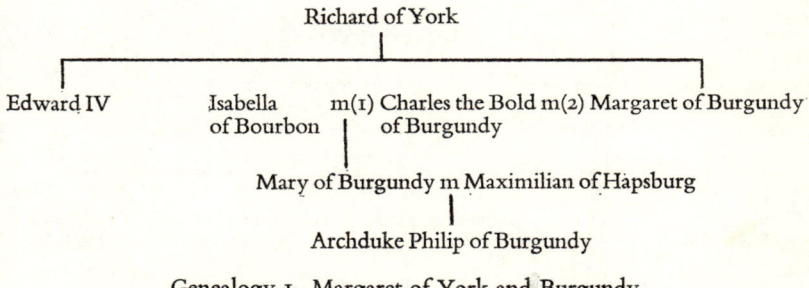

Genealogy 1. Margaret of York and Burgundy

of Burgundy, was as influential against France in the Netherlands as was her step-son-in-law, Maximilian, regent on behalf of Archduke Philip. Thus, the house of York in the person of Richard III ceased to reign after the battle of Bosworth (1485) and Henry Tudor became King of England as a client of France.

The steady success of France over Burgundy, and the apparent permanence of this success, could imply (and perhaps in the last analysis did imply) the permanence of Henry's dynasty on the English throne: if the Burgundian client had defeated and deposed Henry at Stoke (1487), the French would hardly have let the matter rest at that. Yet, in 1485, the Burgundians still possessed the will to fight for the expansion of their 'middle kingdom'; French success of the 1470s, although apparently permanent, had still to be made really so by French arms and diplomacy. Similarly the apparent security of Henry's dynasty had to be confirmed against final Yorkist attacks which might yet win success with the energy of desperation. Henry's defence of his dynasty was largely a matter of domestic politics. But just as the dynastic struggle had been for two decades the concern of other countries, so foreign policy was bound to be important to his success at home. Indeed the first aim of Henry Tudor's foreign policy was to maintain his dynasty on the English throne and thereby to serve the public interest in the best possible way.

The incident of Lambert Simnel emphasised the need to have a foreign policy which would anticipate the machinations of foreign rulers. This negligible imposter, posing as Edward, Earl of Warwick, and announcing himself to the world as 'Edward VI', enjoyed

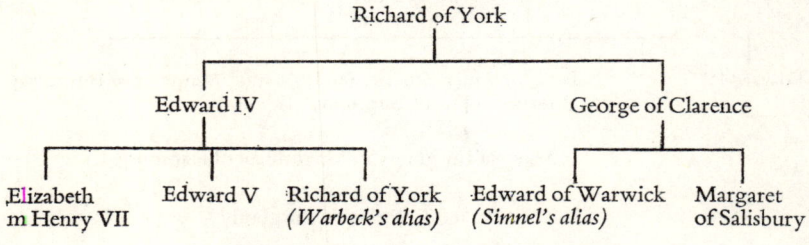

Genealogy 2. Pretensions of the pretenders

the support of Margaret of Burgundy and of Anglo-Irish chieftains (1486). The greatest of these was Gerald, eighth Earl of Kildare, and a direct descendant of Fitzgerald, chief collaborator with Strongbow in the reign of Henry II. This Kildare, a staunch and romantic Yorkist, had been appointed deputy-lieutenant of Ireland by that dynasty and had been accepted as irreplaceable by Henry VII. Kildare recognised Simnel as his sovereign and had him crowned King Edward VI in Dublin (1487). Thus supported, Simnel was able to land in Lancashire and hold Henry to a three-hour battle at Stoke (June 1487).

In November 1491, Henry VII was again in trouble, for Margaret of Burgundy and her step-son-in-law, the Archduke Maximilian (Emperor in 1493), were supporting Perkin Warbeck as 'Richard, Duke of York, second son of Edward IV'. The French with their old Scottish allies were also supporting Perkin, as a temporary embarrassment to Henry while they occupied and annexed Brittany.

Dynastic defence—in danger from Burgundy and Ireland

But the threat of this second pretender provoked Henry to take preventive action in Ireland rather than wait passively until the invader crossed to England.

Henry VII, like his predecessors since 1200, had the title of 'Lord of Ireland', but this lordship had become so indirect as to be negligible. Ireland was an association of warring clans which differed from each other only in that some still lived, and had always lived, under Gaelic chieftains and Gaelic traditions, whereas a few great clans in the south had been Norman feudal lordships since Strongbow's invasion in the twelfth century. But feudal tradition had disappeared in face of Gaelic infiltration which had been hastened by intermarriage between Norman and Gaelic families. Consequently, by 1485, the Anglo-Irish Fitzgeralds of Kildare, Butlers of Ormond, and Fitzgeralds of Desmond differed little from their

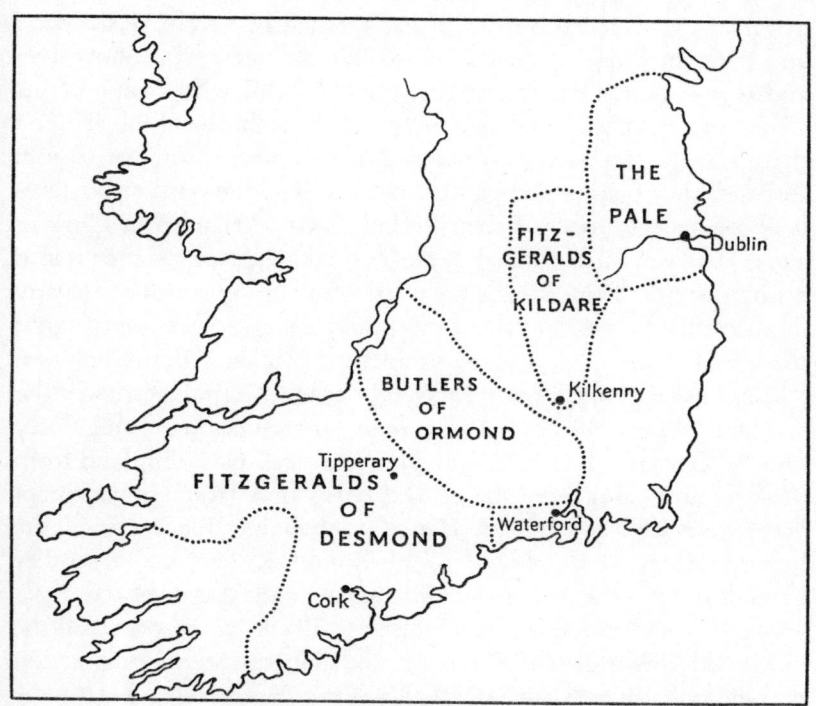

Map 4. Anglo-Irish clans: their areas of influence and intrigue

Gaelic neighbours; between themselves they differed only in that the Butlers supported the house of Lancaster in the Wars of the Roses (rather as the Campbells of Argyll later supported the Hanoverians against Bonnie Prince Charlie and the general consensus of Highland loyalty). Separate from the clans were the towns of Cork, Waterford and Dublin whose burgesses tried to preserve their liberties and their defensive walls against the intrusive blackmail of neighbouring chieftains. The authority of the English king, wielded by his 'Lieutenant' in Dublin, had once been effective over an area twenty miles wide and fifty miles long and known as the Pale. But since Kildare had himself been deputy-lieutenant for many years, England's authority was, by 1491, as dead in the Pale as it was elsewhere.

This was a situation which Henry had been in no hurry to remedy. In the absence of internal communications, the cost of trying to govern Ireland was too great. It had seemed best to leave the clans and their chieftains to themselves to live out their hard, short lives and to fight out their internecine quarrels. But when some of the clans, out of quixotic loyalty or romantic ambition, took it upon themselves to support a claimant to the English throne or to join forces with a continental power, then active intervention by England seemed necessary. When Perkin Warbeck landed at Cork in 1491, Henry at once decided to reoccupy the Pale and to turn it into a military base from which a punitive force might move into any disaffected area. He continued this policy for five years, until 1496; then, in face of more urgent problems elsewhere, the policy was allowed to lapse until it was revived in 1534, this time permanently.

Thus, in 1491, Henry sent an army of two hundred and thirty men to Dublin. They were suitably reinforced from England from time to time, and were the central corps of a larger government force, recruited and led on Henry's behalf by 'Black James' the bastard leader of the house of Ormond.[1] Kildare on the other hand lost his office of deputy-lieutenant and was replaced by a series of loyal but ineffective Dubliners. 'Black James' occupied the Fitzgerald townships of Kilkenny and Tipperary and this action was enough to turn the situation against Perkin who fled to the

---

[1] See Conway, pp. 49–51.

protection of the French king. But in the peace treaty of Etaples (1492), the French king Charles VIII agreed to expel all English rebels, so that Perkin was kept diplomatically on the run and fled back to Margaret in Brussels.

Meanwhile, Henry brought sanctions to bear on Margaret by requiring English Merchant Adventurers to sell nothing in the Netherlands but only in the English market of Calais. This restricted the Netherlanders' supply of semi-finished English cloth, a raw material of their textile industries, and forced them to buy it in Calais subject to English dues and regulations. But the sanctions did not cripple Perkin's prospects. There was every chance that he would return to Ireland in the summer of 1494, financed by Margaret and encouraged by loyal promises from the Desmond Fitzgeralds.

At this point, Henry sent over to Ireland one of his most energetic advisers, Edward Poynings, with an English army which was kept reinforced to a strength of about six hundred men. The new deputy-lieutenant was very different from the inefficient Dubliners. Poynings attacked Warbeck's supporters and pursued them into Ulster (November 1494). Kildare was himself captured and sent to London for complicity in Warbeck plots. Thus Poynings demonstrated that England's military power could be maintained in the Pale and might thence move as a punitive force to any part of Ireland. The chieftains of Ireland accepted the moral: Warbeck's expedition of July 1495, which had lost two hundred men to the militiamen of Kent when it put into Deal, was driven away from Waterford and barely escaped to his other ally, James IV of Scotland.

Kildare in London, shrewd and forceful, convinced Henry that he fully understood the fact of English power and that he accepted its consequences. Henry, for his part, needed every soldier on his northern border to face the menace which now threatened from Scotland; he was also annoyed that Poynings had not financed Irish operations out of Irish taxes. The deputy-lieutenant and his men were therefore recalled. Kildare, chastened and wiser, was restored as deputy-lieutenant to control Ireland with his own forces but in the Tudor interest (January 1496).

Meanwhile, trade sanctions were having their effect in the Netherlands and French victories once more came to the help of the Lancastrians, for Maximilian was so impressed by French progress in Italy that he ceased to relish a quarrel with England; he therefore prevailed on his mother-in-law to come to terms with Henry whereby trade was renewed and all rebels against either government were deported (February 1496). (As part of the price of this treaty, Henry joined the Holy Alliance against France, but without committing himself to war and on terms that showed how fully he realised that his dynasty owed its security to French policy.) In these ways Henry has almost isolated Perkin. But for another eighteen months Henry still failed to detach James IV from the pretender although his efforts were supported, as one would expect, by the French. Unsuccessfully, he offered James a bribe for the surrender of Perkin and England suffered two raids across the Scottish border in support of the pretender (1496 and 1497). But in July 1497 James finally got rid of this client who had become an embarrassment; James made his peace with Henry in the truce of Ayton (September 1497). So Perkin left Scotland with a forlorn following of about seventy men. He gained no reinforcements when he called at Cork, and he landed in Cornwall (September 1497), hoping that this county, which had recently rebelled against Henry, would support a rival claimant to the throne. Recruits did not join him as he advanced to Taunton; he deserted his followers, fled to sanctuary and soon afterwards surrendered to Henry.

Henry's position as King of England was not again threatened, but to secure his personal tenure was not to secure the succession for his dynasty. If England was to remain orderly and strong, a secure and peaceful succession was as important as this single strong king. Security of succession was of great personal interest to Henry, for the day of Henry's death would be the day of opportunity for Yorkist claimants and for the European governments that backed them; Henry's diplomacy was concerned to secure his dynasty against that moment of weakness. He needed to destroy or isolate possible rivals, and to link his heir with a foreign family which would be interested in maintaining the succession, would be militarily strong enough to do so, but would also be sufficiently remote from England to allow England and her new king to remain autonomous. Henry chose the monarchs, Ferdinand and Isabella, of Aragon and Castile to champion and defend the rights of his son and heir; Thomas Savage, Henry's private chaplain and later the Archbishop of York, began to work for the necessary marriage alliance during the trade negotiations at Medina del Campo in 1489, when Prince Arthur, the English heir apparent, was three years old. From that date, Henry slowly created a pattern of circumstances which gave security to Arthur's succession. His negotiations on behalf of Prince Arthur produced a final treaty in 1496 for a marriage in 1500 between Arthur and Catherine, daughter of Ferdinand and Isabella. Prince and princess were betrothed in August 1497. Two years later, Henry executed Edward, Earl of Warwick, senior Yorkist claimant to the throne and son of the Duke of Clarence; this was to reassure Ferdinand that no serious Yorkist rival to Prince Arthur was likely to appear. Arthur and Catherine were married by proxy in 1499, and again in 1500. Finally, in October 1501, Catherine with her dowry reached England for the marriage in November. But the pattern of security was shattered by the boy's death in 1502 at the age of sixteen. The Tudor succession was again frail and precarious, a fact well illustrated by the conversation reported to have taken place among officers of the English garrison in Calais in 1507: 'Some of them spake of my Lord of Buckingham, saying that he was a noble man and would be a royal ruler. Others there were that spake in likewise of your traitor Edmund de la Pole, but none of them spake of my lord the prince'.[1]

After the death of Arthur, Henry was rightly anxious to provide security of succession for Prince Henry his new heir. He tried to transfer to Prince Henry the security which a marriage alliance with Spain might be expected to give. The betrothal of Prince Henry and Catherine was agreed and took place in June 1503; a year later the Pope's dispensation was received to permit this marriage between a widow and her brother-in-law, in spite of canon law to the contrary. (Canon law required one sort of dispensation to permit a second marriage if the first had been consummated, but a different sort of dispensation if the first had not been

[1] Quoted in Elton (a), p. 5.

consummated. In this case, the dispensation was worded to accommodate Spanish diplomatic statements that the first marriage had been consummated. But, to the confusion of future diplomacy, Catherine herself maintained that her first marriage had never been consummated. This was to bring in question the relevance of the dispensation of 1504.)

The marriage plans of Prince Henry and Catherine were thus settled in 1502 and 1504. The speed with which the arrangements were made expressed Henry's anxiety for the succession. He had always been alert to respond aggressively to the least suggestion of a rival successor. Particularly after the death of Arthur in April 1502, he was ready to act on any suspicion, or none; he did in fact arrest Lord William Courtenay and William de la Pole in May 1502. His reaction was similar when Edmund de la Pole, Earl of Suffolk and nephew of Edward IV, arrived in the Netherlands in 1504, a fugitive from Maximilian's court. Henry immediately ordered the

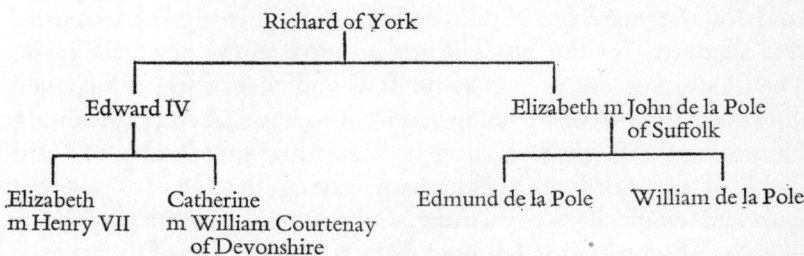

Genealogy 3. Courtenay and de la Pole, families with regal aspirations in 1502

Merchant Adventurers away from Antwerp to trade only through Calais (January 1505). Thus, he imposed trade sanctions on Archduke Philip's Netherlands to show that not the least favour to a Yorkist claimant was to be tolerated. When Philip captured Edmund in 1505, Henry swung from hostility to effusive friendship. Nevertheless, he was finally satisfied only when Philip surrendered Edmund to him in February 1506. Henry was able to extort this condescension because Philip and Joanna were forced into Weymouth harbour by bad weather (January 1506). They became Henry's unwilling guests. The surrender of Edmund (which was

Dynastic defence—in danger from Burgundy and Ireland

subject to Henry's promise not to take the man's life) was an important clause in the general treaty negotiated at that time and known since as the Malus Intercursus.

Besides these anxieties, the central plan of a marriage between Prince Henry and Catherine was storm-tossed and shaken in the following four years by the death of Isabella of Castile (November 1504). This destroyed the unity of Ferdinand's Aragon with Isabella's Castile and rendered Ferdinand too weak to fulfil his appointed role of protector of the Tudor succession. Castile, and most of the power which had been wielded by Ferdinand, was apparently to be inherited by Isabella's heir, Joanna, and to be wielded by her husband Archduke Philip of the Netherlands. Prince Henry was therefore prompted by his father to make a protest of conscience against the Pope's dispensation and to disown his marriage contract with Catherine (June 1505). Eleanor, daughter of Archduke Philip, was sought as Henry's fiancée in place of Catherine. Thus Spanish power (wielded as seemed likely by Archduke Philip) was still to be the guarantee of Prince Henry's succession.

In one sense there had been no change of policy, but merely an adjustment to the circumstances that Philip of the Netherlands was likely to become the effective ruler of Castile. In another sense there was revealed in this proposal a revolution in policy, for Philip the Burgundian was about to be trusted to maintain the Lancastrian dynasty. The Burgundian association with Yorkists was deemed to belong to a dead past, and correctly so, for by 1505 the power of France had reached such proportions that Burgundy must accept allies where she could find them and not indulge in the luxury of patronising forlorn rebels on the strength of past policy or family connection.

However, family circumstances in fact shifted again to restore Ferdinand to a position of central influence; not least of these circumstances was the death of Philip (September 1506) and the aggravation of Joanna's mental instability by his death. The project of marriage between Prince Henry and Catherine had sufficiently survived three years of Ferdinand's weakness for it to be brought forward again. (It also survived the diplomatic cross-currents generated by Henry VII's second foreign policy, described in chapter 7.) The marriage project was fully revived in 1508, so that when Henry VII himself died, Ferdinand immediately offered military aid to secure the succession of Henry VIII (April 1509). In the June following, the new king and his Catherine were married.

Henry VII had thus followed to a successful conclusion the two lines of his dynastic foreign policy: to preserve his own hold on the throne and to secure the undisputed succession of his heir apparent.

7 Henry VII: Defence of the realm—in awe of France and Scotland

The security of the Tudor dynasty was important to the prosperity, order and security of the English people. But even with a stable government, there remained the age-old threat, the straightforward aggressiveness of any strong community towards a weak neighbour. The impulse to conquer one's neighbours was constant in Europe at least from the beginning of the Iron-age, as is evident from Iron-age forts and other relics of warfare. In mediaeval Europe, and also in Tudor times, this impulse found sanction in the idea of 'Empire'. This was the belief that, in God's good time, the spiritual Christendom to which all men belonged would be brought together as a single political reality. Any monarch, brooding over his circumstances, might detect a combination of advantages which seemed to mark him out as God's chosen instrument for this glorious purpose of dominating and unifying all Christendom. Let him therefore act with faith and vigour in order to discover whether he was indeed destined to become 'lord and owner . . . of all Christendom'. Against his campaigns of conquest, neighbouring peoples would of course defend themselves at least as instinctively as he attacked.

Henry VII, ruling in a world of aggressive rulers, was alert to create strategic and diplomatic conditions in which he would be able to defend his people and his area of jurisdiction against foreign conquest. His difficulty was that France, to which he owed his throne, was becoming the most powerful menace in north-west Europe to the independence of other peoples. His ally in foreign policy as it related to dynastic security was more and more likely to become the mortal enemy of English independence, that is to launch upon a conquest of England in the fullness of time.

The threat from France dated from 1453, when English garrisons withdrew from all positions on the north coast of France, except Calais. England was once more as weak as in the invasion years of 1066 and 1216. After 1453 Frenchmen controlled ports from which expeditions could sail against England: Cherbourg, Harfleur, Fécamp and Dieppe, to which they added Boulogne, acquired in 1482, and Le Havre, built in 1516. In 1485 England's fighting merchant ships would not have provided sufficient defence. Defence was in any case difficult against the head-winds which would bring over the invaders. England's control of Calais was indeed an important reassurance to Henry VII, for without Calais, France had no port on the east of the Straits of Dover; she could not easily bring a seaborne force to bear down on London. But since France had

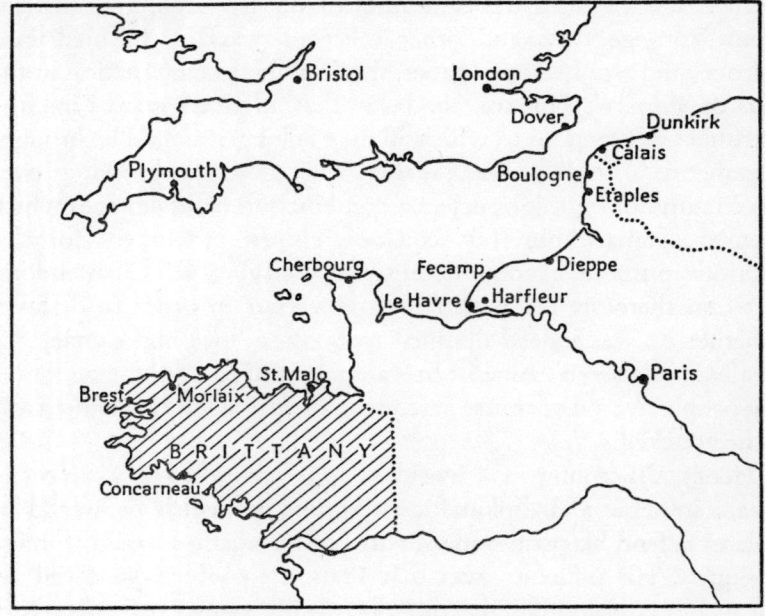

Map 5. The French Channel ports, bases for the invasion of England in 1490, 1545 and 1588 to 1604

conquered Picardy from Burgundy (1482), there was no longer a Burgundian buffer against French attacks on Calais. Henry saw to it that his biggest force of permanent, whole-time soldiers was the English garrison of Calais.

Next to Calais and ports further to the eastward, the most menacing bases for an invasion of England were the ports of Brittany 'a Duchy . . . situate so opportunely to annoy England either for coast or trade'.[1] In 1485 Brittany was an independent territory with minor feudal obligations to the French crown; it was not necessarily available for a French invasion of England. In 1487, Anne of Beaujeu, regent for Charles VIII of France, moved a French army into Brittany; Lord Scales with volunteers from England joined a force from the Netherlands to help in the defence of the province (although Henry denied knowledge of their intention). But a French victory in July 1488 gave France her foothold in the province and a position from which to demand a marriage for the French king Charles VIII with Anne, the heiress of Brittany and immediately afterwards its duchess.

Henry knew that a French annexation of Brittany was a threat to English security and that he ought to prevent it. He saw also that he lacked the power to prevent it. He therefore went through the motions of preparing for large-scale military expeditions against France. This was to convince his subjects of his firmness of purpose. But he wanted also to convince Charles VIII (ruler in his own right from 1492) that although England could be a serious obstacle to French ambitions on her northern frontiers (for example towards Brittany and Flanders), yet she was essentially a friend who would welcome French ambitions in any other direction (for example towards Italy). Henry demonstrated his firmness of purpose by negotiating an alliance with Spain (1489), by asking parliament for £100,000 (1499) and by sending 6,000 men to Brittany who occupied Morlaix and Concarneau. When the French nevertheless occupied more and more areas, and Anne actually married Charles VIII (December 1491), Henry claimed the French crown, took an army to France and began a siege of Boulogne (October 1492). But Henry demonstrated his reluctance to provoke the French, for

[1] Francis Bacon, quoted in Wernham (a), p. 34.

he maintained continuous negotiations with the French government and he despatched his expeditions on a smaller scale than he could have managed. In effect, he conveyed to the French that he would accept their acquisition of Brittany in exchange for a redirection of their aggression to the south-east, and, as this harmonised with the ambitions of Charles VIII, the treaty of Etaples became possible (November 1492). Henry accepted what he could not prevent in Brittany and received compensation of £5,000 a year. In 1494 Charles VIII set out on his great invasion of Italy. French preoccupation with Italy became England's chief security from French invasion. For fifty years French energies and ambitions were expended in southern Europe; consequently, the Netherlands and England were not menaced by France for two generations.

But this was an outcome on which Henry could never rely. France might at any time turn her ambitions towards the Rhine and the north-east. Henry's policy was to discourage such a move, but always to prepare against it. He aimed to secure England against an ultimate French invasion by building up sufficient sea-power and by associating England with allies who could strike across French frontiers. He tried also to deprive France of her 'auld alliance' with Scotland, a policy which involved some early steps towards the consolidation of the British Isles into a single political entity. He developed sea-power by building 'large heavily-armed warships of which the *Regent* and the *Sovereign* of 1487–88 seem to have been the first'.[1] In principle these ships were designed, as of old, to fight by boarding the enemy, yet fire-power was now important also; the *Regent* and *Sovereign* both relied on improved artillery. He also built the dock at Portsmouth, so that a fighting fleet in the Channel could be replenished and repaired without having to return to the Thames. He collected ships' stores and naval armaments at Woolwich and Greenwich so that merchant ships could quickly be equipped for fighting. Naval security was an important motive of his many actions to enlarge the English merchant fleet by the Navigation Acts in respect of Gascon wine (1485) and Toulouse woad (1487), of his struggle with the Hanseatic League and Venice to win rights of access for English ships in the Baltic and the Medi-

[1] Davies, p. 268.

terranean, of his trade treaties with Spain and the Netherlands, and of his patronage of John Cabot, of Sebastian and of other adventurers into the Atlantic. His son, Henry VIII, from the very beginning of his reign, had sufficient naval power to dominate the Channel; this was the strength created and bequeathed by Henry VII. He had brought into being the policy, which has continued for 450 years, of making the most of our 'moat' and defending it.

The re-insurance policy of building an alliance with the neighbours of France was an important aspect of the treaty of Medina del Campo with Spain (March 1489) and of all negotiations with Maximilian, regent of the Netherlands. This policy was launched

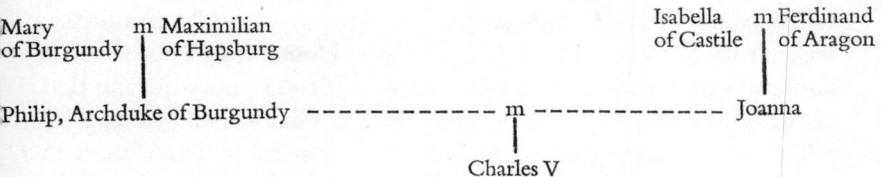

Genealogy 4. The claim of Joanna to Castile on the death of her mother

as soon as France began to threaten Brittany; it lasted, with a number of important interruptions, until the French ruling family, the Bourbons, inherited the throne of Spain in 1700. The policy was, of course, a powerful motive force in Henry's negotiations for a marriage between his heir and Catherine. The policy derived additional strength when Henry's two allies, each impinging on an opposite French frontier, themselves allied in the great marriage of Archduke Philip of the Netherlands with Joanna of Castile (1496). The policy was not put to strain by the death of Prince Arthur, but it was strained by the development of animosity between Ferdinand of Aragon and his son-in-law the Archduke Philip, who began to aspire to the inheritance of Castile on behalf of his wife Joanna. Louis XII exploited this family conflict to negotiate a treaty (1503) for the marriage of his daughter, Claude, to the Charles who was to be heir of Philip as Charles V. When Isabella of Castile died (November 1504), Philip pressed Joanna's claim to Castile and his breach with Ferdinand was complete. Henry judged that his re-insurance policy against France still required the combined stength of Castile and the Netherlands. He therefore shifted away for an alliance with Ferdinand to an alliance with the Archduke Philip, and he abetted Philip's project of an immediate expedition to Castile with enormous loans, £140,000 in all (1505). (This was the cross-current, mentioned in chapter 6, which brought a temporary repudiation of any intention that Prince Henry should marry Catherine of Aragon.)

Philip was proclaimed as regent of Castile (1505) but, in September 1506, he died and Castile reverted to the rule of Ferdinand of Aragon. The Netherlands reverted to the regency of the Emperor Maximilian, acting for his grandson, Charles V. Spain and the Netherlands, which were the two components of Henry's re-insuring alliance, were at loggerheads. In panic or despair, Henry VII proposed that he should marry the insane and widowed Joanna of Castile and that his daughter Mary should be betrothed to Charles V. But English policy was rescued from confusion (as in 1492 and as so often in later years) by the dominant ambition of most European monarchs which was to conquer, plunder and divide Italy. Ferdinand found a basis for reconciliation with the Emperor Maximilian (and indeed with Louis XII of France) in the League of Cambrai which was formed to conquer and divide Venice (December 1508). Henry's two allies were once more allies of each other and might perhaps remain so when they quarrelled with France over the spoils of their wars in Italy.

This prospect moved Ferdinand to a reconciliation with Henry, which was in turn compatible with Henry's continuing friendship with Maximilian. Thus Henry left England reasonably well insured with allies against French expansion across the English Channel. These were the circumstances which revived the marriage agreement of Prince Henry and Catherine of Aragon.

To bring England, Wales, Scotland and Ireland under one ruler had been the recurrent ambition of kings in Westminster (and Edinburgh); it inspired Edward I's conquest of Wales and invasion of Scotland. A more limited aim was to gain such alliances with Scotland as would deny Scottish support to any invader of England. This limited aim often grew into the major ambition. Henry VII's

Defence of the realm—in awe of France and Scotland 65

dynastic policy had forced him to take energetic action to strengthen English influence in Ireland. Meanwhile, in respect of Scotland, Henry had to take over a difficult relationship with James III, king of that country. This was because Edward IV had received Berwick in 1482 at the hands of Scottish rebels against King James. (Yorkists were hand-in-glove with these Scottish rebels, and that was why Henry had the support of a thousand royal Scottish soldiers against the Yorkists at Bosworth.) From the beginning of his reign, Henry spoke in terms of a marriage alliance with Scotland; James on his side was anxious for friendship with England, but Henry could not get an open alliance unless Berwick were restored to the Scots; he could not keep the respect of his own subjects unless it were retained. Things took a turn for the worse in June 1488, when Scottish nobles killed their king after the battle of Sauchieburn; they resented his 'in-bringing of Englishmen'. Henry responded to the new situation by putting all northern defences under a single commander, Thomas Howard, Earl of Surrey (whose first-hand knowledge of the border county was to win the battle of Flodden twenty-four years later). But Henry still believed that alliance with Scotland was a condition of English security against French attacks. He could not wait until the mere passage of time brought the new Scottish king, James IV, to a neighbourly frame of mind. Henry therefore began in 1491 to negotiate with Archibald Douglas, fifth Earl of Angus, who was the leader of a family with some tradition of friendship towards England and of independence towards the Scottish monarchy; (twenty-four years later, his son married Margaret the daughter of Henry VII and widow of James IV; their descendants and connections continued to favour the English alliance throughout the Tudor century). Through Angus, and in spite of continuous Scottish support for Warbeck, Henry began to ply James IV with considerable sums of money (nominally in compensation for English border raids) and with the proposal that James should marry Margaret Tudor, Henry's eldest daughter.

James rejected the proposal and welcomed Warbeck (November 1495) with the consequence that Henry recalled Poynings and his troops from Ireland in order to reinforce the Scottish border. But James was under pressure from the English party among the

Scottish nobility, and also from the French, to give up his quarrelsome posture towards England; he therefore agreed to the truce of Ayton (1497). From this date, relations between Henry and James improved until the treaty of January 1502 established firm peace between the two countries and provided for the marriage of James IV and Margaret. The marriage followed in August 1503 at Holyrood. It gave to Henry VII a sort of security on his northern frontier, but not yet the absolute security which he might need in case of war with France. Nevertheless the hope was born that the frontier had been stabilised and that greater security would be a long-term sequel. In the long term the consequences were in fact various. The marriage alliance itself gave no frontier security during the reign of Henry VIII; it added to the difficulties of Elizabeth by giving to a 'Queen of Scots' a very close claim to the throne of England. On the other hand, it also gave James VI a claim to the English throne and this was the 'great expectation' that held him loyal to England and unwilling to succour the Armada in 1588. At the end of the century, it fulfilled the ancient ambition of bringing England and Scotland under one ruler and so prepared the way for the union of 1707.

8 Henry VIII: Dynastic diplomacy— fulfilling one's role

For the first twenty years of his reign, Henry VIII was not conscious of any major threat of invasion against his kingdom; the rulers of France were wholly occupied with their Italian ambitions; Ferdinand of Spain and the Hapsburgs, both Maximilian and Charles V, were similarly occupied in Italy when they were not diverted by other frontier problems. Inheriting, at the age of eighteen, a kingdom that stood in no danger from any potential conqueror, Henry did not know the obsessive concern for defence which was the preoccupation of Henry VII's last years. Henry VIII did continue to buy and build warships (for example, the *Mary Rose*, the *Peter Pomegranate*, the *Henry Grace à Dieu*), and seven ships inherited from his father became twenty-four by 1514. His admirals were men of sea-going experience. He accumulated ships' stores at Deptford. But all of this sprang rather from a zest for the sea and for weapons of war than from a close calculation of defence needs. Henry revelled in the power of his ships when he watched his fleet in 1512 or when he assisted at the launching of a new ship. He valued sea-power as a means of direct provocation or for the transport of offensive armies, not in order to ensure the safety of his moat: in April 1512, Lord Edward Howard swept French shipping out of the western areas of the English Channel, and in August he provoked James IV by an attack on Scottish ships.

Henry VIII was not obsessed or haunted by any thought of major danger overshadowing his kingdom, but he did cherish, behind his magnificent façade, some doubts about the security of his throne. The security of his heir's succession to the throne—that became truly his obsession, as total as any that mesmerised his father. His doubts about his own security were revealed in the summary execution of Edmund de la Pole, Earl of Suffolk (1513). This violated his father's promise of 1506, but Henry VIII was not to be bound by another man's promise; he had to destroy this claimant to the English throne, before he could set out on his French campaign. Similarly, the prompt destruction of the Duke of Buckingham (1521) revealed Henry's sense of insecurity: the duke had declared that he would inherit Henry's throne because Henry would have no male heir, that he would one day stab Henry as his father had wanted to stab Richard III.

```
                Edward III
                    |
            Thomas of Woodstock
                    |
          Anne m Edmond of Stafford
                    |
       Humphrey of Stafford and Buckingham
                    |
       Humphrey of Stafford and Buckingham
                    |
        Henry of Stafford and Buckingham
                    |
        Edward of Stafford and Buckingham
              (executed 1521)
```

Genealogy 5. Regal aspirations of Edward of Stafford and Buckingham

Whatever inklings of insecurity Henry may have imagined, in fact his security was strongly based on the nation's yearning for a stable dynasty; national acceptance of the new king was confirmed by the unpremeditated gaiety which this young man of eighteen brought to all the activities then expected of kingship. One cannot say that Henry VIII launched his nation into a series of wars in order to rally the nation behind the monarch. One can say that he brought nation and monarch into an intense unity, because he displayed a marvellous personal enthusiasm for the great quasi-athletic occupations of mind and body which his nation then (perhaps all nations always) yearned to associate with their leaders. He demonstrated to them and to himself that he was what both thought he ought to be.

Dynastic diplomacy—fulfilling one's role

They both believed in a king who ventured himself in battle, one who was anxious to blood himself in the field, one who was enthusiastic for the crusading idea and for the claims of his family to the throne of France, enthusiastic also for total self-commitment in the hunting field or tournament. Henry was indeed voracious for the danger and accepted the injuries with rumbustious laughter. Still jousting when well beyond middle-age, he was knocked out and stayed unconscious for two hours; he was then forty-four years old. He loved it all and because he was the man that he was, his subjects ate out of his hand; because he was the man that he was, foreign policy was what it was—at least for the first twenty years of his reign. Thereafter he did perhaps grow to be politic and calculating. For the first years of Henry's reign the man, his policy and his prestige were an indivisible unity.

Henry's only impediment in 1509 was that the alignment of European powers precluded a righteous and Christian assault on France, for France was in alliance with the papacy and also with England's allies, Ferdinand of Spain and Maximilian of Austria. They were all allied for an attack on Venice. Henry had therefore to be content with insulting a French envoy and with ordering his own subjects to be ready for war in 1510.

If immediate fame could not be won in France, the alternative was a crusade against the infidel; here too, the proper opening was difficult to find. But in 1510 a small expedition was planned, and in 1511 was despatched under Lord Darcy to help Ferdinand of Spain in his wars against the Moors—and to strengthen England's alliance with Spain. But Ferdinand countermanded his Moorish expedition and the English force had nothing to do.

1510 and 1511 were given by European rulers to prolonged negotiations in which the alliance against Venice dissolved and a new alliance grew in its place in order to shake French power in Italy. These were also months of vigorous argument in Henry's council between the ecclesiastics who wanted to continue the tradition of minimum warfare learnt under Henry VII and the lay aristocracy who were roused by the scent of war, for they had not yet become 'an elite trained in Greek humanities and arts of citizenship'. Warham, Fox and Ruthal, clearly aware of the cost of war, tried to head the king away from his purposes. Charles Brandon and the Howards urged him on. By March 1510 Pope Julius II had turned against France whose power in Italy threatened the Papal States or at least stood in the way of their expansion. In May England was in friendly entente with Spain against France. Louis XII, on his side, called a general council at Pisa in March 1511 to depose the Pope. Henry was therefore able to present his war-plans as those of a crusade in defence of the papacy against a schismatic France. Thus he satisfied both of his militant enthusiasms at once. He joined the Pope's 'Holy League' in November 1511, in spite of Warham and others who in any case could hardly oppose a war, when the object was evidently ecclesiastical; it was after all a war against a French king who 'would wantonly destroy the unity of the Church'.[1] Henry agreed with Ferdinand to co-operate in an invasion of south-western France (November 1511).

The winter was used to collect large and complex military stores and to prepare for the massing of an invasion force in 1512. In this

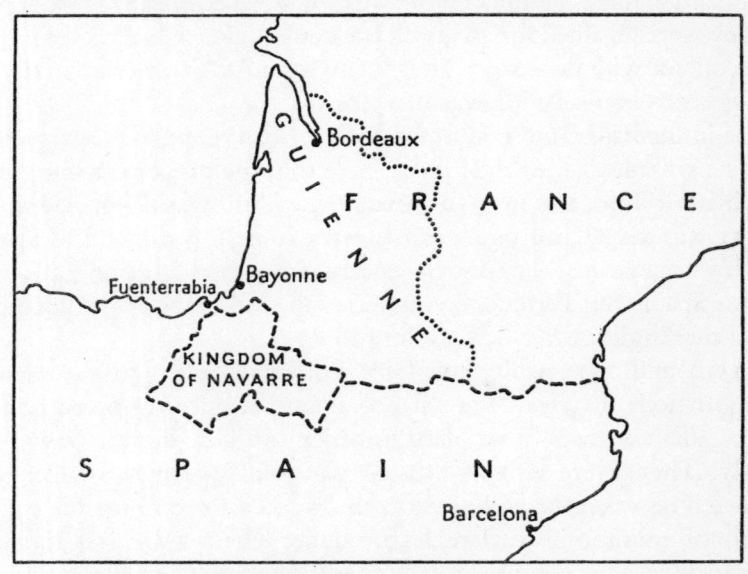

Map 6. The Guienne expedition, 1512

[1] Quoted in Scarisbrick, p. 29.

Dynastic diplomacy—fulfilling one's role

the administrative genius and inexhaustible energy of Almoner Wolsey worked its first miracle. He himself shared with other ecclesiastics a preference for peace which would conserve royal funds and would conform with the ideals of humanism ('can someone be even minutely sensitive about killing a person when mass murder is his profession?').[1] But in 1511, Wolsey could not afford the luxury of a policy of his own, any more than could Richelieu, for example, in 1616. Parliament met in February 1512 to vote supplies of money. In April 1512 Lord Edward Howard cleared the Channel of hostile shipping and in June the English expedition under Thomas Grey, Marquis of Dorset, sailed for the Spanish port of Fuenterrabia. Thence it advanced into Guienne and encamped before Bayonne from June until October. The inactive English army served Ferdinand's purpose, while he conquered Navarre at his leisure, because it outflanked any French relieving force. Ferdinand had never intended that a Spanish army should invade France side by side with an English one. The English force was slowly broken down by inactivity and disease. It returned to England mutinously, contrary to the orders of king and of commander.

Henry's enthusiasm had received a setback, but he was not quite disillusioned, especially as the Emperor Maximilian joined Spain, the Pope and England against France in November 1512. Parliament met again in November 1512 and voted supplies of money. Henry accepted with a good grace Ferdinand's insulting criticism of the English army and negotiated for a Spanish invasion of south-west France in 1513, which Henry would subsidise. Henry, leading his army in person, was on this occasion to attack Northern France, with his own flank protected by Maximilian in the Netherlands. In March 1513 the Pope endowed Henry with Louis XII's title of 'Most Christian King of France', but the honour was to be published only after Henry had conquered France. The great quadruple alliance of Pope, Spain, Hapsburgs and England was finally confirmed in April 1513—by which time Ferdinand had already negotiated a secret truce with France. Moreover Pope Julius II, the enemy of France, had died (March 1513). Such changes of circumstance were dis-

[1] Erasmus, quoted in Hale.

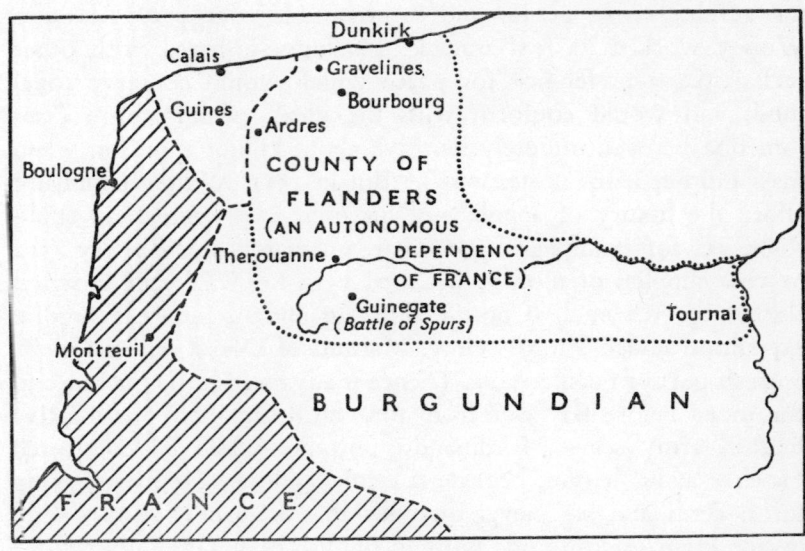

Map 7. The Pale of Calais, 1513

regarded in England. Edmund de la Pole, Earl of Suffolk, was executed to remove a possible danger to the throne. The fleet made an unimpressive attack on French ships off the coast of Brittany. In June, Wolsey's expeditionary force of 25,000 crossed to France in units led by the Earl of Shrewsbury, by Lord Herbert and by King Henry himself with Wolsey at his elbow. The capture of Thérouanne was insured by the battle of the Spurs (August 1513) and the capture of Tournai followed (September). In October 1513 Henry, Maximilian and Ferdinand renewed their alliance and planned an overwhelming offensive for 1514. This alliance was strengthened by an agreement that Charles V should marry Henry's sister Mary and that Henry should again subsidise Ferdinand, in spite of his inactivity in 1513 and in spite of Henry's own financial difficulties, for by 1514 the treasure bequeathed by Henry VII was exhausted. Although England was not in danger of invasion from any powerful country, these exploits against France invited invasion by the Scots in their character of the ancient allies of France. To defend the north against probable invasion, Thomas Howard, Earl of Surrey, moved to the Scottish border. In the consequent battle of Flodden (September), James IV and very many Scottish noblemen were killed. Margaret, the widowed Queen of Scotland, Henry VIII's sister and regent for her son James V, thereupon married Archibald Douglas, Earl of Angus, the son of Henry VII's ally and himself a leader of the pro-English nobility. England's relations with Scotland seemed to have been secured for the next campaigns in France and indeed for the indefinite future (as would have been the case if Margaret had possessed any sense of politics, but she offended all sections of the Scottish nobility, not least her husband for whom she evinced a most bitter hatred).

In honour of the achievements of 1513 and in preparation for the campaigns of 1514, Wolsey was made Bishop of Lincoln and Bishop of Tournai; Thomas Howard, Earl of Surrey, was restored to the old family title of Duke of Norfolk (lost for services to Richard III at Bosworth), and Charles Brandon became Duke of Suffolk.

But the next campaigns in France did not occur, for by March 1514, both Ferdinand and Maximilian had made peace with Louis XII, spicing their treaty with prefatory thoughts of an attack on Henry's continental possessions. This was the news which disillusioned Henry (and caused his first revulsion from Catherine of Aragon, his wife but Ferdinand's daughter). Aggressive preparations were continued; a bargain was made for Swiss mercenaries, and a minor expedition landed near Cherbourg, but this was only a cover for the serious business of peace negotiations with Louis XII, designed to detach him from Maximilian and Ferdinand. This was the sort of policy for which Wolsey himself yearned; he could work with a will, and he was completely successful. By the treaty of August 1514 Henry received Tournai and Thérouanne, with a pension and arrears of the pension provided by the treaty of Etaples. His sister, Mary Tudor, repudiated her marriage agreement with Charles V and confirmed the Anglo-French alliance by marrying Louis XII in October 1514. Charles Brandon, now Duke of Suffolk, attended the wedding in order to propose an Anglo-French invasion of Spain to conquer Navarre for France and Castile for Catherine of Aragon. But Louis XII was interested only in Italy.

9 Wolsey: Peace initiatives of a religious humanist

The entente with France was poor compensation for the exertions of two and a half years; 'experience runs an expensive school' and Henry had learnt his lessons at a cost of over £900,000. Henry 'had learnt much', says A. F. Pollard, 'but his powers were not yet developed enough to make him a match for the craft and guile of his rivals. The consciousness of the fact made him rely more and more upon Wolsey.'

In comparison with the years before 1515 and after 1529, Henry withdrew himself from these diplomatic activities which had brought such expensive disappointment. But his withdrawal was never permanent. He was like the creator and owner of a private business who has decided to retire to the Bahamas and leave his affairs to a salaried manager. Nevertheless, his mind is never wholly detached from his creation; three times a week he is on the trans-Atlantic telephone to be sure that his manager is pressing forward with the right policies; three times a year, whenever particularly urgent or brilliant opportunities seem to offer themselves, he flies into London unannounced to share with his manager the excitement of the moment, even erratically to take control himself. So it was with Henry between 1515 and 1529; the optimistic ardour which he had brought to the throne of England was still warm. He could not wholly surrender his magnificent visions of crusades and conquests after one experience of cynical realism at the hands of Ferdinand and Maximilian. Whenever rivalry provoked him, or opportunity seemed to blow with a freshening breeze, then Henry's old ardour responded, passion and vision returned and he forsook the dance and tennis court to plunge with enthusiastic energy into urgent or visionary projects. The competitive panache of young King Francis roused him in 1515; so did the project of universal peace in 1518 and the imperial candidature in 1519, followed by the papal candidature for his chancellor in 1521. In 1520 he was zealous to win European recognition for his theological learning. In 1523 and 1525 he returned to his first passion, the conquest of France. But these were short moments of irritated or enthusiastic interference or collaboration with his manager. Though optimism remained, so too did the experience of deceit and failure. Lethargy and withdrawal, the fruit of experience, supervened at each first setback.

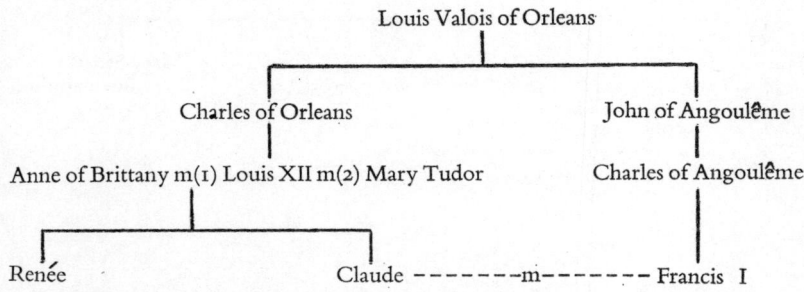

Genealogy 6. French law did not recognise descent through a woman

The first phase of Wolsey's peaceable direction of foreign affairs did not run for many weeks before it was interrupted by the first of Henry's passionate revivals. Unhappily for the French alliance, Louis XII died in January 1515, exhausted by the pace of life set him by his young wife. He was succeeded by his cousin Francis I. Here was a man who might have calculated on the English alliance to secure his northern coast while he pursued his ambitions in Italy, but, instead of calculating the moves of diplomacy, he preferred the open and defiant style of late-mediaeval chivalry. This was altogether the most likely to focus the passionate attention of Henry and raise his hackles, for it was precisely the style in which Henry had himself expected to triumph. Francis trusted an England that was crippled more readily than an England that purported to be friendly. Luck played for the French when Charles Brandon fell in love with Mary

Tudor; Francis skilfully promoted the marriage which was hurriedly completed in Paris in February 1515. Thereupon Francis recovered the jewellery, given to Mary by Louis XII, and mocked Henry with the news that he had lost a marriageable sister who might have been used for a marriage alliance between England and an enemy of France. To complete the immobilisation of England, Francis despatched to Scotland John Stuart, Duke of Albany. This man's father had been the villainous brother of James III, chief promoter of rebellions that humiliated that king in 1482. In the end (1484) the

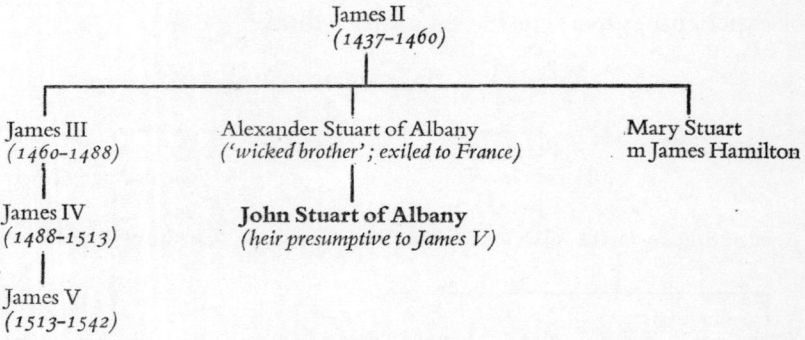

Genealogy 7. John Stuart, Duke of Albany, protégé of Francis I, and heir presumptive to the Scottish throne

old Duke of Albany had had to take refuge in France and there his son John Stuart had grown up. John of Albany, who was sent back to Scotland in May 1515, was thus a cousin of the child-king, James V; he was also heir presumptive to the throne. He rallied the many noble families whom Margaret Tudor had offended. Margaret was deposed from her regency and held prisoner in September 1515; in October she escaped to England from captivity in Stirling Castle, but the English party in Scotland had been utterly overthrown. Francis led his army into Italy, confident that he was unlikely to be invaded from the north. In September he routed Henry's Swiss allies at Marignano and reoccupied Milan. War in Italy was reopened.

The ringing triumphs of Francis stung Henry by their contrast with his own dull performance in the school of European chivalry.

He passionately needed to ruffle, if possible to pluck down, this young cockerel; and so he drove his reluctant chancellor to re-create a coalition of European powers which should be capable of reversing these French victories. But what could Wolsey do? Henry VII's war chest was spent, the parliament of 1515 voted a subsidy early in the year but was concerned to criticise the English clergy rather than wax enthusiastic for war, and Ferdinand himself died in January 1516, leaving Spain to his grandson Charles V who was understandably anxious for two years' peace in which to take stock of his heritage. Wolsey was driven by his master's demands to put on an outward display of opposition to France. This was to save face: Henry's face in the eyes of Europe, Wolsey's in the eyes of Henry. Behind the aggressive façade, Wolsey was instructing his agents to minimise actual preparations for war.

An alliance with Ferdinand had been drafted in October 1515 without committing either party to military action; £80,000 was promised to Swiss mercenaries and to the Emperor Maximilian if they would drive the French out of Milan and invade France. They attacked the French in Milan, received payment and promptly returned to their bases. Wolsey was heartily relieved; he had previously asked his agent, Pace, 'by good wise drifts' to ask the Swiss to petition Henry that they may be 'discharged of persecuting the Frenchmen into France'.[1]

Wolsey and most of the councillors were wholly opposed to this active policy against France and were able to use the withdrawal of Maximilian as their argument for calling off the English invasion of France which had been proposed for May 1516. But such was the ebullient irritation of Henry that the farce of a coalition against France had to be played through twice more, three times in all, before he would really leave foreign policy where he had placed it—in the hands of Wolsey. During the summer of 1516 plans were advanced for a coalition of the Emperor, the Pope and the Swiss, who were to be paid by the English to invade France while Charles V of Spain attacked from the south-west, but Charles V had quite other ideas and entered into the treaty of Noyon (August 1516) with Francis and Maximilian, whereby Francis was to possess Milan and,

[1] Wolsey, quoted in Scarisbrick, p. 62.

at some future date, receive back Navarre; Charles was to marry Louise, the daughter of Francis, and have Naples as the dowry. Henry was isolated. Such a setback was quite unacceptable. Another effort was required of his councillors who sought to create a new alliance between the Swiss and Maximilian which England would finance for an attack on France. This was the treaty of London (October and December 1516). In January 1517, the Swiss accepted a counter offer from France; Maximilian accepted 40,000 florins from Henry to fight in England's interest, 60,000 from the French to join the treaty of Noyon, and 20,000 from the Venetians to surrender Verona, which he was engaged to defend. 'Of what promptitude he is to sudden mutations' said Wolsey.

But by this date (February 1517) Henry's emotional energy had spent itself and Wolsey was free to negotiate effectively with Francis; Francis, for his part, signalled peaceful intent by recalling Albany from Scotland (June 1517). In 1518 Anglo-French negotiations made headway and by the treaty of October 1518 a true pacification was achieved on the basis of restoring Tournai to French suzerainty in exchange for payments of £15,000 a year and a promise of marriage between the Dauphin and Mary Tudor, the two-year-old daughter of Henry. To safeguard this new friendship against future discord, Henry and Francis were to meet each other regularly.

This peace treaty with France was an element in a much wider scheme which Wolsey was promoting on behalf of the whole of Europe. In detail he aimed at a friendly understanding with France guaranteed by other European powers; he was reviving the policy of Henry VII. In wider terms, he was accepting the ideals of international religious humanists—of Erasmus, Colet, More, Contarini. Educated within the ethos which they evoked, Wolsey was ready to act on their belief in the peaceful possibilities of human nature, provided that it were guided by all that seemed best in religion, in the classical tradition, and in the rational notions of enlightened contemporaries. To Henry VIII, Wolsey offered the enormous prestige of leading Europe towards 'humanistic peace' in place of the traditional prestige of European warfare (which, in any case, he could not finance for more than a few years at a stretch).

These ideas began to guide Wolsey's policy once he was clear of immediate pressures from Henry, say from February 1517. Now in March 1518, Pope Leo X called for a crusade against the Turks, proclaimed a five-year European truce, and sent legates to the more important courts of Europe, including Campeggio to England. This *legate a latere* carried with him the authority of the Pope, but Henry refused to admit Campeggio on such terms—unless (as a happy after-thought) his servant Wolsey received the same authority and was made *legate a latere* also. Campeggio was held up at Boulogne through June and July until Leo accorded the honour.

But in the negotiations which followed, Wolsey shifted the emphasis from organising a European truce for the sake of a crusade to organising all European nations into a self-sustaining truce for its own sake, in the service of the ideals of religious humanism, and for the sake of the Anglo-French peace agreement which other nations would be invited to guarantee. Wolsey put his proposals to Francis, Maximilian, Charles V and the Pope (September 1518). The outcome was that the Anglo-French peace treaty of October 1518 was reinforced by a much more ambitious compact of mutual defence against any aggressor, and to this clause other rulers were invited to subscribe. About twenty-four European rulers did so. This was the great treaty of London. It responded to 'the urgent call of Christian humanists for an end to internecine conflict in Europe'.[1] It expressed the hope that the new spirit of critical scholarly reappraisal might open a new era in international affairs as in so many other modes of human activity. The papacy, on the other hand, had been jockeyed from its position of guide and guardian of the European conscience. A reference to an ultimate league against the Turks was all that was left of the original papal initiative. 'From this we can see what the Holy See and the Pope have to expect from the English Chancellor', complained the Roman cardinal who was to become Pope Clement VII. But Henry VII's old councillor, Bishop Fox (retired by this time to his diocese of Winchester) spoke enthusiastically as a disciple of Henry VII, but also as a convinced humanist: 'the best that ever was done for the realm of England'.

The treaty of London was not an empty gesture of self-advertisement. It contained detailed agreements which implied serious intent

[1] Scarisbrick, p. 73.

and it was given the sort of sequel which a continuing struggle for peace might be expected to require.

The death of Emperor Maximilian (January 1519) did not impose any great strain on European amity. In the imperial election which followed, England could stand true to the spirit of the treaty of London and remain impartial as between the two candidates Charles V and Francis. Pope Leo encouraged Henry to stand as a candidate (May 1519), because the Pope preferred a weak Emperor like Henry rather than one with powerful national resources at his command. Henry was stirred to ephemeral enthusiasm and put himself forward as a third candidate, but even this did not alter his impartiality between the other two, for his agents did not poach for votes selectively among the supporters of one particular candidate, and in any case Henry, for all his excitement at the prospect, was hardly a serious competitor. The other two plied the electors with actual bribes, but Henry's agent, Richard Pace, was empowered to offer only promises of bribes to be paid for results, that is after Henry's success in the election. Wolsey could raise little interest in the affair and even Henry made a virtue of defeat and said that he was 'right glad that he had not obtained'. The episode was a distraction from the serious purpose of organising European peace, but it was not in conflict with this purpose: to that Wolsey was giving his mind.

Shortly after the election of Charles V to be the new Holy Roman Emperor, Wolsey was making preliminary suggestions for the first of the meetings of Henry with Francis on the one hand, and with Charles V on the other, which were to be the practical outcome of the treaty of London. For the preservation of peace, the meetings with Francis would be the more critical, because traditions of enmity with France were more deeply rooted. Wolsey was authorised in January 1520 to make preparations for a rendezvous in May and June; vastly elaborate arrangements were indeed provided for the two monarchs and, each supported by 5,000 courtly followers, they arranged to meet where the frontier of France impinged on the territory of Calais. Extensive building (albeit temporary), vast supplies of food, gaiety, colour and minute attention to protocol, indeed every minute item in this Field of Cloth of Gold was as necessary as at our twentieth-century Olympic Games in order to give any chance of good-will where there was such an inheritance of hatred. Wolsey did not want only to anaesthetise traditional hatred for a mere three weeks; he wanted to create the beginnings of permanent amity, to achieve so much good-will that Henry and Francis would be glad to 'repair to such meetings hereafter'. Wolsey's stage-management was so far successful that a strong current of Anglo-French sentiment was running towards new friendliness when the jousting was over and each court moved back to its own national centre. But this proved insufficient for Wolsey's main purpose; long-standing causes of enmity gradually reasserted themselves over the next two years.

For the time, however, a sentiment of solidarity was established between the two kings, and though Henry returned from Calais for an immediate meeting with Charles V—impartiality demanded no less—he gave Charles his friendship without any betrayal of Francis. The meeting with Charles had been arranged for the week before Henry left Dover for the Field of Cloth of Gold, but winds had kept Charles in Corunna, so that he reached Sandwich only a few hours before Henry was to leave. Such hours as Henry could afford were given to the formalities of meeting; but business was left to a later occasion which would have to follow Henry's meeting with Francis. It took place in July 1520 at Gravelines, just beyond the northern borders of Calais. Between Charles V and Henry there was a lavish exchange of hospitality in an atmosphere exuberant with friendship, but neither at Gravelines in 1520 nor during the next twelve months would Henry yield to any pressure from Charles V to weaken his entente with Francis. England was willing to aid either of her two friends if the other became aggressive, but would rather 'stay them both'. Nor would Henry at this time agree to end the marriage treaty between Mary Tudor and the Dauphin. He was bound to Charles by 'fraternal love and consanguinity' and to Francis 'by great concordances . . . in personages, appetites and manners'. In all of this, Henry played his part loyally by the policy that Wolsey had set.

But, in the months that followed, Henry was distracted into two parallel enthusiams by which he hoped to enhance his European dignity, much as he had been excited by the thought of election to the imperial crown. Back in 1518, Henry had turned his agile mind to the refutation of Lutheran heresy. Perhaps Wolsey encouraged this as a harmless exercise of royal energy. Perhaps Wolsey, Bishop Fisher and Sir Thomas More helped to provide the theological argument, but the enthusiasm was Henry's. By May 1521 his book, *Assertia Septem Sacramentorum*, was completed; by August copies were on the way to the Pope. In subsequent months the book acquired European fame, was republished and translated; it added to the king's prestige and it derived prestige from its regal author.

For years Henry had petitioned the papacy for a title to equal the 'Most Christian King' which had been accorded to kings of France. Pope Julius had in 1513 proposed to transfer that title to Henry. Otherwise, Henry's petitions had evoked no response; Pope Leo had carefully evaded every suggestion of an honorific title. But he could not escape the need to recognise this publication and he accorded the title preferred by Henry in October 1521; Henry became 'Fidei Defensor'.

More serious, in terms of possible consequence, was the idea that Wolsey might well become Pope. The suggestion came from Charles V in the course of the meetings in 1520. Here was a proposal to rouse Henry to the highest enthusiasm: to be master and patron of the Pope himself—the prestige of Henry's monarchy could not aspire to any higher status. 'The real thrust and enthusiasm for Wolsey's candidature came from Henry.'[1] Wolsey was sufficiently well informed to estimate his prospect of election as its proper rate; he privately expressed a lack of interest but his public line of conduct was necessarily to humour his master's enthusiasm: 'the mind and entire desire of his Highness... is that I shall attain to the said dignity'. As soon as Leo X died (December 1521) Henry's agents pressed the claims of Wolsey among the cardinals; Charles V too agreed to give his support, but in fact Charles's influence was already exerted on behalf of his Flemish tutor, who became Pope Adrian VI in January 1522 and died in September 1523.

Henry's two ecclesiastical interests had been harmless enough and did not conflict with Wolsey's policy of peace for England and for Europe. But, at a less ephemeral level of his mind, a level at which

[1] Scarisbrick, p. 109.

Peace initiatives of a religious humanist

ideas took root, incubated and persisted, Henry was by now brooding darkly upon a problem which haunted most Tudor rulers. Like his father he had made himself firm and secure on his throne; but like his father he was obsessively concerned for a secure, uncontested succession. His only heir was a minor and a girl. A child-heir was likely to be challenged by the nearest eligible adult; a child-heiress might not get the support even of the well-disposed majority, because they remembered that the last woman to rule England was, disastrously, Queen Matilda. The king's concern for the succession had much greater importance for Wolsey's policy of European peace than had any of the passing enthusiasms to which Henry's spirits rose from time to time. This particular concern was not only persistent; it was the factor in the whole situation which actually overturned Wolsey's own policy of peaceful impartiality.

Henry's yearning for a son was as deep and powerful as any feeling which he could sustain—which perhaps any man could sustain for he was a man whose large passions would shake his whole personality. This yearning is illustrated by the anecdote of the countryman who, in the dusk, came upon a heavily-built man, wearing a penitent's smock and making his way on his knees towards a local shrine; the countryman recognised the penitent as the King of England and the penance as a heartfelt prayer that his week-old son might, in spite of all, survive. Henry's yearning is illustrated also with singular pathos by the commemoration on the great slab of polished slate set in the floor of St George's Chapel at Windsor immediately before the High Altar. This tells us that Henry himself chose to lie in burial beside the only wife who gave him a male heir.

Catherine's last child was born in 1518; it was still-born. By 1521 most men were satisfied that Catherine would have no more children. In that year, Edward Stafford, Duke of Buckingham, began to assert that Henry would have no male heir and to point to himself as one whose succession to the throne might be presumed. Knowledge of these assertions disturbed the deepest of Henry's assumptions. The execution of Buckingham was not enough to give Henry the confidence which he needed. The succession of his daughter Mary must be buttressed and assured by forces greater than the law of England and the good-will of Justices of the Peace. Like Henry VII, he sought foreign support for his heir; like Henry VII, he believed it would be best provided by Spain. The argument will have run as follows: Mary must be betrothed to a powerful foreign prince who will have an interest in securing her succession against all-comers. If the chosen champion be a French prince, the Dauphin for example, then either France will be too weak to secure the succession, or she will have the power and the singleness of purpose to absorb England and convert England into a French province. Let the chosen champion be rather a Spanish prince, for Spain is more likely to have resources necessary to secure the succession; besides, the King of Spain, who is also Holy Roman Emperor, will have so many preoccupations that Charles V will be bound to leave to England at least the degree of autonomy which he is permitting in the Netherlands, and in any case England's prosperity is dependent on her connection with territories already ruled by Charles V, especially the Netherlands and Spain. This was the chief line of thought which influenced Henry in 1521, caused him to throw his influence against Wolsey's impartial neutrality, and so brought English policy from its neutral position to alignment on the side of Spain. Wolsey struggled to preserve an appearance of neutrality or at least to keep open diplomatic routes by which he might return to it. In the event his neutrality was lost in 1521. For all his subsequent struggles, Wolsey was unable to re-establish his chosen policy; he himself became powerless in Europe as soon as England chose one side and ceased to mediate. The prospect for the future of England's independence might indeed seem grave, because the advantage of England to both France and Spain was so great that each was tempted to try to absorb England whenever the other was too weak to prevent it.

Francis became militarily aggressive towards Charles V in 1521. Rebellions in Spain made Charles V so vulnerable that Francis could not resist the opportunity. Charles V appealed to England for help under the terms of the treaty of London of 1518. English foreign policy for the next four years was the outcome of a conflict between Henry's will for alliance with Spain and the will of Wolsey, supported by most of the councillors, for peace; but the limiting factor in any event was the inability of any English government in the 1520s to raise enough money for prolonged military action. Henry wanted to bring England into alliance with Spain, but usually saw that he could not afford to do very much. Wolsey and the councillors wanted to remain neutral and to mediate, but saw that they must humour Henry; unarmed mediation would achieve little, and armed mediation was beyond their resources. All parties were thus reduced to bluffing it out and hoping for the best.

In May 1521, Henry was determined to fight as Charles V's ally, but, because he was short of money, he agreed that Wolsey should offer mediation; this would gain time during which money might be procured. Wolsey accepted the chance to mediate as a genuine chance of restoring European peace and of preserving England's status as arbitrator. He worked exhaustively to bring together a tripartite conference of the French, the Hapsburgs and the English, at Calais in August 1521. He had great difficulty in getting the Hapsburgs to the conference and in keeping their delegates at the table. In fact, Gattinara, their chief delegate, insisted as a condition of continuing to negotiate that England should enter into a firm treaty with Spain which would cover events if the conference failed. In order to keep Gattinara at Calais, Wolsey had to meet Charles V at Bruges and negotiate the treaty by which Henry promised to declare war on Francis in May 1522 unless Francis made peace with Charles V; Henry also promised to keep the Channel clear for the ships of Charles V and to supply an English army of 40,000 for an invasion of France in 1523. Charles on his side agreed to marry Henry's daughter, Mary, to pay Henry the equivalent of his existing French pension and to use his influence on Wolsey's behalf at the next papal election. For Henry, the treaty of Bruges was an accurate expression of the intentions of English policy; for Wolsey, it was an expedient to gain a few weeks for peace negotiations, and, if they should fail, to postpone for at least eighteen months any large-scale English military expedition. Wolsey stated his own view thus: 'I doubt not but by means [of Francis' collaboration] . . . to put over the giving of the said assistance'[1] to Charles V.

Naturally enough, Wolsey's efforts at the Calais conference were not successful. He failed to get even a truce in October 1521. Papal and Hapsburg troops overran Milan, Charles V took Tournai, and

[1] Wolsey, quoted in Scarisbrick, p. 87.

in November Wolsey came back to England. To deter England from overt military intervention, Francis sent John Stuart, Duke of Albany, back to Scotland where he organised the anti-English nobility (November 1521).

In 1522, Wolsey continued to play for minimal involvement. He offered loans to Charles V in exchange for suspending the treaty of Bruges, and got the great expedition postponed from 1523 until 1524. However, Charles paid a prolonged visit to England (May to July 1522) and a declaration of war could not decently be avoided. A small force was raised and Thomas Howard, Earl of Surrey (in 1524 he became third Duke of Norfolk) crossed to France in order to pillage (June to October 1522). Meanwhile a Scottish force under Albany invaded England, but the Scottish troops deserted in fear of a second Flodden, and Dacre the local English commander accepted a truce which Wolsey gratefully offered to extend for sixteen years. (Wolsey added a distant hint that Henry's daughter, Mary, might in the end marry James V.) Albany returned to France in order to bring back 5,000 French troops in 1523.

The three forces in English foreign policy—Henry's will, Wolsey's will, and government penury—danced their ineffective ballet in 1522 and through into 1523. Early in 1523 the Great Enterprise against France was postponed yet another year, that is until 1525. Then, fairly suddenly, Henry's mood changed; he became elated into energetic enthusiasm; overwhelming action was everywhere demanded. The source of this enthusiasm was the revolt of Charles, Duke of Bourbon, the greatest prince aristocrat, against King Francis. It is difficult to understand why Henry should so suddenly have re-assessed the significance of this revolt which was already some months old, and which previously he had regarded with scorn. But, by June 1523, Henry was convinced that Charles Bourbon was offering England and Spain a great opportunity to launch a major offensive in the late-mediaeval style of Henry V or Charles the Bold. This, he thought, was no case of jockeying for minor diplomatic advantage. As in 1513 and 1514, Henry VIII now saw himself as a potential conqueror, about to become King of France in reality as well as in name. A triple offensive was expected to overwhelm France in the course of 1524. Even in 1523, the Duke of Bourbon was to invade Provence from Italy, Charles V to invade Guienne from Spain, and Charles Brandon, Duke of Suffolk, with 10,000 men was to attack Boulogne from Calais, in order to gain this second port for the great expedition of 1524. This 1524 expedition Henry would lead in person. Combined operations on this scale far exceeded the resources of sixteenth-century governments. They could not communicate with each other quickly enough, nor move and supply their troops on this scale. Bourbon was held up in the Alps and retreated to Genoa; Charles V did not get through the Pyrenees. Suffolk, who set out in August, was diverted by Wolsey from Boulogne to deliver a quick knock-out blow against Paris (September) so as to avoid a 'dribbling war'; this change of objective may have been caused by the death of Pope Adrian VI (September 1523), which led Wolsey to seek a way of impressing Charles in the hope that Charles would support Wolsey's candidature for the papacy. Suffolk covered three-quarters of the distance (he got within fifty miles of Paris) and then was forced to retreat to Calais by rain and lack of food (October).

Meanwhile the first parliament for eight years had been summoned to meet in April 1523. Wolsey asked parliament to vote revenues commensurate with the king's extraordinary opportunity. He asked for the unprecedented sum of £800,000. But members of parliament did not share the king's enthusiasm. The failures of 1512 and 1514 were still in men's minds. Thomas Cromwell (in the speech already quoted on page 34) spoke for most men in expecting no success from an attempt to conquer France. As for the suggestion that Henry should lead the expedition in person, members could only deplore so grave a hazard to their king when his only successor was a child and a girl: 'our most gracious Sovereign ... intendeth to go over in his royal person. Which thing I pray God for my part I never live to see. ... How needful is it for us, considering in what case we be (if our monarch should die) to make humblest suit that ever did poor subjects to the Sovereign that he will for our sakes ... desist from that dangerous enterprise'.[1]

Parliament voted only £600,000; the collection was to be spread over two years, so that Wolsey could expect only £300,000 for

---
[1] Quoted in Merriman (b), p. 35.

immediate purposes. In fact £150,000 was the sum actually collected. Though Wolsey vehemently rebuked such a niggardly vote, yet we must believe that he really agreed with the wisdom of parliament; it is difficult to doubt that the speech of Cromwell, his secretary, reflected some part of Wolsey's own mind. Henry's passionate enthusiasms were running at full flood and swept on, undiminished by the cool response from parliament. Wolsey, always preferring a very different policy, was in any case the administrator who had to face the impossible task of mounting a great expedition with insufficient money to pay for it. What could he do but play for time and hope that something would turn up? In March 1524, negotiations were opened for a renewal of the triple offensive against France: this was to satisfy Henry. Simultaneously, Wolsey made suggestions to France that peace might be negotiated. During the next months he worked for peace as hard 'as may stand with my duty to my sovereign, lord and master'.[1] For an invasion of France by an English army there was not enough money. The only offensive came from Bourbon's army in the south. After initial success in August, he too was repulsed and by September was back in Italy. This finally exhausted Henry's hopes; he was once more able to reconcile himself to reality. In September 1524, Wolsey and Henry accepted a formal truce with France and official peace negotiations were opened. These negotiations derived further impetus from the policy of the new Pope Clement VII, for he, fearing the predominant power of Spain in Italy, allied with France in December 1524.

The drift of international affairs was thus generally satisfactory for Wolsey in February 1525. Suddenly every trend was reversed and every excitement was lifted to maximum intensity by the great Hapsburg victory at Pavia, where an Austrian army combined with a Spanish army to overwhelm the French, capturing Francis and killing many of his commanders (including Richard de la Pole, Yorkist claimant to the English throne). Once more Henry was beside himself with enthusiastic expectations. To exploit this tremendous opportunity of French weakness, money must be raised at once, England's vigorous collaboration must be joined to Charles's brilliantly successful initiative. Commissioners were forthwith sent

[1] Wolsey, quoted in Scarisbrick, p. 132.

Peace initiatives of a religious humanist

out into the counties to demand an Amicable Grant—that is a special tax of about one-sixth of lay incomes—which was intended to raise £500,000.

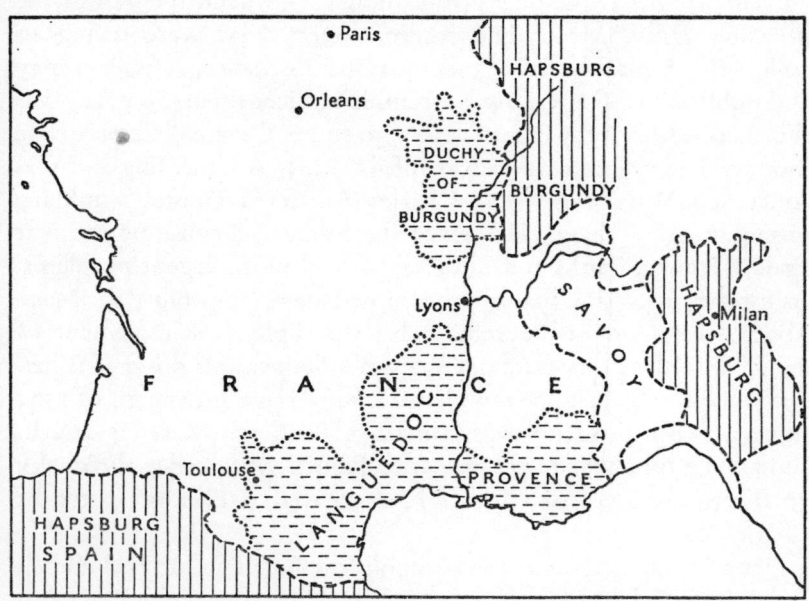

Map 8. Languedoc, Provence and the duchy of Burgundy, 1525: French territories which would consolidate Hapsburg positions in southern Europe. Henry VIII proposed to transfer them to Charles V as soon as he should be crowned king of France

Bishop Tunstall of London led an embassy to Madrid, with magnificent propositions for the exploitation of victory: Charles V and Henry were to make an immediate assault on Paris; Henry was then to be crowned king of France; Charles was to annex Languedoc, Provence and the duchy of Burgundy; Charles was also forthwith to accept Mary Tudor as a resident at his court so that the marriage, agreed upon in 1521, would be completely assured and Charles V could expect, on the death of Henry VIII, to add England and France to his other dominions and so become 'Lord and owner of all Christendom'. Here, in all its glory, was the true late-mediaeval vision of Christendom, translated into a real political structure, the political counterpart of a vast Gothic cathedral. During the following weeks Wolsey had, with difficulty, to restrain Henry for setting out immediately with such forces as could be raised. Reluctantly, Henry agreed that the Duke of Norfolk should command the van of the invading army. Meanwhile commissioners who were trying to collect the Amicable Grant met very stiff resistance, refusals to pay and public abuse from crowds assembled to jeer them. So grave was this that in May 1525 Henry agreed to suspend the collection of the money. The great invasion was off for 1525, as far as England was concerned. What was worse, Charles V rejected Tunstall's military proposals out of hand. He lacked the money to continue the war against France; Turks and Lutherans posed more urgent problems. As for the suggestion that he take immediate responsibility for Mary Tudor, this likewise he refused by the diplomatic expedient of demanding the immediate payment of an enormous dowry. When this could not be paid, he repudiated his marriage agreement of 1521 and married instead Princess Isabella of Portugal (March 1526). In January 1526 he made his peace with Francis, who ceded the duchy of Burgundy to Spain and agreed to marry Eleanor, sister of Charles V.

Henry's magnificent vision of a political Christendom had melted away. Nor did anything remain of Wolsey's ideal of a European peace sustained by English mediation. But the greatest loss of all, since this came within the field of practical politics, was the total disintegration of Henry's plans to secure the succession. Four years previously he had decided to strengthen the family connections of his daughter, Mary, so that, at his own death, she should seem too powerful for anyone to contest her succession. He had chosen a Spanish marriage alliance to achieve this purpose. Now Spain had wholly rejected the policy. His plan was dead. He must needs seek a radically different solution. Not surprisingly perhaps, he again grew hostile to his wife Catherine, for she seemed to be the special representative of Spanish influence in England. In June 1525 he promoted his illegitimate son, Henry Fitzroy, to be Duke of Richmond, Lord Admiral of England and Lord Lieutenant of Ireland, with first precedence amongst English peers. Plainly the boy was being groomed for the position of heir presumptive. Catherine reacted with spirit: king and queen were no longer on speaking terms.

When Charles V decided in 1525 to marry Isabella of Portugal and to repudiate Mary Tudor, this was accepted by most European diplomats as an obvious step which everyone had foreseen. Yet for England the decision contained within itself the genesis of great protagonists and great events. The child of the marriage was Philip II of Spain; the outcome was the annexation of Portugal by Spain in 1580 and the acquisition by Philip of shipyards and harbours in which the Armada could be built and launched. The outcome of this rebuff to Henry's succession plans was the breach with Rome, and the birth of Princess Elizabeth who was to be the chief architect of reformation England and the leader of its defence against Philip and his Armadas.

During the ten years, 1515 to 1525, Henry VIII had intruded upon the work of Cardinal Wolsey on some five occasions: as well as sharing the glory of the great treaty of London, he had tried to curb the mortifying success of Francis, to make himself Holy Roman Emperor, to raise an Englishman to the papacy, to strengthen the prospects of daughter Mary's peaceful succession and, for a second time, to conquer France in the style of Henry V. If English foreign policy possessed any continuity during these ten years, this was derived from Wolsey's consistent hope of building a permanent organisation of European peace, to involve England in warfare only for the limited purpose of buttressing peace.

10 Henry VIII: Dynastic security—diplomatic pressure, 1525–32

The need for a secure, uncontested succession has already been given as the reason why Wolsey was forced in 1521 from his position of neutrality into alliance with Charles V. But the final repudiation of Princess Mary by Charles V in 1525 reduced to bankruptcy Henry's policy of buttressing the succession of his daughter, his heir presumptive. Yet Henry VIII, like Henry VII after the death of Prince Arthur, was more and more obsessed with the need to provide such an undoubted incontestable heir as would exclude all rivals and all possibility of civil war. Since his scheme for his daughter had failed, he felt himself driven forward to more adventurous plans in order to provide the greater security of a son, of a male heir. His consistent yearning for such an heir had already been attested by his recurrent feeling of alienation from Catherine. In the months and years that followed 1525, it was equally revealed in his promotion of his illegitimate male child to highest precedence in the peerage (1525), by his supreme joy at the birth of Prince Edward in 1537 and by his subsequent devotion to the memory of Jane Seymour. The repudiation of Princess Mary by Charles V does seem to have released this yearning from all restraint. Its fulfilment must, of course, involve an annulment of his marriage with Catherine of Aragon, but that would have seemed a small obstacle under reasonably neutral circumstances, because popes were accustomed to wave aside any impediments to the marriage policies of potentates, especially when the peace of a nation was at stake; in any case, the validity of Henry's marriage had been under question, from time to time, since 1503. In 1525 the French Ambassador declared 'God has long ago himself passed sentence on it'.

Dynastic security—diplomatic pressure

The autumn of 1525—when so much of Tudor foreign policy was reconsidered and re-directed—included also the permanent break in Henry's relations with Catherine. From that date his relations with Spain were cool or hostile; his relations with the Pope were wholly concerned with the annulment of his marriage. Positive diplomacy had already established an alliance with France. The treaty of Moor House (Northwood, Middlesex) of August 1525 formally ended the declared state of war between England and France. In May 1526, France, Venice and the papacy joined together in the League of Cognac for the lessening of Spanish influence in Italy. Wolsey at first refused to join; plainly, he was striving to recover for England the status of neutral mediator from which she had stepped down into the fray in 1521. But this was the last time that Wolsey had any room for manoeuvre; it was Wolsey's last vain attempt to formulate and direct English foreign policy. Already the king's mind was firmly set on the need to provide for a male successor. That concern now overrode all other and gave consistent purpose to English foreign policy for the next fourteen years at least.

No one knows when Henry's preference for Anne Boleyn became a decision to marry her—to solve the succession problem by finding here the wife who could bear him a male heir. The decision may have been reached at any time from the earliest weeks of 1526. Thereafter the annulment of his marriage with Catherine was the single aim of English foreign policy; Wolsey continued as the uncomfortable servant of a policy which he had not chosen, until his failure became manifest and he was dismissed. The diplomatic problem had three facets: the first was how best to state Henry's claim that his marriage with Catherine was in law null and void; the second was how to create military conditions in Italy which would leave the Pope free to declare the marriage null, in spite of the opposition of Catherine's nephew, Charles V; in face of failure to create these military conditions, the third problem was nevertheless to create diplomatic conditions which would impel the Pope to make a declaration of nullity in defiance of Spanish armies in Italy.

The first facet of the problem was the least important. The justice and legality of Henry's claim might have been important in the decades which followed the counter-reformation but, under

Clement VII and his immediate predecessors, a marriage was to be declared null in accordance with the diplomatic interests of the papacy or, in the absence of a diplomatic interest, to oblige the great. Thus in March 1527, Margaret Tudor, Queen of Scotland, had her marriage with Archibald Douglas, Earl of Angus, declared null on the grounds that her first husband, James IV, might have survived the battle of Flodden for three years. Charles Brandon, Henry's brother-in-law, was released from three separate marriages by complaisant Church courts and Pope Clement himself confirmed that Brandon's marriage to Henry's sister Mary was itself entirely valid in spite of all the earlier contracts. In Henry VIII's present case Pope Clement was not interested in the justice or injustice of the argument; he valued the controversy because it gave him some influence over Charles V. He was chiefly anxious to postpone a decision in order to prolong the influence. Once he had given his verdict for Catherine, he had one benefit the less which he could offer Charles as a make-weight in any negotiations; if he gave his verdict for Henry, this could only be for the worse in respect of his relations with Charles. Clement's purpose was to postpone the verdict '... in order to nourish the controversy for a while as a means for maintaining in obedience the disposition of the kings'; such was the judgement passed on the motives of Clement by his intimate associate Paolo Giovio.[1]

Though the exact legal basis of Henry's petition may not have been important in diplomacy, it was important to him. He was, in such matters, a man of pedantic scruple who must satisfy his conscience. He insisted that the law of Leviticus, chapter 18, verse 16, forbad marriage between a man and his brother's wife and that it did so with such finality that no papal dispensation could permit an exception. This was, from beginning to end, the basis of Henry's petition and the basis on which Cranmer ultimately declared Henry to be a bachelor, and his first supposed marriage to be null. Wolsey, on the other hand, realised that Pope Clement would never welcome the suggestion that a papal dispensation lacked the power which was claimed for it. In any case, the law of Leviticus could be offset by the law of Deuteronomy, chapter 25, verse 5. In Wolsey's judgement,

[1] Price Zimmermann.

the dispensation of 1503 should be accepted as valid enough in itself, but of no effect in the case of Catherine's marriage with Henry, because it only had legal application if the previous marriage had been consummated. Now Catherine's marriage with Arthur had not been consummated, 'whereof the bull making no express mention',[1] as Wolsey stated the matter to Henry.

Wolsey's line of argument would have been the safer in logic. This was because Henry had already had Anne's sister, Mary, as his mistress. From this he had incurred a degree of consanguinity with Anne which stood in the way of marriage between Henry and Anne. Henry was therefore about to ask the Pope for a dispensation to permit his marriage with Anne, and, at the very same time, to ask the Pope to declare that an identical dispensation, granted by another Pope in 1503 to permit his marriage with Catherine, was not valid—identical except, one must add, in one every precise respect. Leviticus expressly forbad a male person from taking his brother's wife in marriage; it did not expressly forbid a woman from taking her sister's husband or lover in marriage. Henry took his stand on the argument that papal dispensation was not valid against that which was expressly ordered in Holy Writ, but was valid against that which was merely implied. In this detail, as in so much else after 1525, the diplomatic line advanced by Henry was adopted to the exclusion of that preferred by Wolsey.

However much men may have wondered whether the legal aspect of Henry's policy was wisely managed, they were in no doubt that the military situation remained intractably adverse. The League of Cognac (France, Venice and the papacy) did not weaken the Spanish grip on Italy during the summer of 1526. Austrian Hapsburg troops were even more firmly established in north Italy. Only the Turkish victory of Mohacz (August 1526) posed a threat to Charles V's position. The paramount need to weaken Spain in Italy, if Henry was ever to get a papal declaration of nullity, soon forced Wolsey from pretended neutrality into open alliance. From September 1526, England was subsidising the Cognac allies in order to prevent the Pope from becoming the prisoner of Spain. The subsidy developed into the Anglo-French treaty of April 1527 by which Henry was to

[1] Quoted in Scarisbrick, p. 194.

pay heavy subsidies to France and Mary Tudor was to marry the French king's son Henry. But this treaty was of no avail: England's revenue could not provide the subsidies and in any case Rome was occupied and sacked by Hapsburg forces in May 1527; the Pope was blockaded in his Castel Sant' Angelo.

This total collapse of papal government exceeded all expectation and gave Wolsey an unforeseen opportunity. Since the Pope was unfree, Wolsey could fairly suggest that a group of independent cardinals should commission Wolsey to act for the Pope; in this capacity, Wolsey would be able to bring a verdict in the king's matter, and no higher court would exist to which Catherine could appeal. For three months, from June 1527, Wolsey was in France paying court to Francis. Francis, he hoped, would prevail on a sufficient number of cardinals to confer quasi-papal authority on Wolsey. But Charles V defeated this manoeuvre by allowing the Pope to escape in December 1527, so that Henry's cause depended once more on the military defeat of Hapsburg troops in Italy. In January 1528, Wolsey declared war on Spain, but this was a mere gesture of belligerency, uttered without the consent of Henry or his council. No military action resulted; the declaration of war provoked riots in the cloth-making areas of England and, by May 1528, trade had to be permitted with the Netherlands once more. A truce with Spain followed in June. But the gesture may have had some value in giving encouragement to Francis. His army under Lautrec invaded Italy in April 1528 and won a fine series of victories in the Milanese, the Papal States and Naples. There was now a clear opportunity to press the king's case before the Pope.

In fact the king's case had been submitted to the Pope, back in December 1527. This was because Henry who had, from the first, disagreed with Wolsey as to the grounds on which nullity should be claimed, now disagreed as to the best way of getting a verdict. Moreover, Henry had come to distrust Wolsey's zeal, and to suspect that Wolsey wished to postpone the annulment until Henry's ardour for Anne had cooled and had transferred itself to a more suitable lady, such as Renée, cousin of Francis.[1] Consequently, while Wolsey attempted to get a commission from his fellow cardinals to try the

[1] See genealogy 6 on p. 75.

Dynastic security—diplomatic pressure

divorce case, Henry aimed to get the divorce directly from the Pope. In August 1527, while Wolsey was in France, Henry sent his secretary, William Knight (later to be Bishop of Bath and Wells), to smuggle his way into the presence of the beleaguered Pope with propositions which he had been instructed to conceal from Wolsey 'for any craft the Cardinal ... can find'. At that date, Knight failed to extract from the Pope anything likely to advance Henry's affairs, Wolsey recovered control of policy when he returned to England in September 1527 and, under his direction, three more approaches were made to the Pope in 1528. The last two, in April and June, were led by Stephen Gardiner (later to be Bishop of Winchester) and he was able, thanks to French victories in Italy, to wrest concessions from the Pope which might have given Henry his annulment if only the military situation in Italy had remained favourable. The Pope commissioned Wolsey and one other (in the event, Cardinal Campeggio) to investigate the king's marriage and to pronounce their verdict. The Pope also issued a second commission which was to be retained in secret by Campeggio himself; in this the Pope himself condemned the dispensation of 1503 as invalid and thus deprived Catherine, in advance, of the grounds on which she would presumably try to appeal to Rome from the verdict of the two cardinal-commissioners. With these two documents Clement satisfied the insistence of Henry's emissaries, gave himself some respite from their clamour, and all without publicly committing himself to anything dangerous: he had granted so much of Henry's demands that he could hardly be asked for more; yet every outcome must hinge on the second and secret commission. Since it was held by Campeggio, it could, in a moment, be destroyed by him; since it was secret, the world might thereafter never come to credit its existence.

Meanwhile Campeggio played for time until the balance of forces in Europe and Italy should become clear. His departure from Italy was delayed from June until August 1528. His journey to London was dragged out into October. The trial itself was postponed for months: Campeggio tried to persuade Catherine to enter a convent; the Spanish court discovered a second dispensation dated 1503 which covered Catherine's marriage to Henry but was not within the scope of any trial so far envisaged; Pope Clement was rumoured to have died in February 1529 and proceedings therefore stood in abeyance; Clement was later found to have been ill but not dead; in April 1529 Catherine petitioned the Pope to call her case to Rome.

Months before this, Spanish armies had begun to win the victories which drove the French northwards. Before Campeggio's court finally, at Henry's great insistence, began to sit at Blackfriars in June, Campeggio had received the Pope's instruction to avoid a verdict: 'every day stronger reasons are discovered [why a verdict for Henry] involves the certain ruin of the Apostolic See and the Church . . . if so great an injury be done to the Emperor'; so wrote the Pope's secretary to Campeggio. As the case proceeded at Blackfriars, Clement was subjected to the increasing fury of Spanish envoys. The overwhelming Spanish victory of Landriano in June settled the whole issue and the Pope decided 'to become an imperialist and live and die as such'.[1] In July, the Pope revoked Campeggio's power to proceed and Campeggio adjourned his court until October 1529. During this adjournment the Pope cited Henry and his case to Rome. The stream of events had moved strongly and English diplomacy was powerless to deflect them. The Pope made his peace with Charles V at the treaty of Barcelona (June); Francis made his peace with Charles at the treaty of Cambrai (August): Italy was in Spanish control and Henry VIII could do nothing but accede to the treaty of Cambrai three weeks later.

The dismissal of Wolsey in October 1529 did not alter the ends and means of English diplomacy but it cleared the decks for a more convincing display of the means and for the manifest pursuit of ends which hitherto had only been described and defined. Since 1521, Wolsey had been deflected from the neutral policy which he himself preferred; since 1527 he had been by-passed or otherwise prevented from choosing the means for achieving the king's purposes; since that date he had been more and more distrusted. But Wolsey or no Wolsey, there remained only the third expedient, since legal argument was not enough and military dominance was not attainable: the only remaining expedient was to overawe the Pope by diplomatic pressures into a declaration of nullity in defiance

[1] Quoted in Pollard (c), p. 124.

Dynastic security—diplomatic pressure

of all that Spanish arms could threaten on the Pope's doorstep. From the very first, this aim was hopeless and beyond the range of practical politics, yet Henry did not give up hope until he had actually married Anne Boleyn. As late as October 1532, Henry still cherished a distant expectation that Clement would send a papal commission to England with such instructions that its verdict was certain to be in his favour; even at that date, Henry still wanted the Pope's verdict if he could get it, for the prestige which it would have given to his cause in the eyes of his subjects and of foreign rulers.

If the immediate policy in August 1529 was to overawe the Pope into a declaration of nullity, how could this improbable object be at least attempted? The method had been foreshadowed by Wolsey in his many blustering efforts to get concessions from the Pope in the years 1527, 1528 and 1529. He had vehemently argued that, if the Pope did not satisfy Henry, then Henry would strip the Church in England of its privileges and would in the end break away from all allegiance to Rome: 'if the king's desire were not complied with ... there would follow the speedy and total ruin of the kingdom, of his Lordship [Wolsey] and the Church's influence in this kingdom. . . . I cannot reflect upon it and close my eyes for I see ruin, infamy and subversion of the whole dignity and estimation of the See Apostolic if this course is persisted in; . . . the course he [the Pope] now pursues will drive the king to adopt remedies which are injurious to the Pope';[1] such was Wolsey's message to the Pope in 1528. Such threats as these had not induced the Pope to grant Henry his annulment. But without Wolsey, Henry was able to give the threats more weight, partly by voicing them in person and partly by beginning, little by little, to implement them, thus to give the Pope an apprehension that a king who could carry out the lesser part of Wolsey's ominous forecast would not fear to execute the whole. Immediately, in August 1529, writs were issued for a parliament to meet in November. This was a conscious mobilisation by Henry of the national anti-clericalism which had been evident in the parliament of 1515. Parliament was to be permitted to show to the Pope how easily the 'total ruin . . . of the Church's influence in this kingdom' might be effected. Perhaps the Pope would take

[1] Wolsey, quoted in Pollard (b), p. 169.

warning and satisfy Henry, who was the only man who could protect the clergy from the laity. Members of parliament were quick to use their opportunity. Their anti-clericalism was varied in motive and not always coherent, but it was powerful and had a long tradition. Statutes were passed during the first months which reduced clerical fees, limited pluralism and transferred the trial of offenders from Church courts to the Exchequer.

These statutes were an intrusion upon the traditional right of the clergy to manage their own affairs, an intrusion inflicted by Parliament with the assistance of the king in the teeth of fierce opposition from bishops and abbots. They were a mere sample of what king and Parliament might effect if they were provoked and set their minds to the task. This was the diplomatic message which these measures were intended to have for the Pope. At the same time, the charge of praemunire levelled at Wolsey in October 1529 emphasised that papal instructions were operational in England only at the king's permission. A statute of April 1530 forbad papal dispensations for pluralism. In September a proclamation recalled to public notice the 1390 Statute of Provisors. King and Parliament were demonstrating that they had long possessed, and were willing to exert, a practical power to restrict papal authority in England. This was a power which they flaunted clearly enough in the Statute for the Conditional Restraint of Annates (February 1532). The act empowered the king after a lapse of twelve months to reduce the annates, payable to the Pope by a new bishop, to five per cent of the bishop's yearly income; the act required that if someone were chosen for a vacant bishopric he should be consecrated even though the Pope should try to exclude him for failure to pay annates in full. The Pope was intended to understand that, if he did not yield to Henry's wishes, papal revenue from England would be reduced.

Meanwhile Henry seems to have thought that he could bring moral pressure to bear on the papacy. At the suggestion of Dr Cranmer of Jesus College, Cambridge, Henry sent his envoys to invite many European universities to consider the king's case and to pronounce in his favour. Needless to say the response was ambiguous; it varied according to whether the universities were under the jurisdiction of Henry and his allies or of Charles V and his.

Nevertheless the response provided the ground of a portentous display of national solidarity in support of Henry, a demand to Clement, sealed by two archbishops, four bishops, twenty-five abbots, forty-two lay peers etc, that he settle the matter in the king's favour: 'let your holiness declare by your authority, what so many learned men proclaim . . . as you not only can, but, out of fatherly devotion, ought to do'. Of course these expedients made very little impact on papal policy. The most that can be said for their influence is that they may have encouraged Clement to postpone judgement against Henry. He was in no hurry; he held at bay the Spanish demand for an immediate judgement that the marriage was valid; in his schemes, where there was death, there was hope: if he only could play for time, then the death of Henry VIII or of Catherine might dissolve all difficulties without the need of any papal decision. In the meanwhile, he simply showed disapproval of Henry's conduct: in March 1530 he forbad any individual or university to express its opinion of Henry's marriage; in August, a second marriage by Henry was prohibited.

Henry's final species of diplomatic pressure was not quite so empty of possibilities. He hoped that Francis might use French influence with the Pope to extract favours for England. Throughout 1531, Henry's envoys canvassed this suggestion and at last Francis agreed to meet Henry outside Calais on the French frontier where they had met in 1520. The meeting of October 1532 raised an important possibility, for Clement had started to negotiate for a marriage between his niece, Catherine de Medici, and Francis's second son, Prince Henry. The Pope was seeking the solid diplomatic advantage of a marriage alliance; he might be willing to purchase it with a real concession to Henry VIII if Francis chose to include Henry's marriage interests in the scope of the negotiations—and this was what Francis promised to do (October 1532).

Whether this third diplomatic expedient would have induced the Pope to grant Henry the means to nullify his marriage and yet to remain within the Roman Catholic Church we can never know. Long before Francis met Clement in October 1533, Henry had gone his own way, had taken the law into his own hand and had married Anne (January 1533).

11 Henry VIII: Sovereign independence—diplomatic defiance, 1530–34

Of all the calamities which Wolsey had foreseen 'if the king's desire were not complied with', the ultimate calamity was 'the subversion of the whole dignity and estimation of the See Apostolic' in England. When Henry and his Reformation parliament intruded upon the privileges of churchmen in England, they were warning the Pope that men who were already taming the pretension of the clerical estate in England could ultimately defy, and take over, papal authority in England. This was Henry's ultimate diplomatic threat—ultimate in the sense that, once he turned this threat into action, he would not need to fabricate any more threats: his problems would be solved.

The central diplomatic achievement of the Tudor century was the assertion of national sovereignty: the exclusion from England of the Pope's authority and the repulse of all attempts to intrude any other external authority upon this country. The ideas which later generations have expressed in the phrase 'national sovereign independence' interested Henry from the early years of his reign. His ideas were of course cloudy and imprecise. At first he wanted no more than to assert his independence of any imperial authority such as the Holy Roman Emperor could claim over the princes of Germany. Such independence had been claimed by English kings in earlier centuries. With harmless pride Henry kept the claim alive. In 1513 the Admiral's flagship was called *Henry Imperial*; in 1517 Tunstall, later Bishop of London and Durham, said 'the crown of England is an Empire in itself'; in 1525 Henry's new Great Seal showed an emperor's crown; so too, but with more serious intent, did the Great Seal of 1532. But the claim to independent political power left room for the Pope's spiritual jurisdiction in England; for twenty years and more, Henry recognised that jurisdiction. It is difficult to guess what he meant by his statement to More in 1521: 'we received from that see [Rome] our crown imperial'. But his belief that the Pope possessed a jurisdiction in England is clear enough until 1530 at least; he was wholly anxious that the Pope should exert the jurisdiction to declare that the marriage with Catherine was null.

What Henry wanted from quite early in his reign was that his own jurisdiction in England should be fully asserted; he believed that it ought to apply equally and completely to all his subjects without exception. The powers and prerogatives which he possessed in respect of his laity were, he believed, equally valid in respect of his clergy. This was the belief that made him support the anti-clericalism of Parliament in 1512 and 1515. He approved of Parliament's attempt to restrict benefit of clergy. Out of deference to Wolsey, and from lack of confidence in his own judgement, Henry did at this stage deter Parliament from passing new laws in restraint of clerical privilege; similarly, he released from prison the chancellor of the Bishop of London and thus protected him from the furious anti-clericalism of London juries before whom he was charged with murder. However, the drift of Henry's own preference was shown in the pronouncement with which he dismissed this episode: 'we are, by sufferance of God, King of England and Kings of England in time past never had any superior but God; know therefore that we will maintain the rights of the crown in this matter, like our progenitors'. Moreover, Henry, who had stood forth as defender of the clergy in deference to Wolsey, resented this role and disliked Wolsey for imposing it on him. He expressed his resentment by promoting to courtly favour the only clergyman who had been outspoken in defence of the power of king and Parliament to control the clergy, one Friar Standish of London. In 1518 the see of St Asaph became vacant and Wolsey as a matter of course found his own nominee to fill it; however, Henry was in a mind to mortify his Chancellor and Wolsey saw his nominee discarded and Friar Standish promoted to the bishopric; 'for the singular assistance he has rendered for subverting the Church of England', as a bitter cleric observed.

In all this incipient anti-clericalism, Henry intended nothing anti-papal nor any ulterior motive of a diplomatic nature. Henry wanted only the complete assertion of his recognised authority within his own frontiers. But, in turning against the privileges of the English clergy, Henry was in fact turning against the privileges of an international corporation. Sooner or later, if he pursued his anti-clericalism, he must find himself in diplomatic conflict with the Pope who claimed to direct the corporation. This was a realisation or revelation which opened clearly before Henry's mind in 1528 and 1529, and guided his policies in the '30s. He realised that the papal authority that obstructed the civil interests of England and the personal interests of her king was the authority behind clerical claims to be beyond the authority of king and Parliament; these were different aspects of a single intrusion upon the law and realm of England. So long as Henry's main hope was that the Pope might yet do what was right by England and his marriage, he was content to wound and goad by paring away clerical immunities, that is by paring away at the papal corporation. But the ability to wound papal power in England was now clearly associated with the ability to end it. The prospect of ending papal authority became, month by month, more attractive. The notion of a breach with Rome arose as a threat, but it became an object of policy desired for its own sake.

'The crown of England is an Empire in itself', Tunstall had said in 1517, meaning only that the authority of the monarch over the laity of England was free from the supervision of any imperial overlord. But by 1517 Henry was well on the way to a belief that his authority went further than Tunstall would concede, namely that his rights over his English clergy were equal to his authority over ordinary laymen. Luther completed the thought-process by declaring that the authority of a godly prince extended over all his subjects, lay and clerical without exception, that it comprehended all matters, temporal and spiritual without exception, and that it was free from the supervision of any overlord, either imperial or papal. German princes at the diet of Speyer (1526) accepted this statement,

Sovereign independence—diplomatic defiance

and Henry may have been directly informed of events at Speyer. In any case he read, and was excited by, Tyndale's exposition of these same beliefs in his book *Obedience of a Christian man* (1529). 'This is a book for me and for all kings to read', said Henry. Wolsey had warned the Pope that papal authority in England might be subverted; the warning had substance even by 1529. When Henry summoned Parliament for November 1529 in order to release an attack on clerical privilege, he already had in contemplation an elimination of papal authority. For a year Henry allowed this project to rest as no more than a tacit threat. August 1530 seems to have been the month of decision. Perhaps an apparent hardening of Clement's attitude to his marriage hardened Henry in his rejection of papal authority in England. After August 1530, Henry seems to have been convinced that God had created a Christendom of fully autonomous provinces under the rule of 'emperors'. Perhaps he was uncertain whether the autonomy belonged to the community of Christians or was the personal inheritance of the ruler, but he was quite certain that usurpation had been effected during past centuries by the papacy and that he must in England's case reassert the true autonomy of the community or of its 'emperor'. If the Pope had been amenable, Henry might have accepted a Concordat, leaving to the Pope a limited right to define doctrine and heresy, but nothing in the Concordat would have been allowed to defeat the central purpose.

In the autumn of 1530 Henry's purpose became explicit. For the whole community of Englishmen he claimed a traditional right never to be summoned to trial in a foreign court. For himself, he ordered his agents in Rome to declare that he was 'set on such a pinnacle of dignity that we know no superior on earth. By none act [were the English envoys in Rome to] consent, allow or approve the Pope's jurisdiction, but that we may hereafter depart from the same without contrariety in our own acts.' Charles Brandon (Suffolk) and George Boleyn told a papal emissary that 'the king is absolute Emperor and Pope in his kingdom'.

Having presented his challenge to the Pope, Henry had to impose his claims on the English clergy. In January 1531, the charge of breach of praemunire was brought against the whole body of English clergy, who, as part of the price of their royal pardon, were required to acknowledge that Henry was 'protector and only supreme head of the English Church', that he had a 'cure of souls' committed to him by God, and that they themselves retained only those liberties which 'do not detract... from the laws of the realm'. Henry explained to Bishop Tunstall that he was claiming for himself a complete overlordship of the English clergy, except that he would neither preach nor administer the sacraments. The clergy avoided acknowledging a royal 'cure of souls' and a limitation on the liberties of the Church; they acknowleged Henry as head of the Church only 'as far as the law of Christ allows'. Henry had stated his claims clearly but he had not yet been successful in persuading the clergy to acknowledge them. He continued to reject the Pope's authority: 'I shall never consent to his being judge', he said in June 1531. Beyond that Henry seemed to make no headway at all for another twelve months. Parliament, which had been adjourned in January 1531, remained so until January 1532. One wonders whether Henry was at a loss, uncertain what to do next, or, knowing what to do, was frightened that the politically-important JP classes would not stand for it. Did he lose his nerve?

But in January 1532 progress was renewed. King and Parliament began to move more surely; they began to subjugate the English clergy under royal control and so to elbow out the Pope. Thomas Cromwell had, by December 1531, become one of the inner ring of royal councillors; he was undoubtedly the chief navigator of national affairs during England's withdrawal from Roman allegiance in 1533 and 1534. One can guess therefore that it was his judgement that brought about this decision of January 1532 to release the energies of Parliament against the clergy and the Pope. What exactly Cromwell proposed as a policy for ending papal authority can never be known. But let us suppose that politicians can be classified into two types: those of the first type like to start by stating the great principle of action and afterwards fill in the details as best they can; those of the second type like to build from one detail to another until the great principle can at last be proclaimed in order to describe the completed work: the first type likes to issue a declaration of the rights of man and then tries to establish these rights as a reality; the second likes to take practical steps which one by one build up a situation in which citizens enjoy rights which can then be declared. We can hazard a guess that Henry belonged to the first type; his instinct was to declare the authority of the Pope in England to be null and void and then to fill in the details. Henry's homely metaphor was 'if one should pull down an old stone wall, and begin at the lower part, the upper part thereof might chance to fall upon his head'. But a royal proclamation of papal nullity was such a collossal démarche that he may well have hesitated at the prospect, even have lost his nerve. In that case, one would place Cromwell among the second type of politician, the type who would accept the metaphor but would emphasise that the great wall could still be removed stone by stone until none of it remained. Such a suggestion of small steps, one taken after the other, could restore Henry's nerve for action, supposing that he had lost his nerve in what had seemed an all-or-nothing situation.

The first step was to confront the clergy in April 1532 with Parliament's 'supplication against the Ordinaries' (ie. against the bishops). By the 'submission of the Clergy' which was embodied in an act of Parliament (May 1532), all existing canon law was to be valid in England only if it was consistent with the law of the land and received royal assent; new canon law was to be valid only if it received royal assent; the rest of canon law should be annulled. This statute gave to the king a degree of real control over the Church, whereas the previous recognition that he was supreme head 'as far as the law of Christ allows' had been a gesture empty of practical consequence, however splendid the words may have sounded. Thomas More, who recognised the difference, resigned from Henry's service because of the parliamentary act which embodied this submission and because he believed that the Church in England was subject to the authority of the Pope rather than to the authority of king and Parliament.

Archbishop Warham died in August 1532. In accordance with a policy of taking one step at a time, Henry began to cultivate the friendship of the Pope; he even paid the arrears of Annates. In this manner, he secured from the Pope a nomination of Cranmer as the new Archbishop of Canterbury. But by January 1533, Anne was pregnant. We cannot know whether Henry allowed Cromwell to move once more against papal jurisdiction in England because the nullification of his marriage with Catherine was now urgent, or perhaps that he allowed Anne to become pregnant because he was now confident that Cromwell could move effectively against papal jurisdiction in England. Before the end of January 1533 he married her secretly. Parliament was summoned for February and 'An Act that ... appeals ... shall not be from henceforth had nor used but within this realm' was put before the members. This statute cut away from papal supervision all legal proceedings that should ever start in England. Such cases were to be 'finally and definitely adjudged and determined within the King's jurisdiction ... and not elsewhere; ... the English Church [for which king and Parliament had already made themselves effective legislators] ... hath been always thought, and is also at this hour, sufficient ... of itself without the intermeddling of any exterior person or persons to declare and determine all such doubts ... as to their rooms spiritual doth appertain'.

Passed by Parliament in March 1533, this statute went far towards turning England into a sovereign independent nation-state; what remained to be done was added systematically during the next twenty months. Annate payments to the papacy were ended in July. In the early months of 1534 these and all other such payments were, by statute, diverted to the crown. New bishops were to be nominated by the king and consecrated without reference to the Pope. The Submission of the Clergy (1532) was again confirmed by a statute, and this withdrew all diplomatic recognition of the Pope except in his capacity as 'Bishop of Rome'. In the November session 1534, parliamentary statute recognised Henry as supreme head of the Church without the limiting words, 'as far as the law of Christ allows'. Even the definition of heresy was now within his prerogative —the Ten Articles of 1536 were proclaimed on royal authority without reference to Pope or Parliament. Home-brewed statute hereafter supplanted canon law or the conscience of Europe and became the only valid authority for an Englishman: '*your thinking* should not be your trial, but the *law* must define whether you oughted to utter it or not'; so said Cromwell to Bishop Fisher in 1534.[1]

[1] Elton (b).

Sovereign independence—diplomatic defiance

The new position could even be expressed in these extreme terms spoken to Cromwell: 'an act of parliament, made in this realm for the commonwealth of the same, ought rather to be observed in this the same realm than any General Council. And I think that the Holy Ghost is as verily present at such an act as he ever was at any General Council.'

Thus a new diplomatic status had been attained for Henry VIII's England, the status of national sovereign independence. The long-term effects of the change of status, for good or ill, were surely enormous. Some were perhaps coincidental: for example that Elizabeth and not Mary Stuart, Queen of Scots, succeeded to the English throne in 1558. Other effects were strictly consequential on the change of status: for example, that Englishmen were not guided by the Index of the Roman Catholic Church nor very much influenced by the baroque way of life which was the richest harvest of the counter-reformation. Instead, they evolved their native 'Church of England', guided by Hooker, Parker, Cranmer and others in the mellow ways of religious humanism, that blending of the old with the new, of Christian tradition with Greek stimulus and contemporary invention, which, in the days of Erasmus, had been the greatest hope of the greatest minds of Christian Europe. Erasmus and his friends had indeed hoped for international institutions, generating a European way of life, but the only going concern which was also international turned in preference to the anti-humanism of the counter-reformation. Hence the Church of England, with its universities and schools, was the one European establishment which consciously embodied these rich possibilities.[1] This was a Church which for three hundred years did much to help ordinary English folk in their efforts to make some sense of life's experience. One can find glimpses of the rhythm, the enrichment and the direction which this Church imparted to men's experience of life.[2] Even contemporaries were partly conscious of its pervasive force: 'through the cautious humble spirit of Hooker there gleams for one single moment a careful and qualified pride in the achieve-

[1] One might claim that Arminius, in the province of Holland, modified the Calvinist Church to this same purpose.
[2] See Rowse, Trevor-Roper, Jordan, and Laslett.

ment of the English Church'.[1] Because Englishmen derived from this Church a way of life that was unique and seemed indigenous, their great defensive wars always possessed ideological overtones; in 1588 as in 1702 men were defending their own way of life from the intrusion of another way which would have been alien to them; they were never fighting merely to defend a dynasty.

Such consequences as these followed from the breach with Rome. Ironically, the breach failed entirely to bring about its initial purpose; the breach did nothing to solve the succession problem in terms which Henry could regard as satisfactory. Convocation declared the circumstance of his supposed marriage with Catherine to be unacceptable to God; Cranmer pronounced him to have been a bachelor until 1533 and therefore to be truly married to Anne Boleyn; Anne was crowned queen, but her children were a daughter and a still-born son. There was as yet no male heir. Henry only solved his succession problem when he married Jane Seymour (May 1536) and so became the father of an undoubted male heir (October 1537). But this marriage did not require any defiance of Rome. It was valid because his first wife in the eyes of Catholic Europe had died in January 1536 and his first wife in the eyes of English law had been executed eleven days before he married Jane (May 1536).

Meanwhile Pope Clement had cautiously resisted Henry's growing independence. A bull of excommunication was drafted by Pope Clement VII in July 1533; this gave Henry until September to take back his wife Catherine, but deposition was carefully avoided and the bull itself was never promulgated. In March 1534 the marriage with Catherine was declared to be valid. The new Pope, Paul III (September 1534), seems to have hoped for a reconciliation and even to have thought to flatter Henry by raising Bishop Fisher to be a cardinal, but Henry was not attracted and Fisher was executed. Again a bull of excommunication was drafted (August 1535); this did include a deposition of Henry but, again, promulgation was delayed. Unless by rebellion from within or invasion from without, the new status of English independence seemed unassailable.

[1] Rowse, p. 390.

12 Henry VIII: To underpin England's sovereign independence, 1534–40

Papal interdict in the reign of King John had inflicted inconvenience and distress of mind on Englishmen. This distress was never suffered by the subjects of Henry VIII, because almost the whole of the clergy, many of them indeed reluctantly, accepted his claim to independence and rejected the Pope's overriding claim. Acquiescence by the clergy reflected acquiescence by the greater part of the nation: conservative leaders like the Duke of Norfolk or Bishop Gardiner of Winchester, as well as progressives like Archbishop Cranmer and Thomas Cromwell, accepted the need to obey their monarch; they were nationalist enough to reject control from Italy. But an effective minority of Englishmen did reject the change of allegiance and might have revolted against it. The majority, though they acquiesced at this stage and rejected papal leadership as against their king, might yet have rallied to a local patriotic leader if he had managed to formulate the resentment which accumulated as new practices replaced old traditions and every week added offence. In short the majority might have rallied to the minority if the minority had been effectively vocal. For this reason, Henry had to underpin the legal and diplomatic moves which ended his dependence on Rome, by striking down any of the native minority who raised a voice against them: Elizabeth Barton, the Nun of Kent, was executed for treason in May 1534; Bishop Fisher and Sir Thomas More were arrested in May 1534 and executed a year later; Carthusian monks and Observant Franciscans, both groups from London, were executed in 1535. Mary Tudor was forced to renounce her allegiance to the Pope and accept her father's supremacy. In the end, Henry had to face the rebellions in Lincolnshire, Yorkshire and the north which are called 'The Pilgrimage of Grace' (October 1536 to January 1537). At one stage his military position became so precarious that the Duke of Norfolk, in command of loyal militia forces, had to play for time by negotiating with the rebels. Popes Clement VII and Paul III do not seem to have been acutely interested in these signs of native rebellion against Henry. Clement was ageing; as always he was preoccupied by family interests. He gave no guidance or encouragement to actual or potential rebels. Paul III seemed at first to hope for a reconciliation or compromise with Henry. His anger at the execution of Bishop Fisher burnt itself out in the decision to draft a bull of excommunication and deposition. Even this took many months; it was not completed until January 1536. Publication was indefinitely postponed. When the northerners rebelled they received no recognisable encouragement from Rome. Not until they had dispersed was Reginald Pole made cardinal in December 1536 and then *legate a latere* in February 1537; this was much too late to help any rebellion. At no stage did the Pope publish the deposition of Henry or take any steps which might have roused the rebels to such singleness of purpose as would have enabled them to overrun the southern militia.

One must judge from this and from later events that Pope Paul counted on a crusading invasion rather than a native rebellion to bring England back to the Roman Church. This was indeed a possibility which Henry had to fear—a possibility which he had continually to guard against. But, if he feared it, he did not really expect it, because he trusted that all rulers were like himself—fundamentally *politiques* schemers who would put national interest before religious zeal. In this, he differed from Thomas Cromwell (as Queen Elizabeth was to differ from William Cecil), because Cromwell and Cecil (both fundamentally men of religious conviction) believed that in the end Catholic powers would unite in a crusade against England.

The basis of Henry's diplomacy was a total confidence that Francis and Charles V would never trust each other; neither of them would ever allow the other to conquer England; neither would commit an army to the conquest of England while the other was uncommitted. Whatever peace might be negotiated between them, they would be at war with each other again before long. This was the rivalry on which Henry always relied. Already in October 1532 he had met Francis and won his good offices to press for a papal nullification of his marriage. After Henry had broken with the Pope and married Anne, Francis was still willing to earn Henry's support: Henry, naturally enough, was deeply disturbed by Clement's draft bull of excommunication; he could not be sure of the reactions of his subjects. (The Duke of Norfolk, when he heard of the bull, was shocked almost to fainting, because its impact might be to split England into civil war.) At every stage of this contest between king and papacy, Henry seemed to be scared, above all, of internal resistance by his own subjects, whereas the Pope was relying, above all, on external invasion by the French, Spaniards and Scots. Henry's diplomatic response to every bull of deposition was to appeal to a General Council and, when a General Council was called, to reject its agenda as being a denial of natural justice. But in this instance, effective diplomatic assistance came from Francis. Still determined to retain Henry's friendship, Francis prevailed on the Pope to keep the bull unpublished when he met Pope Clement in October 1533. In 1534 Francis offered Henry naval assistance in case Charles V should try to invade England.

Charles V was equally willing to conciliate Henry. He did indeed work for the welfare of Mary Tudor, persecuted as she was at this time; perhaps out of family duty to his cousin, perhaps with an eye to the ultimate restoration of England to the Roman Church, he tried to get for Mary Tudor the protection of a good Catholic marriage with Reginald Pole, or with the King of Scotland, or with Angoulême the son of King Francis, and, when none of these plans won any response from Henry, Charles became party to the first of many Spanish schemes to smuggle Mary out of England (April 1535).

But Charles was entirely opposed to an invasion. Bishop Fisher appealed to him to invade in 1533, and Pope Clement hoped vaguely for a Franco-Spanish crusade; but Charles was convinced that the economy of the Netherlands could not stand an interruption of trade with England. To emphasise this fact Henry himself closed the

Staple at Calais for a few weeks in August 1533. Charles instructed the Pope on no account to lay England under an interdict as that 'would disturb her intercourse with Spain and Flanders'.[1] Not surprisingly, Henry was 'never . . . merrier than he is now' (August 1533).[2]

The election of Pope Paul III (September 1534) revived the ambitions of Francis. He determined to invade Italy once more and to reverse the treaty of Cambrai. As for Charles V, he was preoccupied with the balance of power in the Mediterranean, because Barbarossa, vassal of the Sultan Suleiman, had established himself in Tunis and could harass Spanish communications with Italy. In all the circumstances, Henry, having survived the summer months of 1534, could confidently wait for war to break out in Italy between Charles V and Francis. His confidence was so complete that he even rejected an alliance which Francis offered in September 1534. Fighting in Italy began in April 1536. Charles's ambassador returned to London. England was secure from any threat of invasion for two years, that is until the truce of Nice was negotiated between Pope, Charles and Francis in June 1538.

But, if England was secure, Cromwell and Henry did not take security for granted. In these years began the naval rearmament which was to provide naval defence in 1539 and in subsequent years of crisis. Henry's breach with Rome—an adventurous act of policy—had necessarily to be covered by rearmament and for this large sums of money were needed. The dissolution of monasteries which began in 1536, besides dispersing men who might otherwise support a Catholic invasion by the Pope's allies, was necessary to provide money for defence.

But Cromwell was not satisfied with rearmament; he lacked Henry's confidence in the rivalry of Charles and Francis. He always feared that Charles and Francis would in the end join together in a crusade against England. Consequently, Cromwell maintained a long course of negotiations with the protestant princes of Germany. This was a means of re-insurance against invasion by Charles, for as soon as he committed his forces to an invasion of

[1] Pollard (b), p. 248.
[2] Quoted in Pollard (b), p. 246.

England the German princes could attack the possessions of Charles or his allies in Germany. In times of comparative security, the English were content to maintain a friendly correspondence with potential allies in Germany. In times of acute danger Cromwell would propose a close alliance and would make some show of wishing for a religious union of the Church in England with the Lutheran Churches of Germany or at least with the hybrid Christian-humanist Church of Cleves. But although Cromwell may have had a genuine religious interest in these negotiations, Henry disliked their religious implications and doubted their military value. But he was always aware of what was afoot. Indeed, he had himself originally reopened correspondence with Luther in 1531. Suffice it to say that negotiations were undertaken with Hamburg and Lübeck in the years 1532 to 1534, nominally to achieve a military alliance and a religious union. Again, in 1535, Edward Fox, later Bishop of Hereford, went to Saxony on behalf of the English government. In negotiation with Melanchthon he spun out the 'Wittenberg Articles' of religious belief which might have become the basis of a military and religious alliance between England and the German princes. But at heart Henry was always hostile to any sincere association with the Lutherans.

This was the situation when England and Henry once more found themselves in real jeopardy from France, Spain and the Pope in June 1538. The threat of a Catholic crusade remained acute for ten months until April 1539. In December 1538, Pope Paul pronounced the excommunication and deposition of Henry. David Beaton, a Scottish representative at the French court, was made cardinal and sent back to his native Scotland to organise an invasion from the north whenever France and Spain should invade from the south. (James V of Scotland had recently married Mary of Guise.) Charles and Francis, meeting at Aigues-Mortes, agreed not to negotiate with Henry (January 1539). Both recalled their ambassadors from London in February; English ships in Netherland ports were seized. French and Spanish ships were massed, as for an invasion, at Boulogne and Antwerp.

The response of Henry and his Council was to forbid any English ships to leave home waters. One hundred and fifty ships were organised for coastal defence. Fortresses were built along the south coast, as at Walmer and Dover, at Calshot and Hurst, at St Mawes and Pendennis. The commemorative plaque at St Mawes proclaims, to this day: 'Henricus Octavus Rex Angl. Franc. et Hiberniae Invictus me Posuit Praesidium Reipublicae Terrorem Hostibus'. The dissolution of 'divers and great solemn monasteries' was pushed ahead in 1539 to provide money for the enormous war effort; masonary, quarried from abbey buildings, provided for fortress walls—the stone of Beaulieu became the walls of Hurst Castle.

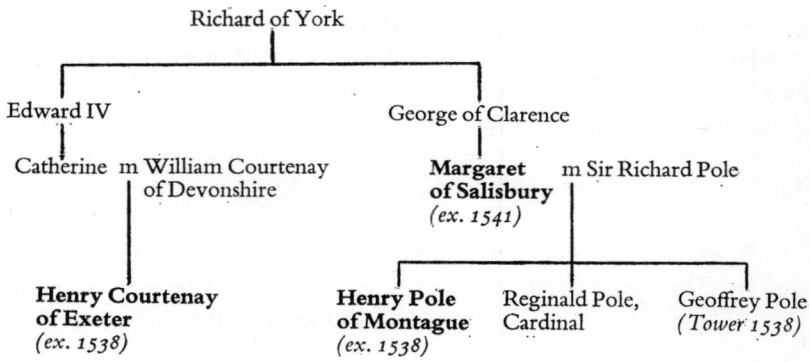

Genealogy 8. Possible contestants for the English throne, executed 1538–1541

The militia of the southern counties, and of the Scottish border counties, was mobilised. National ardour was aroused in national defence. Rigorous preventive action was taken against any who were likely to aid a Roman Catholic invasion or who had a claim to the throne from which Henry was to be deposed by the invaders. Henry Courtenay the Marquis of Exeter, Henry Pole the Lord Montague, the abbots and monks of Reading and Glastonbury were all executed as for treason, and Margaret, Countess of Salisbury, was imprisoned for being the mother of Cardinal Reginald Pole. Even the shrine of St Thomas was despoiled to emphasise that 'he was really a rebel who fled the realm to France and to the Bishop of Rome to procure the abrogation of wholesome laws'.

Meanwhile, as one would expect, negotiations for a religious union with Saxony started again in 1538. It is surely a tribute to

To underpin England's sovereign independence

Henry's religious conviction and to his cold political judgement that the negotiations with Lutheran Saxony came to nothing. But with Duke John of Cleves Henry shared a fellow-feeling; neither monarch was happy to go all the way with Luther; each was developing his own amalgam of religious doctrine. A proposal of marriage between Henry and Duke John's daughter was mentioned in January 1539.

The threat of invasion lifted in April 1539 but it did not wholly disperse. Charles V moved his ships from Antwerp to the Mediterranean. Francis sent his ambassador back to London. Nevertheless, the Cleves marriage project was revived in October. Bishop Gardiner, its chief opponent, was dismissed from the Council. Anne of Cleves arrived in December; Henry married her in January 1540, in spite of his strong and immediate repugnance. This seems to have been an act of desperate re-insurance, pressed on Henry by Cromwell, because Cromwell was fearful of a reconciliation of Charles and Francis. They were indeed meeting in France during this very January. But, by June, Charles and Francis were quarrelling bitterly about the future of Milan; once more Henry felt wholly confident. He could address Charles V as 'loving brother and most cordial friend'. The Pope's great effort had faded away. Henry's status had survived and thereby had acquired respectability. With Catherine long since dead, no family conflict stood between Henry and Charles. England and Spain could work together as they had in 1512. The fall and execution of Cromwell was itself a gesture of reconciliation offered by Henry to Charles in July 1540. Henry felt quite safe—as he had long felt very willing—to have his marriage with Anne annulled.

PART IIB
Between Two Eras

A note on chapters 13 and 14

The foreign policy of the 1540s holds a special interest for ordinary readers because leading scholars disagree in their estimate of Henry's main aim. A. F. Pollard believed that Henry wanted to unify the British Isles by absorbing Wales, Ireland and Scotland into a single 'Greater Britain'. J. J. Scarisbrick argued that Henry was set on the conquest of France and that his actions against Scotland were secondary to his attack on France, although the unexpected weakness of Scotland did cause him to expend more military resources against Scotland than at first he had intended. Scarisbrick has rejected Pollard's ideas not only in their original form but also as 'partly restated in sophisticated form' by R. B. Wernham. The ordinary reader, as an honest juror in face of learned counsel, is thrown back on his own resources for a verdict. As he projects himself into the mind and situation of Henry VIII, he may find that facts which do not speak for themselves nevertheless enable him to say something on their behalf.

13 Towards a 'Unified kingdom of Great Britain', 1530–40

Henry and his England achieved national sovereign independence; they were blessed with a full degree of recognition in that Charles V was willing to join Henry in an old-style alliance. They were blessed also in that the king had fathered a male heir. But Prince Edward was only three years old. The moment of a child's accession could always bring the hazard of civil war. This fact had been emphasised in May 1538 when, for a few days, Henry seemed to be choking to death—black in the face and unable to speak from some infection of the lungs. As Henry lay near to death, men could foresee the possibility of civil war between Roman Catholic supporters of Mary Tudor and men of a protestant inclination supporting the child-heir who belonged on his mother's side, to the protestant Seymours. Where, in such a conflict, would stand the Anglo-Catholic conservatives, Norfolk, Suffolk and Gardiner? They were hostile to Cromwell, who seemed in 1538 to have engrossed all political power under the king. They were not likely to rally to the support of Edward if Edward was to be the pupil of Cromwell. In these late 1530s, Henry saw very clearly that the support of anglican conservatives was necessary to guarantee the peaceful accession of his son. Hence Henry's political operations of 1539 and 1540—the reactionary 'Six Articles', the execution of Cromwell and the marriage to Catherine Howard—look like a manoeuvre or bargain by which he intended to restore unanimity to his council, to reconcile Norfolk with the brothers of Jane Seymour (who were Prince Edward's uncles) and to pledge his conservative councillors to Edward's succession; the execution of Cromwell was the price paid for a secure succession.

The sovereign independence of England, the recognition accorded by Charles V and the new solidarity subsisting between the king and his councillors were all part of the strength of England in 1540. Since monarch and nation found themselves thus suddenly in a position of strength, the question would arise, how best that strength might be applied—what ought to be the role of a country which had in so many respects broken with its past.

Previous events of earlier centuries, and indeed of this reign also, must have kept 'the unification of the British Isles' somewhere on the mental agenda of every English statesman. 'There had not been an English king who had not seriously aimed to unite the two kingdoms' said a sixteenth-century Scotsman.[1] James IV's incursion to Flodden and the later intrusions by Albany must have goaded the mind of Henry and his associates. Henry had used the title of 'Protector of Scotland' since 1514. Thomas Cromwell's brilliant assessment in 1523, even if it was little noticed at that time, must have attracted attention in his years of power when sycophants will have raked over the past to discover his prejudices—enemies to discover words and deeds which might trip up his present greatness. Men must have discovered or remembered his great petitionary speech of 1523: 'if it would please his magnanimous courage to convert first and chief his whole intent and purpose not only to the over-running and subduing of Scotland but also to join the same realm unto his, so that both they and we might live under one Bessaunce (imperial bounty), Law and Polity for ever'. Even if Henry had been disposed to forget Scotland, King James V had the provocative talent to keep Scottish affairs to the forefront of Henry's attention.

From 1533 James presented himself as a suitable candidate for the English throne in case Henry were deposed by the Catholics of Europe and England. In any event, with Mary Tudor and Elizabeth made illegitimate, James was immediate heir, next after his mother Margaret, to Henry. This was not in itself contrary to England's interest, but was rendered so by James's policy of limitless subservience to France: he restored the Franco-Scottish alliance, visited France, and married the daughter of Francis; when she died, he

[1] Quoted in Donaldson, p. 282.

Towards a 'Unified kingdom of Great Britain'

took Mary of Guise as his second wife. Finally he placed himself entirely at the disposal of Cardinal Beaton, an ardent Catholic crusader, a French courtier and an arch-opponent of Henry's breach with Rome. Thus England, at the moment of achieving sovereign independence, was in danger of falling to a ruler under whom she would be reabsorbed into Europe as a Franco-Scottish appendage.

Moreover, events before 1540 did not limit Henry's 'British' interests to Scotland. Wales had recently been brought to better order by Bishop Rowland Lee, President of the Council of Wales from 1534. During his tenure of office, Wales was reorganised county by county, with justices of the peace and members of Parliament, so that the country was fully incorporated with England (1534).

Towards Ireland, Henry had at first continued the policy adopted by his father: the clans with their Norman or Gaelic chieftains were left to fight out their rivalries without interference from England; the English Pale was ruled on behalf of the English government by the Earl of Kildare, with the title of deputy-lieutenant, but also with the advice of English councillors who were variously influential as their personalities varied. Kildare's own clan-lands were immediately south-west of the Pale. In 1520, Henry inflicted on the ninth Earl of Kildare some part of the salutary shock which Poynings had previously been sent to inflict on the eighth earl. Deputy-lieutenant Kildare was relieved of his office by the arrival of Thomas, Earl of Surrey, with a thousand royal soldiers and full powers as Lieutenant for Ireland. For eighteen months England's authority was effective within the Pale and the English councillors were paramount, but a subjugation of Ireland could not be considered. In 1521 Surrey withdrew and Kildare resumed his function of deputy-lieutenant in the Pale, but rather more diffidently. For the most part any early Tudor king expected to leave the Irish to themselves unless they tried to ally with England's enemies or to interfere with the English succession. In 1534, Cromwell's agents in Dublin accused the Earl of Kildare of such intentions; he was summoned to London and put in the Tower where he died. His son, 'Silken Thomas', rose in rebellion. He was defeated by Piers, Earl of Ormond and leader of the Butler clan, who were still unique among

Irish clans for their attachment to the house of Lancaster. 'Silken Thomas' was captured and later executed at Tyburn. Sir William Skeffington arrived from England as deputy-lieutenant, to be followed by Lord Grey in 1537, and Lord St Leger in 1540.

A new and vigorous policy was henceforth applied in the Pale; an effective garrison was always maintained there and the rest of Ireland, though usually left to itself, was always open to intrusion from Dublin. During this time Henry was declared to be 'Supreme Head on earth of the Church of Ireland' in place of 'the usurped authority of the Bishop of Rome ... inasuch as this land of Ireland is the King's proper dominion of England and united, knit and belonging to the Imperial Crown of the same realm'.[1] This statute was obeyed only within the Pale and in Leinster where Ormond's influence was paramount. Elsewhere the old pieties lived on.

The new Tudor deputy-lieutenants also pushed ahead with the policy of 'surrender and re-grant' whereby Gaelic chieftains gave up their traditional rights and accepted the status of freehold tenants-in-chief of the crown with the rights of landlords over their clansmen. These were the general circumstances in which Henry assumed the title of King of Ireland (June 1541) by right of inheritance and conquest. Thus, throughout the 1530s, the government of England involved itself multifariously and persistently with the other three territories of the British Isles. In respect of Wales and Ireland, the assumption behind the statutes was that the constituent territories of the British Isles were theoretically, and ought actually to be, integral with England. Every English statesman, and especially the king, held the idea of the unification of Britain near the forefront of his mind.

[1] Quoted in Curtis, p. 165.

14 A new role or the old?—groping for national unity, identity and role, 1540–50

The role which Henry seems to have chosen for England in 1540 was the role of architect and procreator of a 'Unified Kingdom of Greater Britain'. Once Henry had escaped from the invasion crisis of 1539 and had restored the unity of his Council by executing Cromwell, he launched a major effort to detach James V from his French alliance, from his allegiance to Rome and from his subservience to Cardinal Beaton. Henry wanted to establish James in line of succession to the English throne—second only to Prince Edward as the law stood in 1540—in exchange for an Anglo-Scottish alliance and a Scottish breach with Rome. Henry was showing an equal concern for England's sovereign independence from Europe and for the unification of Greater Britain.

The next year (June 1541) Henry set out for a great meeting with James V at York. The enormous scale and cost of his entourage emphasised the importance of his objectives; it was in fact a military force which could turn from diplomatic display to invasion. Union with Scotland was the object to which Henry applied the resources which seemed to be his at the end of 1540 when, for the first time since Cromwell rose to power, the natural leaders of the nation seemed reconciled to the government and foreign invasion was no threat at all.

Henry at York waited for James V from 19th September 1541 until the 29th. Perhaps James was afraid of being kidnapped. In any case, Henry was disappointed of his hope that England and Scotland could be drawn closer towards alliance and ultimate union. He returned to London to learn that Prince Edward was ill, to be reminded that this son might well die before the father and leave behind a doubtful succession after all. Henry returned to learn also of the many adulteries of Queen Catherine Howard which, while they must necessitate her divorce, must also put a distance between the king and the Duke of Norfolk, so recently reconciled to the king's inner councils. The divisions which this foreshadowed in any possible regency council were frightening. Moreover these divisions reflected growing religious divisions in the country where 'some be too stiff in their old *Mumpsimius*, others too busy and curious in their new *Sumpsimius*'.[1]

The unity and strength which Henry had taken for granted when he went north to York manifestly did not exist. The nation had emerged from ten years of danger, not united and invigorated, but, on the contrary, bewildered and at a loss (like many another similarly emergent nation—Japan for example in this year 1972), lacking any sense of her role in the world. In this condition, the nation was unfit to bear the strain of a truly exacting enterprise, the strain of being bogged down in wars of conquest in Ireland or Scotland. The obvious expedient to adopt, in the circumstances of 1541-2, was a return to the old prescription for national unity, namely the glittering quasi-chivalric contest with France. England would be able to prove herself to herself in the old way, to recover unity in face of the old enemy.

Henry, it is suggested, changed his course at the end of 1541 and gave priority to national unity and security of succession. The nation's leaders, the potential regents, must prove themselves to themselves and to each other in the traditional court of war. The nation was not strong enough to stand the nervous exhaustion of warfare in the mists and moorlands of Scotland and of Ireland, where defeat brought dishonour and victory brought endless tours of duty in remote garrisons; from those areas even conquerors returned with little prestige. The nation needed the tonic of warfare in the familiar battlefields of France; from those areas, commanders could return with renown, even from more or less futile campaigns. The nation could not sustain war with the Scots; it needed war with France. On this hypothesis, one would judge that Henry

[1] Quoted in Pollard (b), p. 336.

had at first believed that he had abundant resources, spiritual and material, and, believing this, he preferred and chose a policy that aimed at the unification of the British Isles. This was the object towards which his energies were directed until the last few weeks of 1541. But when he discovered that his country and government were divided, were spiritually bankrupt and were heading for a civil war of succession, then he changed his aim and chose to bring 'England to herself' once more; he chose to restore the nation's health in the only way that he knew. Through 1542 and in subsequent years, Henry's energies were directed to the maintenance of war with France.

After Henry's return from York in late 1541, and after the divorce and execution of Catherine Howard, Henry entered into negotiations with Charles V for a joint invasion of France. Negotiations continued all through 1542. They were held up because Charles V could not accept a treaty of alliance which referred to Henry as 'Supreme Head of the Church'; Henry could only accept one which did. Nevertheless the great Anglo-Imperial treaty of mutual defence was signed in February 1543 (with the compromise style of 'Defender of the Faith, *etc*'). Charles V agreed to fight to protect England, Ireland and Calais; Henry was to protect Spain and the Netherlands. These defensive clauses continued to carry diplomatic weight until 1559. The aggressive clauses provided for a joint invasion of France by two armies, each of 25,000 men, within two years. Henry was to gain the towns of Boulogne, Montreuil, Ardres, and Therouanne and the provinces of Normandy and Guienne. Charles V was to gain the duchy of Burgundy. (One cannot believe that Henry expected to be able to garrison such large areas or regarded them as real military objectives.) On the basis of this treaty, Henry delivered his ultimatum to France in June 1543. Military operations began at once with the despatch of 5,000 men to help defend the Spanish Netherlands. Henry and Charles, in December, agreed to advance their time-table and attack Paris itself, in June 1544, with 40,000 men each. But by June Henry's expectations had narrowed; he argued with Charles for a limited campaign within range of Calais. Henry's personal military zeal was intense: he insisted on joining his army in the field; he sent

40,000 men to France. But he limited his operations to the siege of Montreuil and of Boulogne.

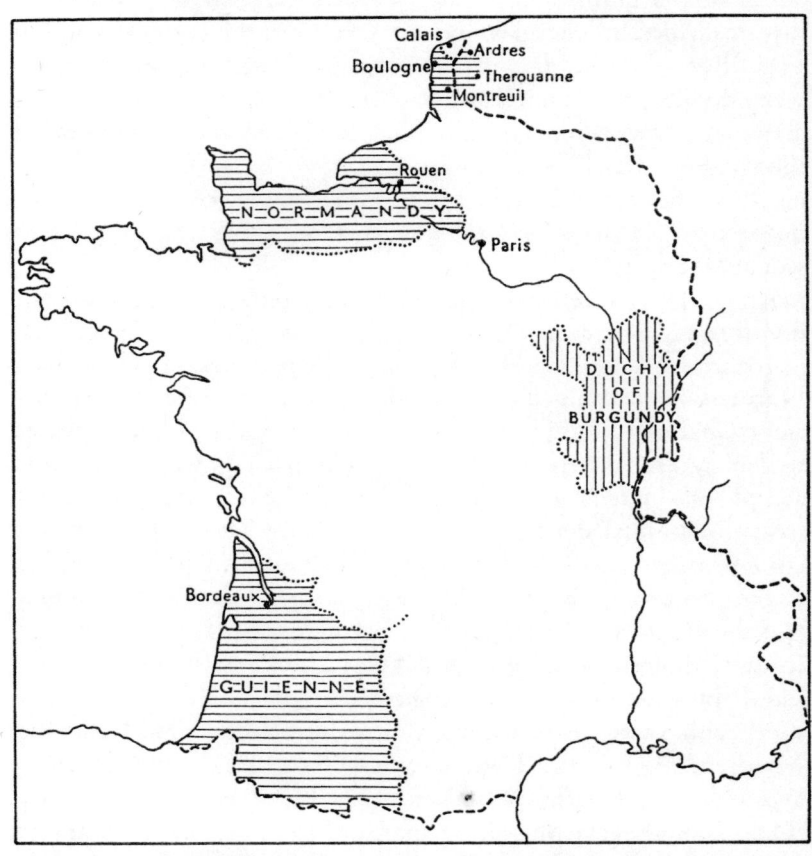

Map 9. Annexation proposed in 1545. To Henry VIII: Boulogne etc, Normandy, Guienne. To Charles V: the duchy of Burgundy

In September 1544, Henry entered Boulogne in triumph accompanied by Seymour, Earl of Hertford, who had been brought from the Scottish border to direct the siege of Boulogne. The major assault on Boulogne was led by Dudley, Viscount Lisle. On the other hand Norfolk's army before Montreuil was badly supplied and was in danger from converging French forces; it had to retreat to

Boulogne. At this critical juncture, and disastrously from England's point of view, Charles V suddenly accepted the peace of Crépy and withdrew from the war. Thus the English people of 1544 found themselves in a situation which foreshadowed Britain's predicament in 1797, 1806 and 1940; the nation was suddenly isolated by the loss of allies in face of a formidable enemy. The garrisons of Boulogne and Calais were out on a limb; England's own defence depended entirely on her own resources. Charles might even ally with Francis. Therefore Henry, in spite of his distaste for Lutherans, re-opened negotiations with German princes as an insurance against Hapsburg attacks.

The French on their side made preparations for a grand assault on England in 1545. Ships were massed at Le Havre; 50,000 men were grouped immediately behind the port; 3,000 men besieged Boulogne and 3,000 entered Scotland by the Clyde to reinforce an invasion from the north. In England military preparations were hurried forward: the harassed Wriothesley raised money by every conceivable expedient (including debasement); armies were mobilised in Essex, Kent and the west of England; Lord Lisle had a fleet of about eighty ships at Portsmouth and privateers further west attacked French ships in the Channel. In the event, the French fleet came out from Le Havre in July, had the better of a minor clash with Lisle but held back as he tried to entice them towards sandbanks. For two weeks or more the English fleet faced a French invasion force of fifty-five ships, twenty-five galleys and 25,000 men. During prolonged manoeuvrings the French fell victims to disease and were consequently forced back to Le Havre. They had not destroyed the English fleet; the invasion was called off and Boulogne, brilliantly defended by Hertford against land-attack—his force was sometimes outnumbered by two to one—could not be invested from the sea. In October, Francis was willing to discuss peace terms.

Henry's councillors were desperate for peace. Another year's fighting could not be contemplated for lack of money. In November 1545 Wriothesley wrote 'I am at my wit's end how we shall possibly shift for three months following'. The councillors were ready to restore Boulogne to the French as the price of peace, but Henry clung to his trophy and negotiations hung fire. At last in

June 1546 Francis agreed to yield Boulogne to England for eight years, after which England would restore it for 2,000,000 crowns. Francis accorded to Henry the title of Supreme Head of the Church of England and Ireland; peace with England carried the corollary that Francis would no longer aid the Scots in their conflict with England.

For although Henry had turned his main attention away from Scotland in 1542, yet he still had to anticipate trouble on his Scottish frontier as soon as he went to war against France. He had to make sure that his northern counties were safe from Scottish attacks. This Henry had been concerned to achieve in the autumn of 1542, as soon as his negotiations with Charles V began to offer good prospects of a joint invasion of France. In September 1542, English and Scottish envoys met in York: the English demanded guarantees that James V would come to England before Christmas in order to negotiate an alliance. This demand was presented as an ultimatum in October 1542, and, when the Scots hesitated, Norfolk led northern militia troops into Scotland to devastate border areas for a week or so. A Scottish force, sent into England on a counter-raid, was routed at Solway Moss (November 1542). Then the death of James V in December 1542 left Scotland with a queen who was only a few days old. The Scottish nobility would have to find a regent or regency council but they were divided into bitter, not to say warring, factions. Thus, within two months, Scotland had ceased to count as a danger to England in face of the proposed war with France. But the extreme weakness of Scotland revived Henry's ambitions for a united Britain, ambitions which he had previously cherished in his months of apparent strength in 1540 and 1541, but had put on one side when the political disunion of his councillors and his people had become more apparent (January 1542). The weaknesses of the English body-politic were not to be cured by the troubles in Scotland; Henry had chosen war against France for reasons which were as valid after the death of King James V as before, and therefore he did not reverse his policy; he did not redirect his whole war effort against Scotland. On the other hand, he intended to exploit Scottish weakness as fully as was consistent with fighting a war in France for the benefit of English unity. If all went well he might

A new role or the old?

achieve the unification of Greater Britain as a secondary side-show of foreign policy.

James Hamilton, Earl of Arran, and heir presumptive to Mary Queen of Scots, became regent of Scotland in January 1543 and arrested Cardinal Beaton. Henry had reason to hope that Arran would favour a breach with Rome, and therefore agreed to open negotiations (February 1543). But, at the same time, Henry's hopes for Anglo-Scottish union were more strongly based on his own

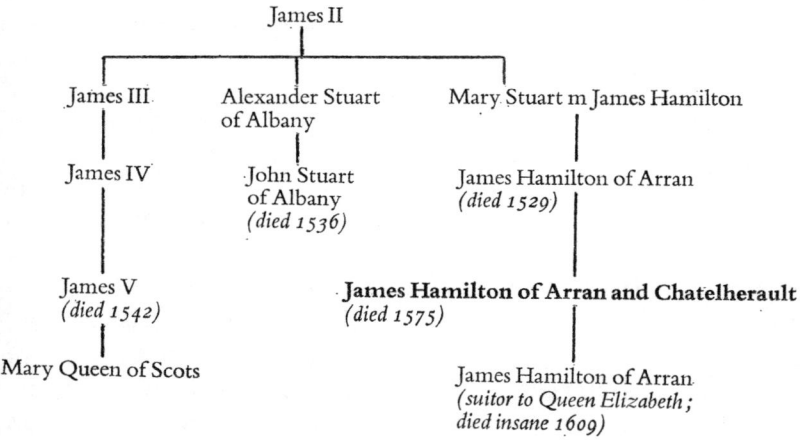

Genealogy 9. James Hamilton, Earl of Arran and Chatelherault, heir presumptive to the Scottish throne

brother-in-law, Archibald Douglas, sixth Earl of Angus and husband of the late Margaret Tudor; the Douglases of Angus had a long tradition of collaboration with England and especially with the house of Lancaster. Backed by Scotsmen who had been captured at Solway Moss and now promised to work in the English interest, Angus moved from Westminster to Berwick and might well have managed to arrest Arran. Henry's intention was that Angus should kidnap Mary Queen of Scots on England's behalf. But Henry, in his confident state of mind, imposed on Angus a set of labours which might have daunted Hercules: the regent Arran must be deposed and replaced by a regency council on which Henry was represented, the Scottish nobility must be induced to admit three

English garrisons, Cardinal Beaton must be transferred to imprisonment in England, and Mary Queen of Scots be sent to England for her education. Meanwhile Henry issued a formal claim to possess 'the true and right title . . . to the sovereignty of Scotland'. Henry was asking Angus to achieve the total subordination of Scotland to England; he was asking far more than could be achieved by any Scotsman however friendly to England.

Henry misjudged the minds of his own chosen agents but beyond that he completely misjudged the power and the interplay of faction in Scotland. He knew that 'the Reformed doctrines had been rapidly spreading in Scotland . . . that greater nobles now strongly desired an alienation of Church property . . . that there were many honest Scots who felt that alliance with a Protestant kingdom must replace the old French league'.[1] Moreover the jockeying for personal power between different Scottish factions was as bewildering and ruthless as anything that confused our observers of the Kremlin in the last days of Stalin and the first of Malenkov, Beria, Kruschev and Bulganin. Henry saw, or imagined, the vicious struggle for regency control that occupied the energies of Cardinal Beaton, James Hamilton of Arran, Matthew Stuart of Lennox, Mary of Guise the Queen Mother, Archibald Douglas of Angus, James Stuart of Moray (illegitimate son of James IV), every one of them (with the exception of Cardinal Beaton) able to assert a claim to the throne as heir of Mary Stuart, the reigning child-queen. Henry may have believed that these Scottish noblemen were so maddened by mutual jealousy and by avarice for Church land that they would willingly accept the firm leadership of an English monarch who could show them how to dispossess the Church and could keep them from murdering each other. But Henry underestimated the Scottish patriotism that underlay aristocratic rivalries and that quickly united the rivals against arrogant intruders; he underestimated the steadying influence upon these turbulent Scotsmen of even a small body of well-disciplined troops. Now the troops which reached Edinburgh in June 1543 were a French reinforcement for Mary of Guise and for Cardinal Beaton whom Regent Arran had already released as a counter-weight to Henry's Angus. The best

[1] Rait, p. 116.

A new role or the old?

excuse that one can make for Henry's misjudgement is that the factors on which he relied to turn Scotland into England's ally were after all the factors which did achieve this in 1560. His misjudgement was to overestimate the strength which these factors had developed by 1543. The truth was that, in July 1543, Henry could get no more from Arran than the treaty of Greenwich: namely, a restoration of peace between Scotland and England, and an agreement for a marriage between Prince Edward and Mary Queen of Scots who would come to England when she was ten. This treaty might give a distant prospect of Anglo-Scottish union; it gave no guarantee against the invasion of Henry's northern counties by the French troops now in Scotland. Such invasion was likely as soon as war should begin against France in Europe.

This possibility became grave in August when Cardinal Beaton prepared to overthrow Arran; it became immediate when Arran repudiated Henry and joined Cardinal Beaton to form a regency coalition (September 1543). The Succession Statute of 1543 was an act of foreign policy, intended to preserve England's independence from France. In the absence of this statute, Mary Tudor and Elizabeth Tudor were illegitimate, so that Mary Queen of Scots was heir presumptive to the English throne next after Prince Edward. This would have been acceptable to Henry VIII, provided that she was wholly detached from the French alliance; she would in that case bring about the union of England and Scotland as an independent 'Great Britain'. But if Mary Queen of Scots became absorbed

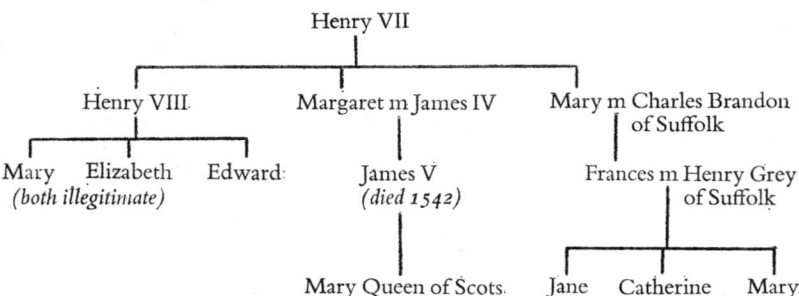

Genealogy 10. Before the Act of Succession 1543: the legal claims of James V and of Mary Queen of Scots to be heirs to the English throne next after Prince Edward

into the French sphere of influence and married a French prince, then England would become a dependency of France. Because the Scots would not hand over Mary their queen for an English upbringing, Henry put as many English heirs as possible between Prince Edward and Mary Queen of Scots—namely, Mary Tudor, Elizabeth Tudor and the descendants of his sister Mary.

As Henry was not willing to shift his major war effort from France to Scotland the most that he could do on the northern front was to secure England against invasion by paralysing Scotland's ability to mobilise invading armies. To this end Seymour, Lord Hertford, was ordered to sack Edinburgh, Leith and St Andrews. Hertford, acting under protest, fulfilled these orders in respect of Edinburgh and Leith. His raiding force left Berwick in April 1544, partly by land under Hertford and partly by sea in Lisle's fleet. Brilliantly organised this 'combined operation' achieved its purpose and was back in Berwick within four weeks. Scottish military power was crippled for the year 1544 and Hertford could be moved to the French front. But the raid also delayed the developments in Scotland which were ultimately to generate the Anglo-Scottish alliance of 1560. It gave the Scots every reason to ask Francis for more French troops. By 1545 invasion of England from the north was again a serious threat; Scotland had recovered and reinforcements had come in from France. An English raid into Scotland was intended to prevent a Scottish invasion of England, but the English were routed at Ancrum Moor (February 1545). Hertford had to go back from Boulogne to Newcastle in order to restore the situation on that front. Some vigorous raiding into Scottish border country secured England's northern counties for the next year. These counties owed their security after that date to a small rebellion by Scottish Protestants who assassinated Cardinal Beaton, captured St Andrew's castle and kept the Scottish regency council busy until July 1547, that is until after the death of Henry VIII.

Henry had given his last three years (1543 to 1546) to war with France and to military diversions on the Scottish border. This warfare must be dismissed as futile if one sets the enormous cost against the territorial gain, a temporary English occupation of Boulogne. But the real gain was quite different, political in the short term and visionary in the long. In the political short term, the war won for England the peaceful succession of Edward in 1547 with a one-party regency council. This was because warfare had tested and proved the nation's leaders in the eyes of the nation. Of the old guard, Suffolk of course had died but Norfolk had been able to demonstrate the incompetence of age; Surrey, his son who might have preserved party rivalry, lost prestige because of his failure as a war-commander. Hertford on the other hand displayed great efficiency on the Scottish front and was then drafted back and forth to whichever front was the most critical. In 1546 he relieved Surrey of his command at Boulogne. The new men, Hertford and Lisle (that is Seymour and Dudley), were the war heroes; they proved themselves and generated the magnetism which seemed then to be of the essence of practical politics—even twentieth-century Americans have been known to elect a president on the strength of war service. Henry was able to put together a one-party regency council with sufficient prestige to rule England; it was led by the upstart uncle of the very young Prince of Wales, supported by other progressives like Cranmer and Lisle. The war had created the reputations which made this council possible; but for the winnowing effects of warfare, faction fights would have been certain and civil war was to be feared—by all who remembered the Wars of the Roses. Who could say whether war in France from 1542 to 1546 was, in real terms, expensive or cheap in comparison with what could otherwise have been feared at the death of Henry VIII?

In the long term, and in terms of national vision, the war carried the nation a great way up the road of self-discovery. Henry had led England to war against France in 1542 after twenty years of internal change but external peace, in order that she should recover her sense of national unity under the inspiration of the old national myth, the myth which saw her role as that of victor on the battlefields of northern France. But the actual experience of the Anglo-French conflict of 1543 to 1546, and particularly the great defensive experience of the summer 1545 (a prelude to 1588), taught Englishmen to see their role in quite new terms. The breach with Rome and the discovery of America had made a great difference to their vision of England's place in the community of nations. They now began to see themselves, not in a quasi-chivalric role, committed to battling out feudal claims in the fields of northern France, but as an island state, detached from Europe, outward-looking and yet defiant of all intruders.

The sense of possessing a national role is a precious asset without which a nation crumbles away. Henry was in some confusion about what the national role was or ought to be, but his arrogant regal instinct saw truly enough that a role was necessary. By dint of pursuing the old role, for lack of a better, he helped his people to grope towards a vision of their new one. In the short term and in the long he may have given his countrymen a better bargain than has perhaps been allowed by commentators who have not tried to rule 3,000,000 people without the aid of telecommuncations or even a standing army.

When Edward Seymour became Protector Somerset in February 1547 he took over a patched-up peace with France and an old-established war with Scotland. He hesitated to give all-out support to the Scottish protestant rebels, because they were a tiny doctrinaire minority, but English ships did take supplies and money into St Andrews. Somerset had a genuine belief in Anglo-Scottish collaboration on the basis of the treaty of Greenwich; he believed in equal partnership between the two countries and in the joint creation of a unified kingdom of Greater Britain. He wanted to negotiate with Arran and other men of established influence. But as things stood between the two countries, Scotsmen could not recognise any possibility of equal partnership. They rallied to Mary of Guise against the old enemy of Scotland. France (ruled since April 1547 by Henry II) sent in the artillery which broke down the defences of St Andrew's castle. The Scots refused to negotiate with Somerset; they thought rather in terms of a marriage between Mary Queen of Scots and the eldest son of Henry II. Somerset decided therefore that as a matter of urgency, he must launch upon a conquest of Scotland. He must establish permanent English garrisons in Scotland and capture Mary Queen of Scots so that her marriage to Edward VI could be assured. In September 1547 he invaded Scotland, won the overwhelming victory of Pinkie, and entered Edinburgh for a second time. Garrisons were established from Arbroath to the

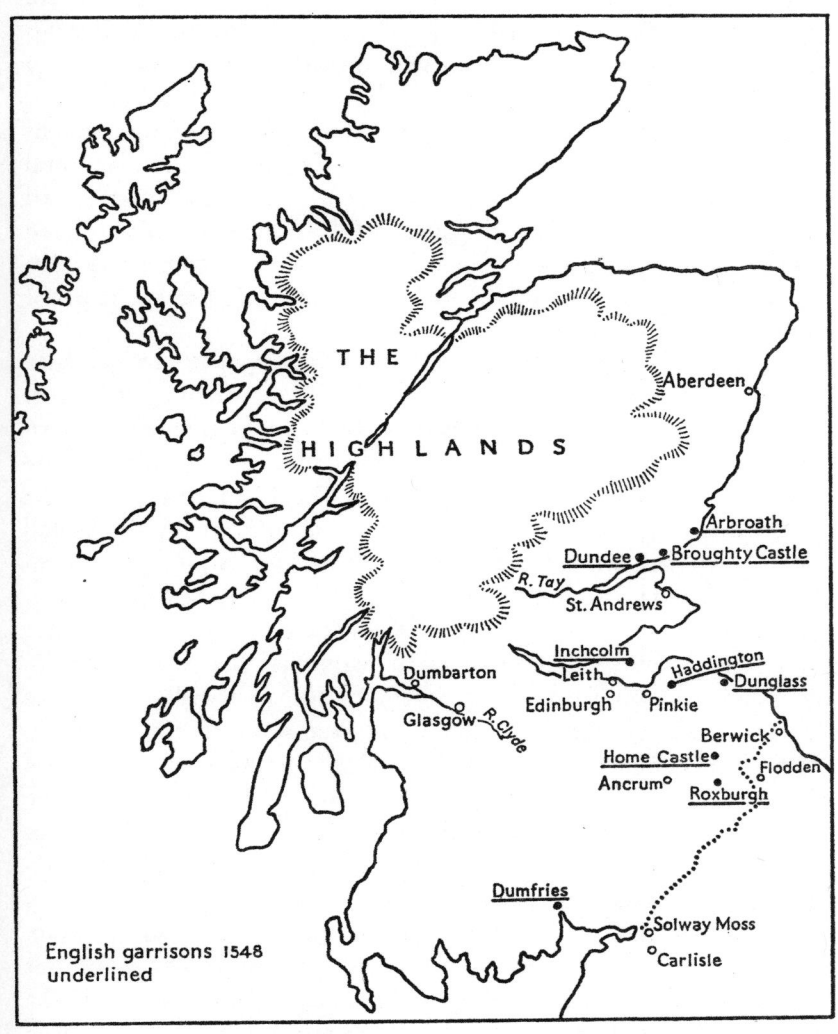

Map. 10. Anglo-Scottish warfare, 1542–49

Firth of Forth and across to Dumfries. Scottish life was dislocated, monasteries were dissolved and Bibles were distributed. But no Scottish government was compelled to negotiate and Mary Queen of Scots was not captured. Somerset himself returned to London in September 1547 and had to direct negotiations from that distant position. He offered the Scots freedom of trade with England and the retention of their own laws in exchange for the marriage of Edward and Mary and for the union of the two crowns. He offered Henry II Boulogne at once in exchange for the 2,000,000 crowns promised in 1546 and for his help in promoting the marriage of Edward and Mary.

But Henry preferred to send heavy reinforcements to Scotland (April 1548). He had been persuaded by Francis of Guise to shift French military effort away from Italy to his own north-eastern frontier. The King of France was persuaded to turn French aggression towards the northern Rhinelands, the Netherlands, and the English Channel. After fifty years of security, England was to fall once more within the orbit of French ambitions (and to remain there until 1815 or 1870). Henry II sent 6,000 men to Scotland whom the English fleet failed to intercept and he offered a promise of a marriage between Mary Queen of Scots and his own Dauphin. The Scottish nobility meeting under the protection of French troops accepted this alliance. In August 1548 French warships took Mary Queen of Scots from the Clyde to Brest; Franco-Scottish troops began to besiege English garrisons. Somerset's efforts to relieve these garrisons were diverted by the English rebellions of 1549 in the south-west, East Anglia and Yorkshire and so England's garrisons in Scotland could not be reinforced. They were withdrawn one by one and with great difficulty before the end of 1549. Scotland was in the control of the French Queen Mother and her French army. Scottish noblemen who had collaborated with the English were hunted down by the victorious faction; collaboration had often been no more than a border truce between Scottish and English marcher wardens, yet about 150 of these noblemen were executed. Others, like John Cockburn of Ormiston, fled to England and were pensioned by Somerset.[1]

[1] See Merriman (a).

A new role or the old?

Meanwhile Henry II declared war on England (August 1549). He attacked Boulogne and was held off with difficulty; his ships harassed English shipping in the channel; he encouraged rebellion in Ulster. Somerset not surprisingly lost the confidence of the regency council. He was sent to the Tower and replaced by Dudley, once Lord Lisle and now Earl of Warwick.

One might say on behalf of Somerset that he accepted the new vision of England's role as a country related to Europe by the needs of defence but otherwise withdrawn from Europe in order to fight for her interests in the British Isles and in continents beyond the seas. However, he asserted this role prematurely without regard to England's resources in 1547 and as a simple-minded idealist who wanted at once to re-establish 'the old indifferent name of Britons'. For, if the government which took over from Henry VIII was more or less united, it was also impoverished by five years of warfare and harassed by religious and social problems. Somerset discovered in 1548, as Henry had perhaps feared in 1542, that although war against France could unite Englishmen by memories of chivalric success, war in Scotland could not; Scottish wars, even if victorious, quickly exhausted men's enthusiasm as well as their money; their divisions became more emphatic. Indeed, Somerset's Scottish campaigns had been financed only by the dissolution of chantries and the sale of their assets.

Warwick was forced to liquidate the whole Scottish project. He negotiated peace treaties with France and Scotland by which England restored Boulogne to France for half the sum promised in 1546 and withdrew all English troops from Scotland. Mary Queen of Scots was safely in France; she was indeed to marry the Dauphin. French troops were in Scotland.

PART IIc
Monarch and People— 'Ourselves Alone'

15 Northumberland and Mary Tudor: Personal interest versus national identity

When Henry VIII died, his fellow Englishmen had already begun to grope towards a new vision of their role in world affairs. In the fulfilment of this role they had discovered a high degree of national unity, a unity which could comprise in a single patriotism men as unlike as Thomas Cranmer and Stephen Gardiner and many thousands of others whose religion gravitated to one of the two poles of belief or hovered uncertainly between them. This patriotism did in fact comprise all Englishmen except those who for private or doctrinaire reasons consciously rejected an overriding idea of national unity. Henry had himself bequeathed conditions within which the succession to the throne followed easily upon his death without disrupting national unity, and he bequeathed from 1543 a Statute of Succession (illogical and indefensible, of course, for how, in logic, could Mary Tudor and Elizabeth Tudor both be legitimate?) that was wholly acceptable to the generality of the nation; the statute was calculated therefore to continue this blessing of an uncontested succession into two more reigns, even though the heirs presumptive were women.

Warwick and Mary Tudor were driven to attack this promising heritage by motives which were personal, if we judge them against the overriding idea of national unity and against the nation's idea of itself as an island state, detached from Europe, outward-looking, and defiant of all intruders. Warwick and Mary Tudor each pushed forward a domestic policy which turned their governments into alienated factions, hostile to and opposed by the nation taken as a whole. In desperate attempts to perpetuate private or doctrinaire interests they were each willing to call in question the Statute of Succession, to take the risk of contested successions and civil wars. To buttress a policy which repudiated national unity, they were each willing to repudiate the nation's own idea of its role in world affairs. Warwick accepted such dependence on France as would lower England to the status of Scotland or Brittany. Mary accepted such dependence on Spain as would lower England to the status of Milan or the Netherlands.

One hardly needs to add that Warwick's motives seem to have been the harsh personal ambition of an able, energetic and intensely selfish politician: 'It seems almost as if there was some fatal taint of crooked self-seeking in the Dudley blood that drove them all towards unpopular and desperate courses'.[1] Mary's, by contrast, were those of a devout woman, self-sacrificing and high-principled; as a person she certainly earned a reverent epitaph: 'as her body, without its inhabiting soul, lay stiff and still in the empty palace of St James, . . . her soul had surely come into peace. For . . . she had . . . trodden, lifelong and manfully, the way that other sinners know.'[2] But by birth and fortune Mary bore the office of ruler and statesman; as ruler and statesman she was necessarily judged. She failed as completely as did Warwick to provide the conditions, or to give the lead, which would enable her people, limited as every people in every age must be, to fulfil themselves, and to serve God and each other, as richly as circumstances would permit. She (and he) had no notion of politics as the art of the best that is possible.

The weakness to which Warwick and Mary reduced England could have been doubly serious because it coincided with Henry II's decision to shift the main area of French interest from Italy towards the Rhinelands, the Netherlands and the English Channel. On the other hand, those who in 1550 detected the beginnings of protestantism in France and in Scotland could not foresee that within ten years this new force would cripple France and would eject the French garrisons from Scotland.

Warwick's aim was to organise a permanent monopoly of political power for his family and for a small group of personal associates.

[1] Wernham (a), p. 193.
[2] Prescott, p. 381.

Personal interest versus national identity 145

His preparatory moves occupied the two years from October 1549 and culminated in his treaty of alliance with Henry II of France (July 1551) and his own promotion to the title of Duke of Northumberland. His main plan of operations occupied the two years from July 1551 to the death of Edward and the failure of Queen Jane in July 1553.

Warwick's policy was bound to weaken the ruling aristocracy by splitting them into rival groups. His purpose was to monopolise political influence and so he was bound to alienate into opposition many eminent men like Thomas Wriothesley, Earl of Southampton, and Henry Fitzalan, Earl of Arundel, who expected to be at the centre of politics. But he also alienated large sections of the non-political multitude and of the central mass of local gentry. This was because he was determined to make himself permanently indispensable to Edward VI, and therefore gave himself the character of the chief champion of Edward's protestant enthusiasms. Throughout 1550, ritualistic instructions were sent out from Warwick's council to the parishes, and these instructions made the church services much too bleak for the multitude of ordinary folk.

Since his ruling faction was small and unpopular, it had to be well armed. Warwick's supporters were expected to recruit armed retainers; they were repaid for this expense by grants from the Treasury and by enormous gifts of crown land. But such expenditure was crippling to a government which had inherited a very large debt from the recent wars of Henry VIII and of Somerset. Since the arming of Warwick's supporters had highest priority, money had to be saved by allowing the navy to fall into disrepair and by neglecting the garrisons of Berwick and Calais.

Warwick's policy entailed chronic, fundamental national weakness in all England's dealings with foreign governments: his own government had no financial assets, the greater part of the nation disliked his policy, the ruling classes of England were divided against themselves. In this situation of total weakness, Warwick provoked Charles V to the brink of military intervention on behalf of Princess Mary Tudor. As the official champion of protestant uniformity, Warwick demanded of Mary Tudor that she should cease to permit the Mass in her household (January and February 1551). Already in the summer of 1550 Charles V had planned to smuggle Mary out of England lest she should suffer persecution at the hands of Warwick's new government. As a part of the plot, the imperial ambassador was recalled from London so that he could sail out of the Thames without attracting special attention. His ship was to turn up the river Blackwater and take Mary on board. In the event, her house near Maldon was too closely watched for her to risk the journey to the landing-place on the river bank.

In 1551 the council's pressure on Mary and her household became more severe. She was browbeaten and berated by Warwick in the presence of the boy king and of the whole ruling council. She stood her ground in the best Tudor style: 'My soul I offer to God, and my body to Your Majesty's service. May it please you to take away my life rather than the old religion.'[1] Warwick dared not order his agents absolutely and physically to prevent the saying of Mass, but some persons who attended Mass in Mary's household found themselves under arrest. These were the circumstances under which King Edward and his council received from Charles V 'a short message... of war if I would not suffer his cousin the Princess to use her Mass'.

When Charles V seemed on the point of military intervention, Henry II let it be known that he might consent to protect England against Spanish invasion if suitable terms between England and France could be arranged. Warwick seized the chance: Henry II was made a knight of the Garter as a prelude to the Anglo-French treaty of alliance (July 1551). The Anglo-Scottish treaty of Greenwich (1543) was dissolved and so was the marriage agreement between Edward VI and Mary Queen of Scots. Edward VI was pledged to marry Elizabeth of Valois, daughter of Henry II. Henry was completing his redirection of French foreign policy from conquests in Italy to conquests in the Rhinelands, in the Netherlands, and on the shores of the English Channel. He was bringing England wholly within the orbit of French military ambitions, where she had not been since Charles VIII marched away into Italy in 1494, but where she would remain until 1815, perhaps until Germany superseded France in 1871.

For the time being in 1551, Henry was poised for his treaty of

[1] Quoted in Prescott, p. 150.

Chambord with the Lutheran princes; he was poised for war with Charles V. England could be left to ripen from weakness to weakness, until Warwick was entirely the client of France and King Edward himself as much a member of the French court as was Mary, Queen of Scots. Somerset, released from the Tower in February 1550, opposed the policy of subservience to France, and the persecution of Mary Tudor which made it necessary. His voice was always for toleration: 'she shall do as she thinks best till the King comes of age'.[1] Somerset's opposition to the French alliance brought about his execution in January 1552. For the immediate effect of the French treaty was very greatly to strengthen Warwick's power in England, and this fact he proclaimed by becoming Duke of Northumberland, while his associate, Henry Grey, became Duke of Suffolk (October 1551).[2]

Northumberland's main political operations during the two years July 1551 to July 1553 did not fall within the field of foreign policy. His second prayer book (1552) was meant to make England so rigorously protestant as would exclude Mary Tudor from ever becoming Queen of England. Thus he was ready to defy the Succession Act of 1543 and to risk civil war and Spanish intervention, in case Edward should die childless before the death of Mary. When Edward was seen to be indeed dying, Northumberland arranged for his eldest son to marry Lady Jane Grey and for Edward to bequeath the crown to Jane to the exclusion of Mary Tudor, Elizabeth Tudor and other lawful claimants.

Henry II meanwhile watched English developments and weighed them complacently. In 1552 Charles V was heavily defeated in Germany; Henry occupied Metz, Toul and Verdun. He asked himself whether the moment was ripe for a military occupation of England. He watched Northumberland's manipulation of the English succession when Edward died; Henry was confident that the new English government would soon be too weak to resist any demands which he might impose upon it. It might very likely become a French client government, dependent on French garrisons to maintain its authority in some parts of England. But Henry's expectations

[1] Quoted in Prescott, p. 120.
[2] See genealogy 10 on p. 133.

were not fulfilled. Instead, English leaders of public opinion quickly generated opposition to Northumberland's new regime. Mary was proclaimed queen and Northumberland was ousted before Henry could rescue him, but not before Northumberland had offered to surrender Calais in exchange for French assistance. The central body of the nation was voting overwhelmingly for the 1543 Act of Succession as the proper foundation of national unity; it was voting against this foreign policy of subservience to France, which so clearly sacrificed the chosen role of national insular independence.

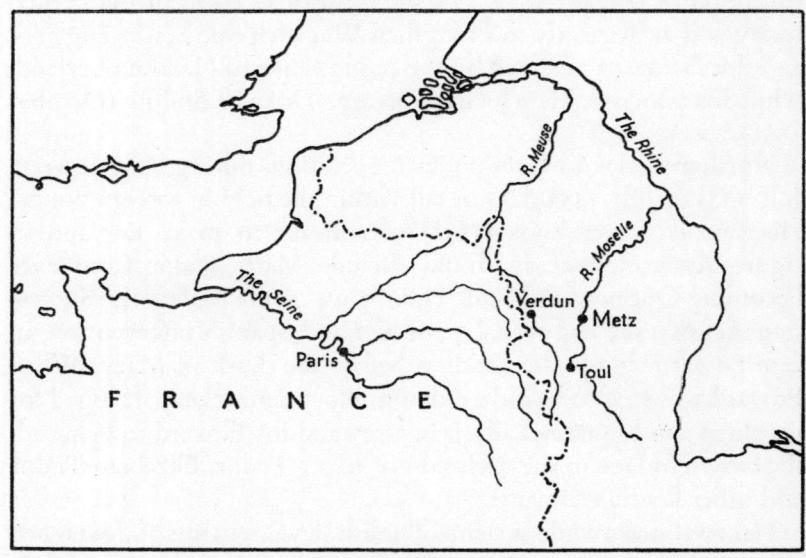

Map 11. Metz, Toul and Verdun. French aggression crossed the watershed from valleys that slope towards the Seine to valleys that slope towards the Rhine

Northumberland had a quick and aggressive mind. In commercial matters (as is suggested in chapter 23), his policy was far-seeing and would have been important, if he had had time and resources for it. But the central concerns of foreign policy are to safeguard a nation's independence and to preserve its sense of purpose amid the many nations, states and political agglomerations that constitute its world. In this sense Northumberland had no foreign policy at all. He lived from hand to mouth; he worked ruthlessly for political advantage and for personal power in England. To that end he sacrificed the wealth, unity and diplomatic influence on which depended England's security and self-determination. In the strict sense he had no foreign policy.

Neither had Mary Tudor. She was even more willing than her predecessor that England should become the dependent client of a greater external power, for Mary was half-Spanish by birth and more than half-Spanish in sympathy (as an understandable consequence of her harsh experience of Englishmen). She had no eye, or concern, for the nation's unity or sense of purpose. Her only concern was to restore England to communion with the Church of Rome. In some respects this might be deemed a foreign policy in itself, but it was conceived in terms of such total submission that it was a policy only in the sense that military capitulation could be described as an act of policy.

Though she was Queen of England, she did not recognise any obligation to act on behalf of her people as the trustee for their many and varied assets—their wealth, commercial opportunities, local cultural heritage, traditional laws and customs. She was blind to her many-sided obligation and to the competitive world in which these assets would soon be exploited and destroyed by other communities and governments (even by the Pope) unless they were cherished with care and protected with 'valour or policy'.

Consequently, the return to Rome was an unconditional surrender, not a carefully bargained concordat, which might indeed have been described as a policy. Yet a balanced concordat, hammered out by tough nationalist negotiators in 1553, could have been permanent, for it could at that date have left scope for Englishmen's insular nationalism and even for a *politique* attitude to religious minorities, as did the Gallicanism of Henry IV in the seventeenth century. But by 1559 England's communion with Rome had grown to be so fully identified with subservience to Spain that any sort of Roman allegiance was politically impossible for a queen or a king of the English. 'Men ceased to go to Mass when they heard of the loss of Calais'.

For just as Mary brought her country back to Rome without conditions, so also she accepted subservience to Spain without equivalent negotiated concessions from Spain to her own people.

Her only concern was that Philip should be ready and willing, in any crisis, to use Spanish power for the maintenance of Roman Catholicism in England. Here again, her one-sided subservience was self-defeating: a well-balanced, carefully-bargained alliance might have been permanent. William Paget, clear-headed politician and nationalist, firmly believed an Anglo-Spanish alliance to be necessary to offset the overweening aggression of France. Charles V, on his side, needed the friendly assistance of England to protect his supply lines to the Netherlands. But the one-sided neglect of England's aspirations made the alliance so unpopular that it died with Mary Tudor.

Mary's reign was the story of national opposition to her policy of subservience to Rome and to Spain. In the form of rebellion and conspiracy the opposition was ineffective, but in the form of parliamentary obstruction and of resistance within the Privy Council it achieved one or two crucial decisions and always, by its delaying tactics, it played for time and thus in one way or another reduced the damage to the interests of the nation as a whole.

Of Mary's two objects of policy, a return to communion with Rome was, of course, first in importance. Nevertheless the alliance with Spain and her marriage to Prince Philip came first in time. Perhaps she was willing that this should be so, because she wanted a powerful adviser to help her with her English councillors; she wanted a husband by whom she could have a child to perpetuate her work; she wanted a princely champion whose Spanish armies would, if need be, control her own subjects and guarantee the succession of her child to the throne; she was already thirty-seven and might die in childbirth. Nevertheless, the order of events was not Mary's choice so much as Charles V's. Charles feared the Pope's political hostility to Spain, he feared that papal influence in London might turn England against Spain and he therefore contrived to keep the Pope's emissary out of England until the marriage between Mary and Philip had taken place. So it was that Cardinal Reginald Pole was appointed papal legate to England as early as August 1553 but did not reach England until November 1554. Perhaps this was unfortunate for Mary, because the early months of her reign were a time during which Englishmen returned spontaneously and happily to Catholic customs and to the Mass. They did not like the idea of allegiance to Rome, but might, at this time, have accepted it, if reasonable respect had been accorded to national aspirations. The Spanish marriage, on the other hand, was deeply opposed from the first at every level of society. Bishop Gardiner led the opposition in the council. Mary's first parliament (October to December 1553) at once petitioned against it. Indeed Charles V's ambassador, Renard, hurried forward his private negotiations with Mary specifically to forestall Parliament; she must be induced to commit herself to a marriage with Philip, before parliamentary pressure could weaken her resolve. The terms of the marriage treaty were signed in January 1554.

By these terms, Philip would cease to have any rights in England if Mary were to die childless; meanwhile he would have the title of King and would help her in the government of the country, but only Englishmen would be appointed to ecclesiastical or civil office in England and England would not be involved in the existing war between France and Spain. If the marriage brought forth a son, he would inherit England, the Netherlands and Franche-Comté (together with Spain, if Philip's existing heir should die childless). These last conditions emphasised the very consequences of the marriage which Englishmen most dreaded. A son of the marriage would be, first and foremost, a son of Philip. As the ruler of Spain and of the Netherlands, he would be first and foremost a continental ruler. England would become a minor dependency of a continental power. Moreover, Charles V flatly refused a request that he should, in accordance with the Act of Succession of 1543, recognise Elizabeth as heir if Mary should die childless. Charles could hardly have accepted Mary Queen of Scots as heir, for she was wholly in the French interest. Men could only conclude that Philip would try to impose himself on England, in spite of the marriage treaty, if Mary should die childless. Reginald Pole, commenting bitterly on the treaty and on his own treatment at the hands of Charles V, observed that Charles could 'not bring himself to believe that I would help him to put my country into the hands of a foreigner'.[1]

Opponents of the marriage organised a rebellion as the only

[1] Quoted in Prescott.

remaining means of preventing it. Simultaneous risings were planned for March 1554, in the south-west, on the Welsh border, in the midlands and in Kent. The conspirators were of differing religious backgrounds; nationalism was their common bond, although Edward Courtenay had the further motive that many would choose him to be Mary's husband in preference to Philip. The conspiracy was discovered in January; the rising had to be launched before the conspirators were ready; only Thomas Wyatt in Kent roused his followers into effective rebellion. Though his force was scattered after ten days, nevertheless he had raised about 4,000 rebels and had occupied London. As in July 1553, so in January 1554, a large part of the nation voted with their feet against a foreign policy of subservience to a continental power.

Moreover, the conflict between the nation on the one side and Mary and Spain on the other did not end with the defeat of Wyatt. It was expressed in a conflict of wills about the fate of Princess Elizabeth. Mary and the Spanish ambassador, vigorously supported by Charles V, wanted the execution of Elizabeth as an outcome of the rebellion. The nation wanted her as the heir who would exclude Philip from the throne if Mary should die childless. Paget in the council was able to persuade Mary that an execution without trial would provoke widespread rebellion; a London jury, by acquitting the conspirator Nicholas Throckmorton, demonstrated that the queen was not likely to get a conviction against Elizabeth (the jurors were imprisoned for six months for their independence of mind); finally, Mary's second parliament (April to May 1554) resolutely insisted on maintaining Elizabeth's rights of succession to the throne and on refusing to give Philip the protection of England's treason laws. Parliament did however accept the marriage treaty. Philip married Mary in July 1554 in time for him to preside over England's return to Rome. His task was to make the return permanent by begetting a son and by means of Spanish power.

In November 1554, Cardinal Pole reached London and England was formally reconciled to the Church of Rome. The only concessions asked of the Pope were those which Charles V demanded on behalf of his adopted subjects; the Pope guaranteed to laymen the possession of any Church lands which they had acquired and the

Personal interest versus national identity

Pope acknowledged the authority of Parliament so far as to permit Parliament to repeal Henry VIII's law against papal authority.

As Warwick used the first eighteen months of his regime to turn himself into the Duke of Northumberland, so Mary used the first eighteen months of her reign to restore Roman Catholicism and to establish Philip as her husband and protector. The rest of Northumberland's regime was a vain attempt to give permanence to his own authority; the rest of Mary's reign was a desperate struggle to give permanence to the Roman Catholic restoration. Under both rulers, foreign policy became a secondary, hand-to-mouth activity that lost all national support.

Above all, Mary wanted to retain Philip in England. This would give her the greatest possible chance of bearing a child; it would strengthen Philip's will to maintain the Roman Catholic restoration at the critical moment of Mary's death. But the same parliament (November 1554 to January 1555) which restored the authority of Rome again refused to have Philip crowned King of England, again stood by Elizabeth's rights of succession if Mary should die childless, and utterly refused any assistance to Spain in her present war against France. Parliament yielded only to the extent of giving Philip the protection of English treason laws and of giving him the regency in respect of Mary's child in case that should be necessary. Disappointed by Parliament of the inducements which she thought might keep Philip in England, Mary tried desperately to mediate peace between France and Spain in the war which was enticing Philip away to the battlefields. At least he waited patiently during the months of 1555 when Mary was believed to be pregnant, but that hope disappeared in August and a fortnight later he left London for Dover and the Netherlands.

In January 1556 Philip became ruler of Spain, Spanish America, Naples and the Netherlands. He had little time for English affairs unless England would give him what he wanted. But the fourth parliament (October to December 1555) had again refused to support him in war or to crown him as king. Moreover the new Pope, Caraffa, now to be Paul IV (May 1555), was a Neapolitan and therefore an implacable enemy of Spain's occupation of Italy. He allied with France in July 1556. Warfare between France and Spain had been interrupted by the truce of Vaucelles (February 1556), but France now attacked the Spanish Netherlands with new vigour. Philip demanded English help in accordance with the terms of the alliance in 1543. The Privy Council refused to yield to Mary's desperate demands. Ultimately, the council did agree to meet their treaty obligations to the extent of sending 6,000 men to support Philip (January 1557). But his own desperation served Mary's purpose to the extent that he himself returned to England in March 1557 to try to extract a full declaration of war from the council. The councillors resisted all pressure until Henry II's folly did Philip's work for him.

Henry II, of course, had anxiously watched events in England. In 1553 he had been preoccupied with critical events in the Netherland and the Rhinelands, which followed upon the death of his ally, Maurice of Saxony. Nevertheless, Henry's assistance was at the service of any plot for the overthrow of Mary Tudor. He assisted the promoters of Wyatt's rebellion in 1554; he grieved at the marriage of Mary and Philip; he encouraged the plot of Sir Henry Dudley in 1556. But in the crisis of April 1557, he allowed Sir Thomas Stafford to mobilise a small force in Dieppe for a private invasion of England. Stafford landed at Scarborough, was captured and hanged. But, in face of this provocation, the privy councillors could not still reject Mary's insistent demands for a declaration of war. War was declared by England against France in June 1557.

The nation lacked any will for war. Its morale had been drained away by four years of unpopular government. The Spanish connection was deeply resented. The decision to burn heretics meant the martyrdom of a hundred ordinary citizens each year; it alienated thousands who had little sympathy for protestant doctrine and who blamed Philip for the policy of his rival, Cardinal Pole (since March 1556 Archbishop of Canterbury). Meanwhile Pope Paul had completed men's bewilderment by excommunicating Philip and by summoning Cardinal Pole to Rome on a charge of heresy. In these circumstances war loans were difficult to raise and Parliament when it met in January 1558 voted very little money. Recruits were difficult to find and often deserted. German mercenaries hired by Mary's agents, and arms bought in Antwerp for her forces, were commandeered by Philip. The English declaration of war did, of course, lay Calais open to attack. Partly as a consequence of Philip's interference, the garrison was left without winter reinforcements; the fleet which might have supported the garrison from the sea was laid up to save money. When the attack was launched in January 1558 by Francis of Guise comparatively little resistance was offered. After seven days the town surrendered, in spite of the bitter resistance of a neighbouring garrison at Guines. Neither the English themselves nor their Spanish allies were able to mount any effective counter-attack in 1558. The main combatants were exhausted after sixteen years of heavy warfare. Peace negotiations started at Cateau-Cambrésis in October 1558. The death of Mary in November enabled Philip and Henry to agree on peace terms whereas previously Philip could not in honour sign away his wife's Calais nor could Henry give up such a notable conquest. On the other hand, by November 1558, Philip had neither the will nor the resources to obstruct the working of England's Act of Succession. The most that he asked was that Princess Elizabeth should be given in marriage to a Spanish grandee. Princess Elizabeth was carried to the throne by the assumptions and acclamations of the privy councillors, of the squirearchy and indeed of the whole people. Mary's strenuous efforts to serve Philip and Spain had lost the sympathy of her people without gaining the purpose for which she yearned.

[The policy of Mary Tudor in Ireland was detached from the main lines of her policy in England and was strangely continuous with the policy of Henry VIII. Perhaps any established European government, whether it were Protestant or Catholic, must have reacted similarly to the problem of establishing law and order among the wild Irish clans. Their ideal, bred and perpetuated by Gaelic bards, 'was that of an aristocracy who still lived in the heroic age, in the atmosphere of battle and foray, and who were expected by their poets, historians and followers to be warriors rather than statesmen. Numbers of them fell in the forefront of useless battles, while the wise man who let the others do the fighting and kept himself in power for a long life was rare.'[1] Some of the wildest of these ancient clans lived in the difficult country of Offaly

[1] Curtis, p. 180.

Map 12. Ireland in the second half of the sixteenth century, showing King's County and Queen's County (the first plantations), and the Lordship of Shane, Turloch and Hugh O'Neill, Lords of Tyrone

and Leix which lay immediately to the west of the Pale. Raids into the Pale were incessant. Under Somerset and Warwick the two areas were annexed to the crown and the landowners were dispossessed under charges of treason. In Mary's reign, by a decision of 1556, the native inhabitants were granted the western third of this area. The rest was allotted to settlers, 'English subjects born either in England or Ireland'. Two settlements were established, known as King's County and Queen's County and administered from Philipstown and Maryborough respectively. The whole area remained disturbed for the rest of the century, but these, the first of the 'plantations of Ireland', were thus completed. Plantation was the process which did in the end bring some sort of temporary pacification to Ireland.]

16 Elizabeth: Patriotic constraints on policy

For fifty years after 1494 Italy suffered as the vortex of European warfare. For England, a thousand miles away, foreign policy was a luxury in which she could choose to indulge or not, as her governments preferred. By 1558 the vortex had shifted to Flanders and the English Channel. England, a little country of three million people, was bound to be drawn in, was likely to be broken and impoverished, even to lose her identity and to suffer the fate already suffered by the Neapolitans and soon to be suffered by the southern Netherlanders.

The forty-five years of Elizabeth's reign was a time of pessimism, of insecurity and of agonising national danger under the overshadowing power first of France and then of Spain. Englishmen had discovered the role which they wished to fill, but could hardly believe that they would ever be free to fulfil it. They had been divided against each other by the factious ambitions of Northumberland and the narrow zeal of Mary Tudor; they had now to live under permanent threat of invasion after half a century of immunity. In the days of the Armada, and afterwards, Englishmen were impressed, not by the magnitude of their victory, but by the permanence of their peril and the certainty that the enemy would return: 'their force is wonderful great and strong'; 'their fleet consisteth of mighty ships and great strength'; 'all the world never saw such a force as theirs was'.[1]

From 1558 until 1600 all visible probabilities seemed to weigh against England's newly-chosen role of national independence and

[1] Quoted in Mattingly (a), p. 352.

transoceanic enterprise. The most that men could hope was to take one step at a time, to survive one year at a time and so to wait upon the Lord and discover whether, peradventure, He would sustain this people after all. The legendary popularity of Drake represented a momentary release of pent-up anxieties, a feeling of relief that somewhere some victory had been won; certainly it did not represent confidence that any victory could be final. In retrospect, men have come to think of Elizabethans as 'sea-dogs and singing-birds', but their own song was the song of their Litany: '. . . from plague, pestilence and famine; from battle and murder and from sudden death, Good Lord deliver us. From all sedition and privy conspiracy; form all false doctrine and heresy . . . Good Lord deliver us. . . . Remember not, Lord, our offences, nor the offences of our forefathers, neither take thou vengeance of our sins: spare us, good Lord, spare thy people . . . and be not angry with us for ever.' Meanwhile those who did chance to prosper expressed their uncertainty in their dress: 'mannerist clothing with no resemblance to human form, intellectually fantastic but not passionate, a style that arises in a world of unhappy politics, uncertainty and pessimism, and expresses itself in a thousand different forms; houses as big as could be, based on late mediaeval timbered barn-like motifs, decorated in the gargoyle, bargee, style, and containing heavy, tactlessly carved furniture'. After 1598 danger from Spain was no longer acute, but by then chronic rebellion in Ireland and chronic poverty at home prolonged the sense of weary apprehension.

* * *

In 1558 the new queen and her ministers did not need to discover and define an acceptable role for the nation. But they did need to express it in ways that respected the nation's acquired preconceptions. That need imposed limitations on their freedom of action. The experience of the previous five years caused most Englishmen to associate papal catholicism with the subordination of England to foreign interests; they remembered 'the late days of Queen Mary when . . . the Pope's authority was wholly restored and for the continuance thereof a strange nation . . . brought into this land to lord it over us'. Elizabeth might be tempted, simply in terms of foreign policy, to accept a reconciliation with Rome whereby the Pope would declare her to be legitimate and England would remain in communion with Rome. But such a policy was excluded by Elizabeth's need to lead Englishmen away from past humiliations, if she was truly to establish unity between monarch and people. Such considerations also excluded a marriage alliance between Elizabeth and Philip II, however useful that alliance might seem against French aggression. In any case Elizabeth was splendidly alert to emphasise national independence against every intrusion; 'mere English' was her self-conscious claim, based on a hundred years of her own English ancestry.

The critical problem through all the years of Elizabeth's reign was to provide for the defence of realm and monarch against foreign enemies and to do so within terms which did justice to the nation's role as an independent people, with aspirations that looked outward from Europe. The problems of home defence, however desperate, usually left the government and people with surplus resources for an aggressive economic policy in the Baltic, Mediterranean, Atlantic, Pacific and Indian seas, and for plantations in Ireland and America. Their outward-looking aspirations were thus expressed in action (see chapter 23). On the other hand, ideological foreign policy was excluded by the need to limit England's commitments in Europe and to avoid subordinating England to European interests, however friendly they might be; alliance with Calvinists of Scotland, France or the Netherlands could be accepted only in so far as it helped England's strategic interests, narrowly conceived; it could not be ideological in essence.

A first prerequisite to any effective foreign policy was the achievement of national unity on the home front. Englishmen might be generally united in opposition to foreigners and in their notion of the nation's role in world affairs; yet even so they could never act effectively if they were divided into bitter factions at home, or confused by conflicting theologies. Elizabeth and her ministers had the problem of discovering in home affairs that middle ground which would content the inarticulate yearnings of the great majority and would attract the acquiescence of many who were both articulate and opinionated. It is beyond the scope of an essay on foreign affairs to describe the creation and growth of the Church of England, and the establishment of a way of life and a tempo of living which served the majority of men and women for about three hundred years. One can only observe that the discovery and occupation of this middle ground was necessary in 1558 if the nation was to find sufficient national unity at home. In 1558, this Church of England was needed as a foundation of national strength; fifteen years later, as circumstances grew more acute, it came to be the only dyke holding back the flood-tide of civil war—for the Protestants who in 1558 had seemed to be no more than humble craftsmen of the Lollard tradition, were, fifteen years later, visibly aggressive, Calvinistic, men of affairs; meanwhile the old quiescent Catholic families of 1560 were being overtaken by new fanatical missionaries from Douai. As Protestant and Catholic polarised into growing fanaticism, civil war must have ensued in England (as in France), if Elizabeth and her ministers had not already defined the middle ground and cajoled most men into an increasing acceptance of it. Thus, the extremists always lacked in numbers what they possessed in zeal. Majority acquiescence grew into national unity, whereas faction and confusion would otherwise have grown into organised conflict and civil war.

17 Elizabeth: Succession, the prerogative of Time

Very important limitations were then imposed on Elizabeth, if she was to fulfil the nation's own idea of its role, to develop the unity of the nation and to maintain unity between monarch and people. All of these limitations converged to render insoluble one of the central problems of all Tudor foreign policy, in so far as foreign policy was consciously conceived from 1490 until 1558. This was the problem of succession. Henry VII had been obsessed with the need to leave an heir whose succession to the throne could not be challenged. Henry VIII had disturbed all Europe for twenty years lest England should fall into civil war over a contested succession when he himself should die. Northumberland and Mary crippled the independent strength of England in attempts to distort the succession or to guarantee it against any possible challenge. Elizabeth seems shrewdly to have observed that these expensive efforts achieved little of their purpose: Henry, in spite of years of diplomacy to the contrary, had in the end accepted the notion of Mary Tudor as a likely queen of England; Northumberland and Mary had entirely failed to attain the ends for which they worked. Elizabeth found herself queen, in spite of her mother's execution, in spite of solemn parliamentary declarations of her illegitimacy, in spite of Northumberland and in spite of Mary Tudor. Elizabeth might have ascribed her succession to the illogical statute of 1543; more accurately she ascribed it to luck and fate: 'Time hath brought me hither' she said. Like her predecessors and like her anxious subjects, Elizabeth knew well enough that the peace and prosperity of England would be ruined if the succession were contested at her death, but Elizabeth

Succession, the prerogative of Time

was alone in her conviction that present efforts to provide an undoubted royal heir to the throne were wasted efforts, for the future would take charge of itself: Time, which had brought Elizabeth hither, would do the same for her heir whatever well laid schemes men might build.

But present efforts would not only be wasted in their future consequences; they would, more likely than not, destroy present unity and strength. She could not herself provide the heir unless she married. If she married an English nobleman she would acquire a special relationship with his relations; she could not remain equally the monarch of her whole nobility; she would generate faction, would weaken the unity which was essential to any foreign policy and would give foreign enemies a greater chance of finding powerful allies within the English body politic. If she married a foreign prince, she would bring England into danger of future subordination to a foreign power. Like every good administrator, Elizabeth had on her desk one tray labelled 'Too difficult'; into that tray she put this particular problem and there she left it. From the very beginning of her reign Elizabeth seems to have decided that the succession problem, undeniably a problem of desperate gravity, was yet insoluble and that efforts to solve the insoluble would do immediate harm to national unity. As she said to Parliament in 1559: God 'will so work in my heart and in your wisdoms as . . . good provision by His help may be made . . . whereby the realm shall not remain destitute of an heir . . . peradventure more beneficial to the realm than such offspring as may come of me'.[1]

She was reluctant to marry because that would divide the nation and reduce its independence; she was reluctant to name an heir presumptive for the same reason: 'I know the inconstancy of the people of England, how they ever mislike the present government and have their eyes fixed upon the next to succeed'. Whatever evils an uncertain succession might one day bring to England, the present consequence of uncertainty was that Englishmen rallied all the more ardently to their reigning monarch and England's enemies were more divided against each other in jealousy of the others' claims. That was why Elizabeth hesitated to execute Mary Queen of Scots.

[1] Quoted in Neale (a), p. 49.

If she did so, 'the King of Spain, having a title, might affect the kingdom for himself'; alternatively, Elizabeth might have to fear 'the danger she stood in of the son [James VI], after the mother should be taken away'. England's present difficulties were always so great that every present advantage must be seized and the future must be left to itself, or to divine providence. The Spanish ambassador's survey of England's prospects had once reached this conclusion: 'the more I reflect ... the more I see that all will turn on the husband which this woman chooses'. Elizabeth entirely agreed: she chose her husband in accordance with this opinion.

Great pressure was brought to bear on Elizabeth, by Parliament and by her privy councillors, to persuade her to marry and give the country an heir. Occasionally deep personal loneliness seemed to move her to the same conclusion. But from the beginning of her reign her own political decision was against marriage and against naming an heir. Exceptional circumstances might change this decision; probable circumstances would not.

In 1558, Mary Queen of Scots had the strongest claim to be Elizabeth's heir as Queen of England. Indeed, those who believed that Henry VIII had married Catherine of Aragon must regard Elizabeth as illegitimate and a usurper; in that case, Mary Queen of Scots was already the lawful Queen of England, unjustly deprived of her rights. Under the terms of the statute of 1543, Mary Queen of Scots was indeed excluded from the succession, whereas Elizabeth had been included and the next heir would be Lady Catherine Grey, sister of Lady Jane Grey and grand-niece of Henry VIII through his sister Mary Tudor. But all observers agreed that Lady Catherine lacked the qualities necessary in a monarch; her marriage in 1560 to Edward Seymour, Earl of Hertford, made her the focus of faction rather than of national unity. Mary Queen of Scots was without a real rival as Elizabeth's heir and yet her accession would be a national disaster, driving protestant Englishmen to civil war and subordinating England to France. No wonder patriotic Englishmen hoped that Elizabeth would marry and have a son.

Philip II was the first suitor to be refused. His proposal came before the end of 1558; its serious purpose was to guard against an Anglo-French alliance, and to that purpose it did contribute.

The most promising Hapsburg suitor was the Archduke Charles, younger son of Emperor Ferdinand. Such a husband would bring the advantages of a Spanish military alliance with the least likelihood of England and Spain becoming in the end a single monarchy. This marriage continued to enjoy desultory consideration until 1567. But the Archduke Charles insisted on religious concessions which Elizabeth was unwilling to grant. Of all foreign suitors, James Hamilton, son of the second Earl of Arran, seemed to offer the greatest diplomatic advantages.[1] He was in line of succession to the Scottish throne; he would not necessarily subordinate England to France or Spain. Cecil observed complacently enough that 'the best felicity that Scotland can have is . . . to be made one monarchy with England'. Unfortunately Arran was already half-mad and was evidently growing worse. After 1566 he was not capable of any sort of public life. If loneliness and love had driven Elizabeth to marry against her political judgement, then she would have married Robert Dudley, son of Northumberland, in the course of 1560. William Cecil was desperately afraid that she would do so. No one was more anxious for a royal marriage and a royal heir than was Cecil, but he also knew that marriage with Robert Dudley would utterly destroy the queen's prestige among her own people. The Dudley family was an object of general and of aristocratic hatred; Robert was thought by many to have procured the murder of his wife, Amy Robsart, in order to be free to marry the queen.

With no prospect of a husband, Elizabeth had to face the demands of Parliament for an immediate marriage and the demands of Mary Queen of Scots for immediate recognition as England's heiress. William Cecil was terrified that Elizabeth would yield to this demand, for he regarded Mary's accession to the English throne as an ultimate calamity: 'God send our mistress a husband and by time a son. . . . The matter is too big for weak folk and too deep for simple. The Queen's Majesty knoweth it and so I will end'.[2] However much Elizabeth may have prevaricated, her policy towards Mary was

---

[1] The second Earl of Arran was commonly called the Duke of Chatelherault after 1548, and his son was, in courtesy, called Arran even during his father's lifetime. For Arran claims to the Scottish throne, see genealogy 9 on p. 131.

[2] Quoted in Read (b), p. 221.

clear enough: to preserve Mary's hope of peacefully gaining the English throne so that her supporters would not be driven to the extremity of civil war and invasion, but also to hold Mary very firmly at arm's length. Elizabeth refused to meet Mary on her journey to Scotland in 1561, or even to allow her to travel through England. A meeting between the two queens was again rejected by Elizabeth in 1563. Nor was she willing to name Mary as her heir as part of a bargain in which Mary would surrender her claim to be Queen of England so long as Elizabeth was alive. For Elizabeth to name her heir was to point forward to her own death and that she consistently refused to do: 'the desire is without example to desire me to set my own winding sheet before my eyes'. Elizabeth's last word on this subject, given on 5th March 1565 was: 'The Queen's Majesty . . . to offer to the Queen of Scotland gentleness etc., but not to meddle with her title until she be married herself or be determined not to marry.'[1]

Meanwhile, Parliament had been in a fever of anxiety for their queen who had almost died of smallpox in October 1562. They petitioned her to name her successor in January 1563, but she evaded the request with only an acknowledgement that 'the grave heads of this House did right well consider that she forgot not the suit of this House for the succession, the matter being so weighty'. She was at this time as near to a succession policy as she was likely to get; she was cherishing the thought that, if Mary were married to Robert Dudley, England's interest might be safeguarded. She was not to be shifted from her intentions by parliamentary pressure: to name Mary as successor was, for Elizabeth, unthinkable in advance of this marriage; to name anyone hostile to Mary would prevent the marriage. 'The matter is so deep, I cannot reach unto it,' said Cecil. 'God send it a good issue.' In 1566 Parliament held up the voting of new taxes when Elizabeth forbad a discussion of the succession, but, in face of parliamentary discussion, Elizabeth once more avoided naming Mary as her successor but yet kept her hopes alive by refusing to name anyone else.

After the flight of Mary Queen of Scots to England and her imprisonment there (1568), Elizabeth left the problem of a successor

[1] Quoted in Read (b), p. 315.

totally in abeyance until James VI began to grow to maturity and to present himself to the minds of more and more Englishmen as England's future ruler. Elizabeth entered marriage negotiations with Henry, Duke of Anjou, in December 1570. When he grew unwilling, negotiations were shifted to his brother Francis, Duke of Alençon, but in each case the negotiations had a purely strategic purpose: to secure French support against Alva in the Netherlands, but to restrain intervention by the French if they seemed likely to grow powerful there. The marriage negotiations led, as was intended, to the treaty of Blois (April 1572) which provided for an alliance without a marriage.

Later marriage negotiations in 1578 with Alençon may have had more serious intent. Elizabeth had just been shocked out of long-established habits of mind by Robert Dudley's sudden marriage to Lettice, daughter of Sir Francis Knollys. She was lonely and was stung into a hope that new life might begin for her too at the age of forty-five. In origin the French negotiations had the same strategic purpose as they had possessed in 1570, but on this later occasion Elizabeth seemed to be genuinely excited at the prospect of marriage. William Cecil (now Lord Burghley) treated the prospect very seriously. He himself was as concerned as ever for the provision of an heir; he anxiously noted in his memoranda: (1579) 'her Majesty ... having no ... lack of natural functions in those things that properly belong to the procreation of children, but contrariwise, by judgement of physicians that know her estate in those things and by the opinion of women, being most acquainted with her Majesty's body in such things as properly appertain, to show probability of her aptness to have children, even at this day'.[1] Yet he was opposed to the marriage because Elizabeth was too old, because any son of Alençon (known as Anjou, after his brother's accession as King of France) would probably be sickly, and because Alençon 'hath showed himself an enemy to the professors of the gospel in France' and 'no nation can be more misliked than a prince of France'. Burghley was anxious to preserve an alliance with France, but he did not want this marriage and was afraid of it. Yet Elizabeth was genuinely excited by the prospect and Walsingham

[1] Quoted in Read (a), p. 210.

was therefore despondent: '. . . matters of love and affection be not guided by wisdom. God send this cause better success than I hope after'. Anjou was in England in August 1579; thereafter Elizabeth urged her council into the task of drafting a marriage contract. Perhaps it was the deep distress of the loyal populace that diverted Elizabeth from her course. *Discovery of a Gaping Gulf whereunto England is like to be swallowed by another French Marriage if the Lord forbid not the banns* was published by John Stubbe in August. His presumption was punished by having his right hand chopped off, but his message took root in the queen's mind, so that, in the end, she accepted Sir Philip Sidney's proposition that she ought to prefer English Protestants 'your chief, if not your sole, strength' to 'the son of a Jezebel of our age that . . . himself did sack La Charité and utterly spoiled [the Huguenots] with fire and sword'.[1] By January 1580, Elizabeth had decided against the marriage. An appearance of courtship was maintained until 1584 because this brought strategic advantages to both sides. Anjou was again in England from October 1581 until February 1582, but each side knew that marriage was being postponed indefinitely by each demanding unacceptable conditions about worship and so it continued until Anjou died in June 1584.

During the first twenty years of Elizabeth's reign no progress was made, either by the government or by popular consensus, towards the identification of her successor. Meanwhile King James of Scotland, born in 1566, was attaining a precocious maturity and the status of chief candidate for the position of heir presumptive to Elizabeth. If James had possessed ordinary modesty, he would not have asserted any claim to the English throne as long as his mother, Mary Queen of Scots, was alive to assert her own claims which, though unacceptable to most Englishmen, were very difficult to refute. But the self-assurance of James and his ambition were so overweening that he soon asserted his own position without regard to the prior claims of his mother. In two respects he could become acceptable to Englishmen as she could not: first because he was a protestant, and secondly because his self-assurance would reject any subordination to the Guise family or to France. Elizabeth on her

[1] Quoted in Read (a), p. 217.

Succession, the prerogative of Time

side 'personally . . . prevented the Act for the Queen's Safety (1585) from involving James in his mother's downfall. But for her, his title would . . . have been forfeit'.[1] Hence Elizabeth was able to conclude a treaty with him in spite of her furious dislike of the 'double tongued scoundrel'. At the treaty of Berwick, in July 1586 and six months before Mary's execution, James accepted £4,000 a year and an understanding that Parliament would not be allowed to impede his accession to the English throne; in exchange, he accepted a league with England 'in matters of religion, wheranent we do fully consent the League be defensive and offensive'. Not a single reference was made to Mary Queen of Scots and her claims. When she was executed in February 1587, James made his formal protest, but he had already expressed his real thoughts precisely enough to Leicester: 'how fond and inconstant I were, if I should prefer my mother to my title'.

Though Elizabeth prevented members of Parliament from speaking against the succession of James, she would certainly not allow any member to speak for it; Peter Wentworth she sent to the Tower for his *Pithie exhortation to her majestie for establishing her successor* and there he remained from 1593 until 1596. Whenever a Scottish emissary asked for assurance about the succession, he received 'nothing but negative answers, the matter being of so sour a nature to the Queen'.[2] Philip II had also claimed the throne by virtue of his direct descent from John of Gaunt and of the will of Mary Queen of Scots. More recently he had passed these claims on to his daughter, the Infanta Isabella, wife of the Hapsburg Archduke Albert. Elizabeth could still reckon on some diplomatic advantage from emphasising uncertainty and keeping hopes alive. Even Jesuits were less likely to plan for violent rebellion when they could set their hopes on the peaceful accession of a Roman Catholic to the English throne. In the event, uncertainty helped to divide English Roman Catholics against each other because the Jesuits favoured Isabella whereas the more patriotic 'Appellant Catholics' preferred James. Even a negotiated peace with Spain might be eased by the distant prospect of winning Elizabeth's support for a Hapsburg successor.

[1] Neale (b), p. 135.
[2] Quoted in Black, p. 442.

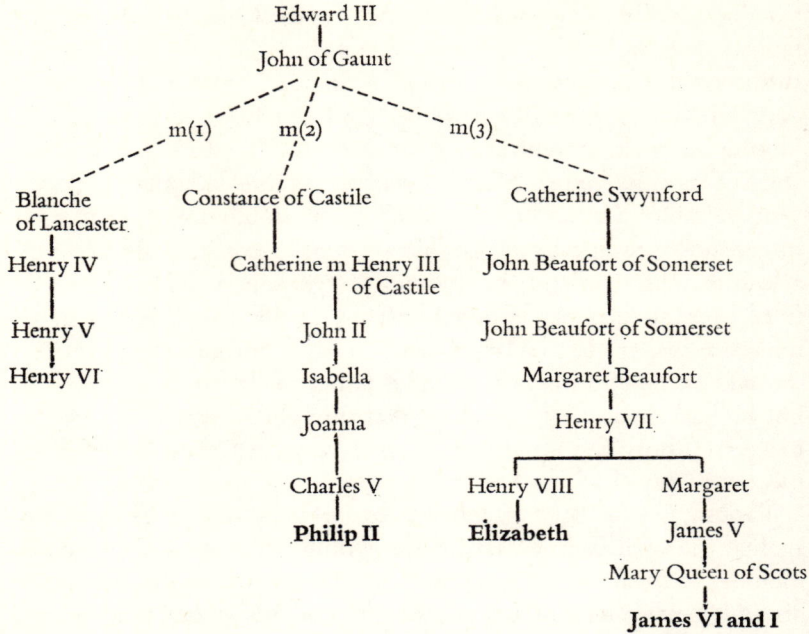

Genealogy 11. Claims to the English throne: a comparison of Philip's claim and the claims of Elizabeth and of James VI and I

Perhaps Elizabeth reckoned also that James's good behaviour was secured better by the tantalising probability of succeeding to the English throne than by the certainty of this happy event. If this was her reckoning, she may have misjudged her man, for his patience was sometimes strained to the very brink at which negotiation turns into war. His memorandum of 1592 on the English succession contemplated military intervention in order to guarantee his rights to the throne. In 1599 he told the Scottish Parliament that 'He was not certain how soon he should have to use arms; but whenever it should be, he knew his right and would venture crown and all for it'.[1] To this impatience the Earl of Essex appealed when he warned James in 1600 that Robert Cecil supported the Infanta and opposed James for fear that the son of Mary Queen of Scots would take vengeance for her execution on the son of William

[1] Hurstfield.

Cecil. With these arguments the Essex faction urged James to invade England in 1600–01 in order to sustain his own rights and to restore the personal prestige of Essex. Finally, Essex recommended his own ineffective *coup d'état* with the battle cry: 'For the Queen! The crown of England is sold to the Spaniard'. Luckily for England, James was too cautious to move at this juncture. But Robert Cecil was worried that James would try to seize the throne before the queen died. Consequently Cecil began a secret correspondence with James in spite of the queen's extreme distrust of any such liaison. This soon convinced James of the folly of 'entering that kingdom by violence as a usurper' since he was assured that he would soon 'enjoy the fruits at my pleasure, in the time of their greatest maturity'. From 1601 the two men, future king and minister, drew closer together and jointly planned the succession which followed so easily in March 1603.

Thus, the queen in one way, and the minister in another, ensured that nothing final would be proclaimed by the English government or done by the Scottish until the last hours of her reign and until almost all men had found their own way to an acceptance of a Stuart heir. 'I do assure myself,' said a cautious observer, 'that the King of Scotland will carry it, as very many Englishmen do know assuredly. But to determine thereof is to all English capitally forbidden and therefore so I leave it. The queen herself slowly advanced backwards, never willing to acknowledge that her heart had accepted the verdict of Time; never willing, until the very end, to define her successor so that only one person could be intended. 'My throne hath been the throne of kings; neither ought any other than my next heir to succeed me'—this was the imprecision of her statement in January 1603. But in March and in her own final exhaustion she at last relaxed her regal grasp so far as to name her successor in a single phrase: 'I have said that my throne was the throne of kings and I would not that any base should succeed me. I will that a king succeed me and who but my kinsman the king of Scots'.[1]

Thus did Time, and many an 'answer answerless', solve the insoluble, so that 'whereas it was the expectation of many, who

[1] Quoted in Black, p. 496.

wished not well unto our Sion, that upon the setting of that bright Occidental Star, Queen Elizabeth of most happy memory, some thick and palpable clouds of darkness would so have overshadowed this Land, that men should have been in doubt which way they were to walk and that it should hardly been known who was to direct the unsettled State, the appearance of Your Majesty, [King James I] as of the Sun in his strength, instantly dispelled those supposed and surmised mists and gave unto all that were well effected exceeding cause of comfort'.[1]

[1] From the dedicatory epistle of the Authorised Version of the Bible.

18 Elizabeth: Defence of monarch and realm— in awe of France, 1558–1603

Elizabeth and her advisers faced urgent problems of national defence in almost every month of her reign. The defence of the realm, and the defence of Elizabeth as queen, were two aspects of one problem; in the circumstances of the time, the nation could lose its independent status and become the appendage of a great empire through a *coup d'état* which deposed the queen or through a general invasion. The queen's only evident successor in 1558 was Mary Queen of Scots, wife of the Dauphin and the embodiment of French interests. The deposition of Elizabeth must entail the accession of Mary Queen of Scots or the outbreak of a civil war which would open the country to invasion from Europe; and this might well cause a war between France and Spain with England as the battlefield and as the victor's trophy, in fact as a second Italy.

In November 1558 French and Hapsburg and English negotiators were at Cateau-Cambrésis terminating the most recent and, in the event, the last of the great wars between Hapsburg and Valois. These negotiations could have generated supreme peril for England and Elizabeth. This was because the spirit of counter-reformation was so lively that zeal for a crusade against heretics might change from lip-service to action. By the terms of the treaty, Philip II was to marry Elizabeth Valois, daughter of Henry II. If so much could be achieved by old enemies, might they not settle their remaining differences in an agreed partition of the British Isles from which all heresy would be eliminated? This policy might seem to be foreshadowed by their agreement at Cateau-Cambrésis to reduce 'all Christian Europe to a true accord'. Such dangerous moments were recurrent in Elizabeth's reign. Elizabeth and William Cecil, her principal secretary, differed, not in their aims, but in their estimate of this particular danger. Cecil, like Thomas Cromwell before and Oliver Cromwell after, believed that religious motives would prevail, that Roman Catholics would in the end unite to launch their crusade and that protestants must ally with their brethren in self-defence. Elizabeth, like Henry VIII, believed that *politique* motives would prevail, that the territorial rivalries of France and Spain would push them apart, however much religious agreement might draw them together—unless an aggressively protestant foreign policy should drive them into alliance.

During the negotiations, therefore, Elizabeth did her best to fan the rivalry of Philip II and Henry II; as soon as each monarch proposed a marriage alliance with England, Elizabeth was careful to report this to the other. She also softened, rejected, or stood deaf to the demands of parliament for radical changes in religion—so deaf, that, as the date for the dissolution of Parliament drew near, the Spanish ambassador could note: 'I see the heretics are very downcast' (March 1559). But at this time news arrived of a peace settlement which included England in its terms. The queen could feel more secure: 'either in the night watches of March 23rd-24th . . . or between 9 a.m. and 1.0 p.m. on Good Friday, the Queen changed her mind. Instead of going to Parliament to end the session, she had it adjourned over Easter to April 3rd, and, in so doing, altered the pattern of the Elizabethan religious settlement'.[1] Bishop Grindal recalled: 'We were indeed urgent from the very first that a general reformation should take place. But the Parliament long delayed the matter and made no change whatever until a peace had been concluded between the Sovereigns, Philip, the French king and ourselves.'

But, in order to have England included in the general peace terms, Elizabeth had had to recognise that France would not restore Calais. England had to be content with a face-saving clause: France would pay 500,000 crowns for Calais or restore the town to England after eight years, unless there were any acts of aggression

[1] Neale (a), p. 69.

between England and France in the meantime. The loss of Calais made the problem of English defence more difficult: French expeditions to the Firth of Forth or against England's eastern harbours would not any more have to run the gauntlet of the Straits of Dover; Calais gave France a base for commerce-raiding very close to the main shipping route between London and Antwerp: 'The French king bestriding the realm, having one foot in Calais and the other in Scotland'.[1]

Critical events in the months of 1559 were frequent; Elizabeth and her advisers must often have wrestled with decisions in the night-watches. About fourteen days after Elizabeth had adjusted her parliamentary policy to the peace of Cateau-Cambrésis, protestant rebellion broke out in Scotland. If Philip and Henry II were united with any crusading zeal for Roman Catholicism, this rebellion must surely move them to action. Two months later, during the tournaments in honour of the marriage between Philip and Elizabeth Valois, Henry II died of a jousting injury. The government of France passed nominally to Francis II, aged fifteen and married to Mary Queen of Scots, but really to Francis, Duke of Guise, the brother of Mary of Guise, regent of Scotland, and the uncle of Mary Queen of Scots and of France. Mary Queen of Scots forthwith displayed the arms of the Queen of England. Europe was faced with the massive prospect of a Guise empire, comprising Scotland, England and France, and unified from Cape Wrath to the Mediterranean. This empire was symbolised by the person of Mary Queen of Scots, whose eldest son by King Francis would rightly claim to be heir apparent to the totality of it. By this empire, Hapsburg dominions would be neatly sliced into two details. If Philip wondered whether to work with or against Henry II, his father-in-law, he had no hesitation in respect of the Guise family. So long as the Guise were powerful and could cherish such great ambitions, Philip was the enemy of their ambitions and of all that was symbolised in the person of Mary, Queen of Scots. Elizabeth as Queen of England, and England as an independent country, stood in jeopardy of Guise power already established north of the Scottish border and south of the Channel, but both Elizabeth and England could

[1] Armagil Waad, civil servant, quoted in Neale (a).

rely on the support of Philip against Mary's claims to be Queen of England.

Moreover, Guise power, even in these months of terrifying potential, was weakening at the hands of Scottish rebels. Back in the 1540s Scotsmen had been alienated by England's armies and garrisons, but they had continued to yearn for the 'great commodity and quiet life and civil justice'[1] which they thought could best be got by religious reformation and by collaboration with England. By 1559 French garrisons were hated quite as much as the English had been: there was an outbreak in Edinburgh between French troops and local people as early as 1548. Ten years later the Earl of Argyll compared Scotland with 'the exampill of Brytanny': ...'the France ar cumin in and sutin down in this realm to occupy it and to put furtht the inhabitantis tharoff and siclik to occupy all uther menis rowmes pece and pece and to put away the blud of the nobilitie'.[2] Many of the nobility of Scotland covenanted together in 1557, as 'Lords of the Congregation', to set up a reformed Church in Scotland; in May 1559 they rose in arms against the regent Mary of Guise, occupied Edinburgh and drove Mary of Guise and her French troops into Leith. The Lords of the Congregation, led by Mar (alias James Stuart, illegitimate son of James V), Argyll, Morton, James Hamilton of Arran (heir presumptive) and his son James, declared themselves joint-regents for Mary Queen of Scots.

Maitland of Lethington (secretary of the regency council) gave Cecil prior notice that rebellion was intended; Cecil, through the English ambassador in Paris, engineered Arran's escape from France so that he could join the rebels. But Cecil could only give effective help if Elizabeth was willing and this rebellion soon showed how his attitude differed from the queen's. Cecil was afraid of a Catholic crusade for the destruction of protestantism; consequently, his policy was to seek maximum collaboration with protestant rebels in Catholic countries. The queen was relying on the fundamental rivalry of Valois and Hapsburg; consequently her policy was to make the greatest play of balancing one power against the other. This Scottish instance offered an urgent opportunity of strengthen-

[1] Merriman (a).
[2] Quoted in Donaldson, p. 285.

ing England's 'postern gate'[1] and of weakening her enemy. The opportunity was also very precarious, because the rebels had sufficient supplies to remain on a war footing for only a few weeks and they had insufficient siege artillery to take any fortified position by assault. 'The Scotch,' said Cecil, 'for lack of ability cannot expel the French out of the town. . . . If they gain it not before new succours come from France . . . they shall be compelled to recant.' Not surprisingly, Knox wanted to know what aid would be sent: 'I require you, Sir, to make plain answer what they may look for.' Cecil was only too anxious to 'nourish and entertain the garboyle in Scotland' but he 'had such a torment herein, with the Queen's majesty, as an ague hath not in five fits'. Elizabeth had sent money to the rebels, £2,000 in August and £3,000 in November. But the French had sent a thousand men to Leith and had another 9,500 ready. The Scots had neither ships to prevent the landing nor guns to take Leith. On 16th December 1559, queen and council began to yield to Cecil's persuasion: Admiral Sir William Wynter was sent to Scottish waters with instructions to get blown into the Firth of Forth and to intercept the French 'as of your own courage'. English troops and guns were mobilised at Berwick, but Norfolk refused to lead them northwards. Elizabeth opened marriage negotiations with the Archduke Charles in order to insure Hapsburg neutrality.

The immediate crisis passed when the French expeditionary force was wrecked by December gales off the coast of Zeeland. But respite was momentary. In February 1560 the Guise were mobilising another force for Scotland and Elizabeth at last entered into formal alliance with the Scots rebels, but only after Cecil asked to be allowed to resign 'with a sorrowful heart and watery eyes'. This alliance was the treaty of Berwick (February 1560): the English would help the Scots against the French so long as Mary Queen of Scots was married to a Frenchman, and the Scots would help the English against any French invasion. In March 1560, an English army of 8,000 advanced towards Leith. But in this same month the feverish energy of the crisis weakened, for there occurred in France the first tremor of the civil wars which later blunted this acute French

[1] Neale (a), p. 85.

threat to England's independence. The 'tumult of Amboise' was a revolt of a section of the lesser Huguenot nobility against Francis II and the Guise family. The outbreak was so helpful to Elizabeth's Scottish diplomacy that her ambassador Throckmorton has been suspected of promoting it.[1] An English assault on Leith was repulsed, but the French were unable to send reinforcements; in Leith French supplies began to run low and Mary of Guise was herself dying. Consequently Cecil, who had travelled up from London in May, was able to drive negotiations to the triumphant conclusion in the treaty of Edinburgh (July 1560): the French and English agreed to evacuate Scotland and not to reoccupy it; Mary Queen of Scots was not to display the arms of England but was to recognise Elizabeth as Queen of England and Ireland; Mary was to negotiate a religious settlement with the Scots Parliament; France acknowledged that concessions to Scotland were concessions in which England also had an interest. Although Francis II and Mary Queen of Scots refused to ratify this treaty, it nevertheless remained the basis of affairs between Scotland, France and England. 'The peace of Edinburgh was', says Conyers Read, 'one of Cecil's greatest achievements and one of the greatest achievements of Elizabeth's reign.' Cecil himself concluded: 'the benevolence (of the Scots) at this time towards England is so great . . . as I see not that in long time the French shall recover the mind of Scottishmen against us'.

(Just after the treaty was signed, Cecil received a note from Elizabeth ordering him to insist on the restoration of Calais as a condition of peace. One wonders why.)

In December 1560 died Francis II King of France. This event weakened the power of the Guise, lifted Catherine de Medici into the position of French regent, brought French civil war nearer and so contributed even more to the security of England. But it did also bring Mary Queen of Scots to her decision to return to Scotland as queen rather than to remain in France as queen-dowager. The return of Mary to Scotland in August 1561 did indeed raise the possibility that her charm might capture 'the mind of Scottishmen' and that her French loyalties might restore these minds to the French and against England. Roman Catholicism was still the dominant creed

[1] See Sutherland.

in north-central Scotland, from Aberdeen to Skye, so that the basis of a French party always existed.

Although for the time James Stuart, now Earl of Moray, remained the effective head of state, and in 1562 crushed Earl Huntly of Aberdeen and the Roman Catholic Gordons, it was still incumbent on Elizabeth to detach Mary from her French affiliations, if that were possible. For this reason Elizabeth encouraged, in every way short of formal recognition, the belief that Mary was her natural successor. For this reason also Robert Dudley—'some person of noble birth within our realm . . . such as she would hardly think we would agree to'—was suggested to Mary as the most suitable husband. Elizabeth expressed anger when Mary married Darnley in July 1565, but it was Elizabeth who permitted Darnley's father, the Earl of Lennox, to return from England to Scotland in 1564 and allowed Darnley to follow him in February 1565. Perhaps Elizabeth believed that Mary Queen of Scots would at least be detached from France by her marriage to Darnley.

However, Moray and his protestant associates were dismissed from office and fled to England after an unsuccessful rebellion (which Elizabeth subsidised) so that the general trend of events in Scotland was moving against England's interest. But the trend was turned to political chaos by the collapse of all affection between Mary and Darnley. Darnley in association with the protestant James Douglas, Earl of Morton, murdered Rizzio, who was Mary's favourite and secretary (March 1566). The assassins recalled Moray and his allies, but Darnley had acquired momentary support rather than political power and Moray before long went back into exile, for Mary gathered about her another faction led by James Hepburn, Earl of Bothwell, who between February and May 1567 murdered Darnley, kidnapped Mary and married her, all equally, as it appeared, with her consent. In the popular reaction to this multiple outrage, Morton raised a force which won the battle of Carberry Hill (June 1567); he drove Bothwell into exile, captured Mary, forced her to abdicate in favour of her infant son James VI and recalled Moray to be regent. A year later (May 1568) Mary escaped and fled to England. Any chance she may have had to 'recover the mind of Scottishmen' for France had been lost.

Perhaps Elizabeth ought to have adopted the policy of openly convicting Mary of murder and bringing her quickly to execution. In fact, no verdict ever emanated from the enquiry which was held at York. Factions which advocated the claims of Mary were thus allowed to revive in Scotland where they harassed Moray and the Scottish supporters of the English connection; they revived also in England where they launched their many plots to assassinate Elizabeth. The Marian revival in Scotland culminated in the assassination of Moray in January 1570 and in civil war between James Douglas, Earl of Morton, who led the protestants, and Maitland of Lethington who led the Marians. Morton drove the Marians back into Edinburgh castle and Elizabeth supported this protestant counter-attack by recognising Morton as regent of Scotland and James as king in place of Mary (April 1570); she gave the protestants total victory when she sent in an English siege-train which broke down the defences of Edinburgh castle for Morton in May 1573 (although this military reoccupation of Scotland was in violation of the treaty of Edinburgh of 1560). The Marian revival in England quickly led to the Rising of the Northern Earls (1569) which might well have established a dangerous conjunction with the Marian revival in Scotland. Both movements were dangerous but both were crushed and Mary's seven years in Scotland wholly failed to restore the Franco-Scottish alliance. For the future she was important, not as the symbol and creator of the French threat to England's independence, but as a pawn in England's protracted defence against Spain, against the threats implicit in the arrival of Alva in Brussels with 25,000 men (August 1567) only one month after Mary had abdicated.

For the possibility of a French conquest of England had receded. Widespread civil war and heavy fighting occupied the energies of France from March 1562 when the Duke of Guise usurped the government by a *coup d'état* and Condé, Coligny and the Huguenots took up arms against him in defence of their religion and the monarchy. At first, Elizabeth and her advisers could not be sure that France had ceased, for the time, to be any threat to England. They had to fear an all-out Guisan victory and they were fully aware that a united France had the power to invade England. Consequently they felt bound to take advantage of these French wars to re-establish English occupation of at least some of the Channel ports from which invasion was to be feared. Cecil reckoned that 'the perils growing upon the overthrow of the Prince of Condé's cause' might include the conquest of England by the Guise. He urged England's ambassador in Paris to 'continue your writing to put the Queen's Majesty in remembrance of her peril if the Guisans prosper'. Ambassador Throckmorton, for his part, argued that 'the protestants ... may be moved to give us possession of Calais, Dieppe, or Newhaven [Le Havre], perhaps all three'. When Huguenot fortunes had sufficiently declined in 1562, they made just such a humble concession to Elizabeth as the price of her help. By the treaty of Richmond (September 1562) Condé received the help of a large English loan and 3,000 troops, but at the price of handing over Le Havre to an English garrison as a pledge that Calais would be restored. But during the next ten months shattering losses afflicted both the Huguenots and the Guises—Antony of Navarre was killed, Condé taken prisoner and Francis of Guise was assassinated—so that Catherine de Medici was able to reassert royal authority and negotiate a settlement. Frenchmen of all parties rallied against the intrusive English. The garrison of Le Havre, reinforced but dying of plague at the rate of seventy men a day, was compelled to surrender in July 1563.

Elizabeth accepted the peace of Troyes (April 1564); by her military intervention she forfeited her right to the restoration of Calais and by this treaty she recognised this loss for a payment of one-third of the price which had been agreed in the treaty of Cateau-Cambrésis. This was a humiliation in terms of diplomacy; it was not a disaster in terms of military strategy. Elizabeth had intervened on the assumption that the wars might create an aggressive Guisan France; in fact they exhausted France and established the comparatively pacific government of Catherine de Medici. Renewal of civil war in October 1567 and then again from September 1568 until the peace of St Germain (August 1570) maintained the state of exhaustion, advanced Coligny to a central position in the government of France, and reduced the influence of the Guises.

The years 1568 to 1570 were years of transition in English foreign policy. Englishmen began to recognise that Spain, England's traditional ally, had great armies newly established in the Netherlands, and therefore presented a new and acute threat to English independence; they began to recognise that France, who had previously presented such an acute threat to English independence, was divided and exhausted and might even serve as a temporary ally. Elizabeth's policy towards France had to serve two aims. First, since French exhaustion was temporary, and since France had been and would again become England's chief enemy, Elizabeth's first aim was to ensure that France should never be allowed to gather strength from Spain's defeat—as the Earl of Sussex summarised the matter once and for all: 'the case will be hard with the Queen and with England if ever the French possses or the Spaniards tyrannise in the Low Countries'. But, equally, Elizabeth had to counter the unpleasant truth that the weaker France became the stronger was the likelihood that one French faction or another would discover advantage in handing over the French Channel ports to Spain. There was a danger to be feared from Spain and this must be enlarged if ever Spaniards should occupy the notorious French invasion ports. To keep Netherlands ports out of the hands of the French and to keep French ports out of the hands of the Guises and the Spaniards—these were the long term and the short term objectives of Elizabeth's attitude to France from 1570 until 1603.

These would seem to be the motives which prompted Elizabeth in December 1570 to seek an alliance with the newly established *politique* government of Catherine de Medici, Charles IX and Coligny. Her suggestion was that she should marry Henry of Anjou, the French heir presumptive, and this suggestion became a firm proposal from the French side in March 1571. Marriage was never a likely outcome because Elizabeth seems to have been indifferent and Henry was a bigoted champion of catholicism. But the negotiations created a collaborative atmosphere and this, as far as it went, was likely to strengthen a French government which would not admit Spanish forces to French ports. But Elizabeth's great anxiety at this time sprang from the aggressive plans of Coligny and Charles IX. Their object was to intensify the new-found unity of France and to take advantage of Spain's difficulties in the Netherlands by launching a French invasion of the Low Countries. This seemed to be the ideal time, and this the natural area, for victorious French aggression. Elizabeth was apprehensive of the long-term consequences for England of French armies and fleets in the ports of the Netherlands. She opened negotiations with Alva (March 1572) and even offered to help him if he would promise autonomy to the Netherlands. She ordered the Dutch Sea Beggars out of Dover with the consequence that they captured and occupied Brill and Flushing; thus they anticipated and precluded the French and fulfilled Cecil's anxious hope that 'it were done rather by themselves than by others (i.e. the French) that percase would not suffer them long to enjoy their liberty when it should be recovered'. Sir Humphrey Gilbert took English troops to hold Flushing, as well against the French as against the Spaniards (July 1572), and also to prevent the Dutch from becoming so desperate as to call in the French, which they were likely to do if, as Walsingham said, 'there be no assistance given underhand by her Majesty'.

But all the while, Elizabeth was also moving towards a defensive alliance with France, even discussing a possible marriage with Alençon, the younger brother, when Anjou, the elder, proved to be intractable. This alliance, by the treaty of Blois (April 1572), provided for mutual assistance if either country should be attacked by a third power (Spain). It was just the sort of association which has sometimes enabled one country to apply restraint to its ally and may have been intended to give Elizabeth a restraining influence if France should move towards war in the Netherlands as soon as the marriage of Henry Bourbon and Margaret Valois (a Huguenot prince and a Catholic princess) had confirmed the new *politique* solidarity of Frenchmen. Instead, the massacre of St Bartholomew's Eve (August 1572) renewed their civil wars and their international impotence. Elizabeth had many weeks of anxiety on account of these civil wars, lest the outcome should prove in one way or another fatal to English independence, but as one war followed another during the 1570s she did not in the end feel driven to intervene, except that she permitted volunteers to help in the defence of La Rochelle in 1573.

Her problem became acute in the intervals between the wars,

for at those times Henry III of France (lately the Duke of Anjou) revived French plans for an invasion of the Spanish Netherlands, or his younger brother Anjou (lately the Duke of Alençon) planned to aid the Netherlanders on his own account. At all such times Elizabeth felt bound to help the Dutch if only to forestall the French and irrespective of whether, at the moment, the Dutch were in desperate straits or were holding their own. Elizabeth offered the Dutch £100,000 in December 1576 rather than have them become allies of France. As in the Anjou courtship of 1571, so in the courtship with his brother in and after 1578, the diplomatic motive was to establish a hold on a young man who was intent on winning the Netherlands for France (although in this case an actual intention to marry may have developed). After 1578 the Dutch rebels were under desperate pressure from Don John and later from Parma. They needed help. Elizabeth would give very little and then only to dissuade the Dutch from offering the sovereignty of their country to a Frenchman. The younger Anjou was able to mobilise some troops, though probably not enough to capture the country permanently for France. Elizabeth concluded that a confused and tentative policy was the least objectionable in a confused situation. She herself gave the Dutch sufficient aid to preserve her own diplomatic influence with them; she gave this second Anjou moderate encouragement with his own plans of intervention and tried to establish a strong limiting influence upon them.

On these terms her courtship developed in 1578. Anjou's first army disintegrated south of the Netherlands' frontier in December 1578 without achieving anything except temporarily drawing off a part of the Spanish army. In 1579 and 1580 the courtship continued, with Anjou himself in England for a part of the time. But the desperation of the Dutch ran ahead of Elizabeth's hesitations and, by the treaty of Plessis le Tours, they offered and Anjou accepted the sovereignty of the Netherlands (September 1580). Thereupon Elizabeth's diplomacy of courtship was renewed with very great vigour; a vastly impressive French commission arrived to negotiate in April 1581; it was entertained with fantastic ceremonial and at great expense. It achieved no conclusion, except to demonstrate Anglo-French friendship. Anjou himself arrived in England in

October 1581. When he left in February 1582, he took a loan of £50,000 and with that he was able to do a little to distract the Spaniards until he fell out with the Dutch in January 1583 and then retreated back to France (June 1583). At his death in June 1584, Henry Bourbon became heir to the French throne. The prospect of a Huguenot king intensified the French civil wars, so that for some years French intervention in the Netherlands need neither be expected nor feared.

For the next ten years, Elizabeth's desperate concern was to keep the French Channel ports from the use of Spanish fleets—to keep the Channel ports out of the power of the Guises who in their weakness had become clients of Philip and would put these ports at his disposal.[1] Elizabeth's task was the more difficult, because the northern hinterland was Guise territory and because Henry III, whose governors controlled the harbour fortifications, was never far from becoming a Guise-puppet. In 1586 and 1587 Elizabeth was tempted to give powerful aid to Henry Bourbon in the forlorn hope that he might work the miracle of defeating both Henry III and Henry of Guise. But that policy would have forced Henry III into total alliance with the Guise. She resisted the temptation and sent only minimal aid to Henry Bourbon. Henry III, on his side, evaded Guise pressure in one way and another, until at last he submitted to it in the 'Edict of Union' in July 1588. He agreed to crush the Huguenots and to end negotiations with England. But July 1588 was too late to serve the Armada. When the Armada appeared in the Channel during this same month, Royalist governors, who did not favour the Guises, still controlled the French ports—Brest, St Malo, Le Havre, Dieppe, Boulogne and Calais. Medina Sidonia could not count on hospitality; when he anchored off Calais, Gourdan the governor permitted only the minimum courtesies and refused all military supplies. The Spaniards had not got from France the advantage which would most grievously have threatened England's defences: deep-water harbours, fairly near the English coast, with prevailing winds coming offshore.

The fiasco of the Armada encouraged Henry III in the assassination of the overmighty Henry of Guise; this death permanently

[1] See map 5 on p. 60.

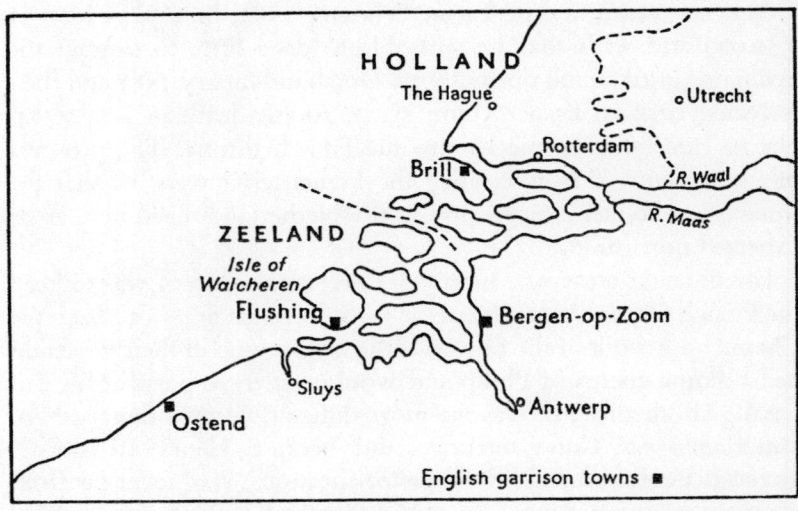

Map 13. Ostend, Flushing, Brill and Bergen-op-Zoom, English garrison towns in 1594, as much against France as against Spain

weakened the Spanish faction in France. Nevertheless, the French ports which were vital to England's defence in 1588 continued to be so for another five years. That is why 4,000 men were sent to help Henry Bourbon in Dieppe in 1589; another 3,000 helped him at the unsuccessful siege of Rouen in 1591 and were maintained in Henry's service until 1593; an expeditionary force of 4,000 was maintained in Brittany from 1591 to 1595 in order to deny the use of Brest and St Malo to Spanish fleets. For the Spaniards had landed troops in Brittany and were 'become as a frontier enemy to all the west part of England.' On the other hand, the belief of English strategists was that unless Spaniards held the ports of northern France or of the Low Countries 'our dangers cannot be great'.[1] As Henry IV began to unite the whole of France, Englishmen ceased to fear that Spain would ever be allowed to use French ports.

As the acute fear of Spain lessened, so the old long-term fear of France returned. In the long run, France would want to invade England; England would be difficult to defend against a country

[1] Quoted in Wernham (b).

which controlled the ports of the Low Countries as well as the French Channel ports. At the end, therefore, Elizabeth returned to her long-sighted opposition to French expansion in the Netherlands. English garrisons were maintained in Ostend, Flushing, Brill and Bergen-op-Zoom until 1594, nominally to keep out the Spaniards but equally, in truth, to keep out the French. She objected strongly when Dutch sovereignty was offered to Henry IV in 1590 and when a triple attack of Dutch, French and English was proposed in 1596 to drive the Spaniards out of the Netherlands. In 1598 and again in 1599 she was in trouble with her Dutch allies, because her fear of France was profound and her hostility to Spain was limited. Her fears of Spain never swamped her conviction that France would be the ultimate enemy. She would never have aided and abetted Mazarin against the Spaniard 'to the unspeakable prejudice of all Europe in general and of this nation in particular'.[1]

[1] Colonel Edmund Ludlow's comment on the foreign policy of Oliver Cromwell.

19 Elizabeth: Defence of monarch and realm from Rome and Spain, at low tension, 1568–73

Elizabethan statesmen reckoned Spain to be England's natural ally in principle and in the long term. Circumstances might bring temporary alliance with France, but in the long term England would have to fight for survival against her old enemy of Crécy and Agincourt. Circumstances might bring friction and even war with Spain, but unless actually conquered and absorbed by Spain, England would return to the old Spanish alliance—to the old 'Burgundian alliance' as Elizabethans liked to call it.

Philip II accepted this general estimate of the probable relationship between England and Spain. He hoped and expected that Spain would either absorb England into her system of client territories or retain her support as an ally. Philip may for a few weeks in 1559 have inclined to a crusading alliance with Henry II of France against heresy, but in any case he returned to traditional Hapsburg fear of France as soon as Henry was killed in July 1559. Philip's attitude to Elizabeth was friendly, tinged only with regret that her government and country were not in communion with Rome. He would defend Elizabeth as Queen of England rather than have Mary Queen of Scots in her place, for Mary belonged to the house of Guise and would unify London, Edinburgh and Paris in a single imperial system. Spain's sea communications with the Netherlands required the friendly neutrality of England's ports and of England's privateers if ever France was hostile. Philip offered to marry Elizabeth in accordance with these calculations and, for the same reason, he maintained a friendly policy after he was refused. His ambassadors for the first ten years were of a friendly disposition: de Feria until 1559, de Quadra from 1559 until 1564 and de Silva until 1568: 'we are the best of friends' said de Quadra of Cecil; de Silva 'happened to be a Spaniard with whom she [Elizabeth] got on well';[1] she 'was genuinely sorry to see him go'.[2] The foundations of this friendly association of England and Spain were, however, weak in two respects. First, Philip's disposition depended on his belief that France, and in particular the house of Guise, was a threat to his dominions; future events might weaken France; Philip would then reconsider his need for an English alliance and might decide to do better without it. Secondly, Philip was willing for the time to accept English friendship in order to strengthen his strategic position, but this strategic position would be much more secure if he could absorb England into his dominions and this would also serve his imperial belief that all Christendom ought to be brought into political unity. Philip's policy of an English alliance might at any time become a policy of imperial conquest which would be in absolute conflict with Elizabeth's commitment to national independence.

The policy of friendly collaboration was maintained, with little interruption, for ten years; in particular, Philip restrained the Pope from excommunicating Elizabeth and from declaring her to be deposed. Friction arose, strangely enough, from the attempts of John Hawkins to enlarge and exploit the friendly situation. Hawkins believed that, under cover of general Spanish benevolence, he could induce Philip to admit English traders to Spain's Caribbean settlements. Hawkins' expeditions of 1562–63, 1564–65 and 1567–68 failed to achieve this diplomatic purpose. They ended in the disaster of San Juan de Ulua. But neither the intrusion nor the disaster were likely to cause a breach between Elizabeth and Philip, much less to be a *casus belli* in Europe, for all that Elizabeth was determined to find opportunities for her countrymen overseas and Philip was determined to maintain Spain's overseas monopoly. The two rulers were likely to find a compromise between Philip's exclusive claims and Elizabeth's refusal to recognise Spanish sovereignty except where Spain was in 'effective occupation'. In any case, France and

[1] Neale (a), p. 140.
[2] Read (b).

Spain had recognised at Cateau-Cambrésis (1559) that acts of war to the south of the tropic of Cancer did not constitute a *casus belli* for governments in Europe. Consequently Philip and Elizabeth contented themselves in 1568 with diplomatic protests and, for the rest, gave practical recognition to a doctrine of 'no peace beyond the line'.[1] The exploits of Hawkins scarcely disturbed Anglo-Spanish relations in Europe. Indeed Hawkins' own personal agents were dealing directly with Philip in 1571 on matters associated with the affairs of San Juan de Ulua.

The first breach in Anglo-Spanish relations occupied the years 1568 to 1573. The manifest cause of this breach was the arrival of Alva in Brussels in August 1567 with 25,000 Spanish troops. There followed five years of conflict which foreshadowed, experimentally and in minature, all of the items which constituted the great twenty-five-year crisis of 1578–1603: Englishmen fighting in the Netherlands, an attack on Spain's bullion shipments from America (alias 'a silver blockade'), a Catholic revival in Scotland, Catholic assassination plots on England's home-front, and rebellion in Ireland—every item of the later crisis except that no Spanish Armada was mobilised specifically for an assault on England. The years 1568 to 1573 served as a dress-rehearsal to the greater conflict of the 1580s, with this difference that in 1568 Philip was in two minds: he felt some hostility to Elizabeth but he still regarded her as a bulwark against Guise power in Europe. By 1580 he had come to regard the Guises as subsidised dependents of Spain; he no longer needed a bulwark against their influence; he was single-minded in his hostility to Elizabeth.

For a decade before 1567 there had been resistance in the Netherlands to Spanish influence, partly patriotic resistance led by famous Roman Catholic aristocrats (Egmont, Horn and William the Silent) and partly religious resistance led by Calvinist fanatics. Elizabeth had little sympathy with either type of rebellion: 'when the colour of dissension began first to kindle between his subjects of the Netherlands and him—I mean not Holland and Zeeland only, but of Brabant and the other provinces which are now in the Archduke's possession, then I gave them counsel to contain their passions and

[1] Mattingly (b), p. 145.

rather by humble petition than by violence or arms to seek ease of their grievances. . . . I was so far from forgetting the old league that lasted long between the race of Burgundy and my progenitors . . . as I dissuaded them'—so the queen recalled, truly enough, in 1601.[1] But a Spanish army, a Spanish military presence in the Netherlands, was an act of war against England, total and overwhelming to the minds of Elizabethan statesmen. They knew that the imperial idea was the accepted idea of European policy; they knew that every powerful government accepted the ultimate aim of creating Christendom by conquering Europe; they knew that a government, which was able to conquer, would do so; that England could expect no more than 'the courtesy of Polyphemus to Ulysses, namely to be the last devoured'. Finally, they doubted whether Englishmen could prevent seaborne invasions from the Netherlands, 'the very counterscarp of England', or could repel a veteran army once it had landed in England. Elizabeth and her councillors were clear that the Spanish government would use the Netherlands as a base for the conquest of England. They were especially concerned about the island of Walcheren that controlled the approaches to Antwerp.[2] In due course, members of Parliament reached the same conclusion: 'if the Low Countries . . . were subdued by the King of Spain . . . the Low Countries shall crown him Aeolus and Neptune of the winds and the narrow seas'.[3]

Elizabeth's government never acquiesced in Spanish military presence in the Netherlands; but Spanish political presence they wanted to keep, because an independent Netherlands would be a small weak country that invited conquest by France. A Spanish military presence in the Netherlands was intolerable; a French one would be worse. The aim of Elizabethan policy was to persuade Philip that Spain had more to gain from the trade, the resources and the military support of a semi-autonomous Netherlands than from prolonged warfare for Spanish domination. Elizabeth wanted Spain to withdraw the Spanish army and to permit a *politique*

[1] Quoted in Neale (b), p. 429.
[2] See map 13 on p. 186.
[3] Quoted in Neale (b), p. 180.

degree of toleration for the sake of public order, but Spain was also to retain suzerainty over the Netherlands and be ever-ready to invade France across the Pyrenees if the French dared to invade the Netherlands. Elizabeth's aim was to prevent Spanish victory in the Netherlands (but not to cause Spanish defeat) until Spain had come to accept this conclusion. By the ultimate conclusion of 1609 and 1648 Spain preserved a weakened military presence in the southern Netherlands, but had no deep-water ports, and this arrangement gave England in practice the sort of security for which Elizabeth strove: Spain was not able to use the Netherlands as a base for an invasion of England but at the same time her military presence in the southern provinces helped to keep France out.

In 1568 Alva and his troops seemed likely to win a quick and easy domination in the Netherland. Elizabeth had to prevent this, to impose on Spain a long stalemate. Cecil was in correspondence with Dutch rebels in 1568; he was also in correspondence with Coligny. The three together were able to arrange a blockade against Spanish shipping in the English Channel which did not however commit the English government to war with Spain. Huguenot privateers from La Rochelle, William Hawkins and his associates from Plymouth, de la Marck and his sea-beggars based on Dover, closed the Channel to Alva's supplies; his reinforcements had to come across country from Italy. An early consequence of this privateering was that four Spanish ships took refuge in Plymouth in November 1568. They were carrying £85,000, a loan from Genoese bankers; it was to pay for Alva's army. Elizabeth provided a military escort to bring the money by land to London and then arranged with the Genoese to take over the loan herself. This action upset Alva's military operations and drew him into violent counter-measures against England which reduced his resources even further. On the advice of de Spes, the new aggressive Spanish ambassador in London, Alva confiscated all English goods and ships that were in the Netherlands. Elizabeth replied against the goods and ships of Spain. Philip in Spain took similar action against English assets there. The balance of loss went against Alva because the Channel was still blockaded against his shipping, whereas English merchants in 1569 diverted their cloth exports to Hamburg. Alva declared that he would destroy the English convoy en route for Hamburg, but it was safely escorted out and back.

By this date Cecil was arguing for outright military aid to William the Silent in support of the Dutch rebellion, but this was not undertaken. But in another direction a new and experimental type of aggressive pressure was attempted against Spain: this was the pressure which came to be known as the 'silver blockade'. Drake, presumably with the connivance of his government, attempted to prevent the flow of bullion from America to Spain.[1] His exploit of 1572-73 at Nombre de Dios was highly successful and may have contributed to Spanish financial difficulties in 1574 and 1575, which in turn caused the great mutiny of unpaid Spanish troops in the Netherlands in July 1576. Meanwhile the Spaniards, harassed by the Channel blockade and distracted by the threat of French invasion from the south, did not establish their authority over the northern Netherlands. In March 1572, Elizabeth began to disengage from direct conflict with Alva. In order to encourage negotiations, she ordered de la Marck out of Dover. He seized Brill and Flushing. At a single stroke Elizabeth was disembarrassed of her association with Dutch rebels and a revolt was started in coastal towns to which William of Orange would come with reinforcement from the hinterland. To these coastal towns went Thomas Morgan, Humphrey Gilbert and three or four thousand volunteers in support of Dutch religious freedom. The greater were Alva's immediate difficulties in the Netherlands, the greater was his willingness to negotiate with Elizabeth. In April 1573 trade between England, Spain and the Netherlands was restored by the treaty of Nymegen. By the end of 1573 all English volunteers had been brought back to England. (Thomas Morgan, the original leader, himself returned to England in January 1574.)

But others besides King Philip came into open conflict with Elizabeth during these five years. The most important of them were the Pope and the anti-English party among Spanish officials, men like Granvelle in Brussels and de Spes in London, who had no patience with Philip's hesitations. By 1568 the Pope had ceased to hope that Elizabeth would return to communion with Rome; he believed

[1] See map 2 on p. 25.

that she ought to be deposed in favour of Mary Queen of Scots. This opinion was shared by conservative leaders of opinion in northern England (commonly known as the 'northern Earls') and by leaders of the counter-reformation in Ireland. An attempt to depose Elizabeth would be supported by a growing Marian party in Scotland, by de Spes and ultimately by Alva. Thus, at the time when the realm of England seemed in jeopardy from the Spanish army newly arrived in the Netherlands, the queen was herself encircled by religious and personal opponents who were working for her deposition or assassination just as similar groups were to work for the more famous 'Enterprise' of the 1580s.

De Spes tried to master-mind the forces of opposition. He was an ambassador of a new type, a product of religious fanaticism, of the counter-reformation and its Calvinist parallel. Earlier ambassadors of the sixteenth century had developed a tradition of civilised intercourse which reduced the occasions and the asperities of international conflict, but these new men were primarily organisers of sedition, standing firmly on the proposition that no faith should be kept with heretics. De Spes was 'a truculent crusader, intent on recovering England for the old faith'.[1] He was in communication with Mary Queen of Scots even before he reached England. In 1568 he established contact with Northumberland, Westmorland, Norfolk and others who were opposed to Cecil and intended that Norfolk should marry Mary Queen of Scots. De Spes encouraged Alva to plan an invasion. In September 1569 Elizabeth forbade marriage between Norfolk and Mary. Norfolk submitted to this veto. But in November the northern Earls took up arms on behalf of the Catholic religion and in defiance of the queen and her Council of the North. They were rapidly suppressed by Henry Carey, Lord Hunsdon.

One group of opponents had taken to arms and been suppressed, before the others had moved—but only just. In January 1570, the regent Moray was murdered by supporters of Mary Queen of Scots; his successor, Lennox, suffered the same fate in March 1571. Mary's supporters seemed likely to dominate the country. Once more 'the postern gate' was open to England's enemies. But John Erskine,

[1] Read (b), p. 409.

Defence of monarch and realm from Rome and Spain

Earl of Mar, reorganised the protestants. He was heavily subsidised by Elizabeth and drove the Marians back into Edinburgh Castle by the end of 1570, where they held out for two years, until Elizabeth sent in cannon to force a way into the castle (April 1573). The Earl of Mar had died in November 1572 and James Douglas, Earl of Morton, was recognised as regent.

Meanwhile, the Pope broke loose from Philip's restraining hand and made his own decision to excommunicate Elizabeth. His bull was published in England in May 1570. This brought demands from Parliament that English laws against Roman Catholics should be intensified, but Elizabeth stood her ground for the time and played for the loyalty of the Catholic community in spite of the Pope's verdict of deposition.

While the Marians were still at large in Scotland or were holding out in Edinburgh Castle, Roberto Ridolfi planned to give a cutting edge to the Pope's proclamation. His plot for the assassination of Elizabeth involved de Spes, Mary Queen of Scots, the Duke of Norfolk and, in the imagination of Ridolfi, many thousands of discontented Catholic Englishmen. He sought for the collaboration of Alva in Brussels and of Philip in Madrid, because a Spanish army might be necessary to complete the operation. Alva and Philip did not reject Ridolfi's proposal out of hand, but they both remained unenthusiastic—Alva because he now doubted the chance of success, Philip because he doubted also the wisdom of displacing Elizabeth for the benefit of a Guise. Both men were rather more impressed by de Spes' assurance that John Hawkins would support a Catholic invasion with all the fighting ships he could control. Hawkins was however in the role of a double-agent collecting information for Cecil. When Ridolfi's plot had collapsed and Norfolk had been executed (January 1572), Philip observed to de Spes with some relief —for the unwisdom of displacing Elizabeth for Mary still seemed paramount—'the thread of the business now being cut, there is no more to say to you about it'.

In December 1571 de Spes received his dismissal at the hands of the queen's council and in January he departed. Parliament, which demanded the death of Norfolk, was clamant also for the death of Mary Queen of Scots. But Elizabeth could see that Philip feared a possible Guise empire and that he therefore feared to see Mary as queen in place of Elizabeth. Mary, alive and also in English custody, was the best guarantee that Philip would try to restrain the Pope. Mary was important to Europe as the symbol of a French European empire. Therefore her significance in the political calculations of Elizabeth depended in part on her significance in the calculations of Philip. Because France was potentially Europe's most important political unit, political calculations in all neighbouring countries reflected the fortunes of the warring parties in France. In 1570, and even more after Guise power was revived by the massacre of St Bartholomew's Eve, Mary was the best guarantee that Philip would restrain the Pope and his own agents from any attempt to depose or assassinate Elizabeth. The restraint which Mary generated through Philip was at least as important in 1570 as the encouragement which she gave to assassins of Elizabeth. She was even a partial counterweight to the menace of a Spanish army in the Netherlands. Mary, alive and in English custody, was an important pawn; Mary, dead, could serve no purpose. For this reason, if also out of cousinly sympathy, Elizabeth rejected the demands of Parliament and of the commissioners from Scotland, but she kept Mary under secure arrest.

Irish affairs provided the final set of episodes for this 'rehearsal' in the 1570s, as it did also for the great crisis in the 1590s. During the 1570s Irish opposition to Tudor interference began to acquire a nationalistic sense of purpose and a conscious self-association with Spain and the counter-reformation. An earlier rebellion, by Shane O'Neill in Ulster (1558 to 1567), had been only an old-style Gaelic rising, the effort of one chieftain to establish kingship over neighbouring chieftains: 'I care not to be an earl unless I be better and higher than an earl. . . . My ancestors were kings of Ulster and Ulster is mine and shall be mine'. O'Neill's efforts had only an incidental hostility to Tudor government in Dublin and to the extension of English influence, but his immediate enemies were his Gaelic neighbours and by them he was defeated and murdered. Quite a different affair, 'modern' rather than 'Gaelic', was the revolt in 1569 of Sir James Fitzmaurice Fitzgerald, the leader of the Desmond Geraldines of Munster. This was the revolt of established Anglo-

Irish landowners against legal decisions of 1568 which declared the rightful owners of their property to be certain English-born intruders—Peter Carew, Walter Raleigh, Humphrey Gilbert and others—men who could claim descent from the earliest Norman landowners of these Irish estates. Established Irish landowners, besides hating these the new intruders, had also felt the influence of counter-reformation missionaries. They had begun to send their sons to colleges in Spain or the southern Netherlands, there to be taught a new zeal for the old faith. Between 1570 and 1573 Fitzmaurice Fitzgerald was worn down by Carew and his associates. Small units from the English garrison in Dublin helped them to capture Munster fortresses one by one. At last, in 1573, Fitzmaurice Fitzgerald left for Europe in the belief that he could organise the forces of the counter-reformation for the liberation of Ireland. But Europe was not, at the time, ready to listen to him. Elizabeth and Alva, Elizabeth and Philip, were once more on speaking terms and at peace. English volunteers were being recalled from the Netherlands; the magnificent defence of Leyden restored Dutch morale; Alva was recalled to Spain. Between the Dutch rebels and de Requesens (the new Spanish governor) Elizabeth did her best to mediate a settlement, (1573-74).

During these five years, the chance of war with Spain had seemed great. Yet even at the height of tension (January 1569), Cecil had retained a confidence that England and Spain would remain on terms with each other: 'I cannot think it convenient either for the King of Spain or for us to bring this unkindness to a flat falling out. But in the meantime the Duke of Alva seeth just cause of repentance'.[1] The anti-English party among Spanish officials, which included Granvelle and de Spes, believed that the 'unkindness' ought to be brought 'to a flat falling out', because Spain (they thought) would not conquer the Netherlands until she had first conquered England. This was an opinion to which Philip listened and to which he himself did in the end move. But by 1570 he was not yet persuaded that Spain's interests would be served by an attack on England and Elizabeth. His assessment of Spanish policy in Europe depended in 1570 (as in 1560 and 1580) on his assessment of the potential strength of the Guise household. In 1560 they seemed

[1] Quoted in Read (b), p. 435.

very strong indeed, prevented only by Elizabeth from establishing political control of a massive trans-European empire. By 1580 the Guises had become so weak that they were Philip's dependent clients; by 1580 a Guise territory would be a Spanish satellite; to put Mary Queen of Scots on to Elizabeth's throne would add one more satellite to the Spanish imperial constellation just as a Guise king of France would add another.

In 1570, however, the situation was transitional and uncertain. Momentarily, the Guises were much weaker than once they had been, yet not so weak but that they might recover. Philip was therefore hesitant and doubted whether he would be wise to weaken Elizabeth and to advance Mary Queen of Scots. When the Guises recovered in the immediate aftermath of St Bartholomew's Eve, Philip saw that his caution was justified, that it was indeed not yet convenient for the King of Spain to bring things 'to a flat falling out' with the Queen of England.

Elizabeth fully appreciated his restraint. Consequently, when Drake returned from Nombre de Dios and his first 'silver blockade' in August 1573, he received no royal acknowledgement of his brilliant exploit. He was relegated into obscurity—hustled off to the fighting in Munster, according to popular legend. The contrast between this reception in 1573 and his reception at Deptford in 1580 is the measure of the great change, sudden and abrupt, which reversed Elizabeth's relations with Philip at some point between 1573 and 1580.

20 Elizabeth: Defence of monarch and realm from Rome and Spain, at high tension, 1578–1603

The great twenty-five-year struggle between Spain and England (1578 to 1603) comprehended every area of conflict that had found a place in the five-year rehearsal (1568 to 1573), namely the Netherlands, the English home-front, Scotland and Ireland. The rehearsal, the early bout of low-tension sparring, was transmogrified into a war for survival by events in France and in the mind of Philip II. As Philip reassessed developments in France between 1575 and 1580, so he changed the perspective of his foreign policy. In this new perspective, Elizabethan England ceased to be Spain's essential ally against the Guises and became instead a central objective of Spain's European ambitions. 1580 was Philip's year of decision, when he redirected against the Dutch, the English and the Huguenots, forces which had previously been concentrated against the Turks: 'In August 1580 ... an agreement between the Ottoman and Habsburg empires to end almost a century of great wars [led to] Spain turning north and west to engage the English and their Dutch allies'.[1]

From 1573 until 1578, Elizabeth's relations with Philip were amicable. These were the years between Alva's departure from the Netherlands (November 1573) and Parma's arrival there (January 1578). During these years the circumstances in the Netherlands developed slowly if erratically towards the compromise that Elizabeth always wanted: Spanish suzerainty, with a moderate degree of *politique* toleration, and without any Spanish army of occupation. De Requesens, governor-general of the Netherlands in succession to Alva, negotiated with William of Orange for the restoration of

[1] A. C. Hess: 'The Battle of Lepanto' in *Past and Present* 57, Nov. 1972.

local provincial autonomy; he sought Elizabeth's favour by expelling English refugee-Catholics and by giving immunity to English protestant traders. But de Requesens also refused the religious toleration demanded by Zeeland and Holland and he kept up military pressure against them. This was so effective that Dutch resistance seemed not far from collapse at the end of 1575 and they themselves seemed likely to call in French help as an act of final desperation. Consequently, in the spring of 1576 Elizabeth began secret shipments of arms to the Dutch. But Philip, perhaps as a remote consequence of Drake's exploit in Nombre de Dios (1572-73) had already in 1575 suspended interest payments on his debts. He was unable to raise money to pay his armies. In March 1576 de Requesens died, and so the Spanish troops in the Netherlands, without pay and for nine months without a commander, drifted into a series of mutinies which culminated in the great sack of Antwerp, commonly called the 'Spanish Fury' (November 1576).

These prolonged disorders united all Netherland provinces, Catholic and protestant alike, into a single determination to clear their country of Spanish garrisons. By a joint declaration, the Pacification of Ghent (November 1576), they recognised Philip as their sovereign but they demanded autonomony as in Charles V's reign together with the withdrawal of Spanish troops and a negotiated religious settlement. They refused to recognise Don John, their new governor-general, until he had accepted the Pacification. Elizabeth, to strengthen Dutch bargaining power, gave them an immediate loan of £20,000. In February 1577, Don John issued his 'Perpetual Edict', accepting the Pacification; Spanish troops withdrew to Italy. If Elizabeth could have mediated a permanent settlement between Don John and his various subjects on these terms, she would have been well satisfied. But Don John would make no permanent concessions, because his own ultimate ambition was intense and magnificent: he meant to subjugate the Netherlands, to invade England and to marry Mary Queen of Scots. The Netherlanders were divided between Calvinist and Catholic, with the Catholics, then as now, divided between Walloon and the self-consciously Flemish: Don John, in July 1577, withdrew to the Walloon area. Flemish and Dutch rejected Don John and themselves appointed the Archduke Matthias as their governor-general. Philip, treating this as rebellion, ordered the Prince of Parma to bring the Spanish troops back from Italy and these men, in January 1578, routed the united Netherlands' army at Gembloux. For Elizabeth, the prospect was once more quite as bad as ever it had been: England seemed likely after all to be faced with that gravest of threats to her existence, a powerful military presence in the Netherlands.

English volunteers had already moved back to their old battle front: Sir John Norris took over 3,000 men in July 1577 and remained in command for seven years. Elizabeth, reluctant as ever to spend money or to help rebels, nevertheless stood security for a Dutch loan of £100,000 and sent in arms and munitions, but Don John and Parma quickly re-established their hold on the southern Catholic provinces. These split away from the northerners and constituted the Union of Arras in January 1579. They made peace with Parma, agreeing to permit only the Catholic religion in exchange for a promise that Spanish troops would be withdrawn and political rights honoured. The northern provinces drew together in the Union of Utrecht (January 1579). Don John died, but the northerners were now at war with Parma, his very able successor. The threat of this situation to England was seen to be as ominous as it had been in 1568, because the defence of England was, in the opinion of Elizabeth and her council, inseparable from the defence of the Netherlands. As in the years from 1568 to 1573, so also in the years after 1578, the danger from Spanish troops in the Netherlands was reinforced by danger on three other fronts: once more papal agents collaborated with the Spanish ambassador and with Mary Queen of Scots and English Catholic zealots to overthrow Elizabeth by assassination; once more the Catholic cause in Scotland had a revival and threatened to open England's 'postern gate'; once more Irish resistance invited European intervention. But there was a new dynamic factor in the revived conflict between England and Spain, namely Philip's reassessment of the balance of forces in France. He began to foresee and fear a powerfully united *politique* France, even a protestant France. The Guise party which once had seemed to him to be dangerously powerful now began to seem dangerously weak. On the other hand Philip also perceived that the Guise

party in France could owe everything to Spanish support, could be a Spanish client. The Guises, in their weakness, themselves turned to Philip for help in 1576; in 1577 Don John turned to the Guises for assistance in the Netherlands; by 1580 Philip and the Guise family had established habits of mutual support, which were regularised five years later in a treaty of alliance, the treaty of Joinville (January 1585). By this treaty the Guise party became subsidised dependents of Spain.

In the same way, Mary of Scots, the Guise claimant to the English throne came to be thought of as Spain's puppet. Mary could become Philip's dependent ruler in England, his agent in a policy for the general unification of Christendom under Spanish presidency. In this perspective, Elizabeth was seen as an obstacle to Philip's policy, not in the Netherlands only but in respect of the unification of Europe. Thus the status of Mary in Philip's political schemes, and the status of Elizabeth, were reversed by his reassessment of the prospects of the Guises in France. Mary, reassessed by Philip, necessarily acquired a different value in the calculations of Cecil and Elizabeth; Mary had been an asset to Elizabeth, imposing restraint on Philip, but now she was a liability, a claimant on whose behalf Philip could invade England just as she had once been a claimant on whose behalf Ridolfi had planned assassination in 1570 (contrary, at that time, to Philip's better judgement).

The Netherlands, the home-front, Scotland and Ireland were all areas of danger for Elizabeth in the years after 1578 as they had been from 1568 to 1573, but after 1578 every danger derived supercharging energy from the policy-decisions of Philip II, whereas before 1573 every danger had been reduced by the restraining influence of Philip who at that time doubted the wisdom of deposing Elizabeth to make way for a member of the Guise family.

After 1578, plans for the assassination of Elizabeth were wholeheartedly supported by Philip as they had not been between 1568 and 1573; they were supported by a greater number of dedicated Englishmen than were available between 1568 and 1573. Cardinal William Allen and his missionaries from Douai seriously influenced English Catholicism in the late 1570s. These zealous men were reinforced by the great Jesuit mission after 1580 when

Pope Gregory gave his blessing to this new Catholic initiative. Instructions to these missionaries excluded political action and Gregory also issued an *explanatio* which relieved Catholics of their duty under the bull of 1570 to act against Elizabeth's government, but the *explanatio* applied only until such time as the bull was about to be enforced by an invasion. English Catholics were thus instructed to hold their fire until sedition could evidently be effective. In fact, the religious enthusiasm of the missionaries infected many young laymen with seditious zeal, and these laymen took their cue from the spirit and letter of Cardinal Allen's *Admonition to the Nobility and People of England concerning the present wars*. His admonition told them that Elizabeth was 'a most unjust usurper, a depraved excommunicate, the very shame of her sex and princely name, the only poison and destruction of our noble church and country'. English Catholics were in any case encouraged to sedition and assassination by papal arguments in favour of tyrannicide and by papal promises of plenary indulgence for any sins that might be committed in connection with the assassination. The papal secretary, Cardinal Como, gave this moral directive for the encouragement of heroic conspiracy: 'Since that guilty woman of England rules over two such noble kingdoms of Christendom and is the cause of so much injury to the Catholic faith, and loss of so many million souls, there is no doubt that whosoever sends her out of the world with the pious intention of doing God service, not only does not sin but gains merit, especially having regard to the sentence pronounced against her by Pius V of holy memory. And so if these English nobles decide to undertake so glorious a work, your lordship can assure them that they do not commit any sin' (1580).[1] This was not empty encouragement. It 'gave boldness and ability to two murderous Popish wretches to take the life of that worthy Prince of Orange' in 1583.[2]

Assassination of Elizabeth became the acknowledged object of a zealous minority of English Catholics. Their purpose was to release Mary Queen of Scots and make her Queen of England. They counted on the support of Mary's cousins in the Guise family and on the

[1] Quoted in Black, p. 178.
[2] Quoted in Neale (b), p. 44.

support of Philip who was now patron of Guise interests. Among a number of minor conspiracies, two great schemes were dramatically defeated by Elizabeth's secretary of state, Francis Walsingham; the first was associated with Francis Throckmorton in 1583 and the second with Anthony Babington in 1586. Throckmorton was arrested in November 1583 by Walsingham's agents. He revealed under torture that Jesuit leaders, in association with Mary Queen of Scots and Mendoza (Spain's ambassador since 1578), had plans for the assassination of Elizabeth, for an English Catholic rising and for a Guise invasion supported by Spanish troops. The Spanish ambassador had his agent even in Walsingham's counter-espionage department. The notion of a sudden rising by 'incredible numbers' of English Catholics may, in retrospect, seem unrealistic; but Catholic enthusiasts looked back to the popular rising of 1553 which carried Mary Tudor to the throne in place of Lady Jane Grey. They expected a repetition of that episode.

Once Walsingham had uncovered the details of the plot, Mendoza, like de Spes in 1572, was interviewed by the council and expelled from England (January 1584). This second ambassadorial expulsion had deeper implications than the first because in the first instance the ambassador was working without his master and the misdemeanours of de Spes did not strain relations between Elizabeth and Philip. In the second instance Philip and his ambassador were in sympathy; the Guise associates of the ambassador were Philip's clients. The ambassador was rewarded for his labours by an appointment to Paris, whence he would be best able to direct further operations against England. English Catholics and a Spanish ambassador had been involved in what amounted to acts of war between governments.

The Babington plot of 1586 followed the previous formula of assassination: Catholic rising, release of Mary, and an invasion from abroad. It was less important in its foreign associations, but more important for the complete involvement of Mary Queen of Scots.

Papal aggression against Elizabeth was thus much more active after 1580 than it had been before. Her government reacted as best they could. Walsingham's secret police were energetic and skilful. The government intensified its laws against Roman Catholics.

The fine for being absent from Church was raised from 1/- to £20 a month (1581). The conversion of any of the queen's subjects to Catholicism was given the status of treason (1581) both for the missionary and for the disciple; the mere presence in England of Jesuit or priest was made treason by the act of 1585. On the other hand, the queen always remained confident that more than half of her Catholic subjects were loyal to her regime. Sir Thomas Tresham and a group of fellow Catholics evidently rejected the Pope's policy: 'We for our parts utterly deny that either Pope or Cardinal hath power or authority to command or license any man to consent to mortal sin... Much less can this ... purpose by any means be made lawful, to wit, that a native-born subject may seek the effusion of the sacred blood of his annointed sovereign. ... We do protest before the living God that all and every priest and priests who have at any time conversed with us have recognised your Majesty their undoubted and lawful Queen'. Part of Elizabeth's counter-strategy against the papacy was to take full account of the loyalty of the majority of English Catholics and to cherish it. Laws were therefore not always enforced. A Catholic family whose loyalty was suspect could be destroyed by ruinous fines, but many families were not molested. 250 priests and others were executed for treason, but usually because of their response to the 'bloody question'. This question asked how a man would act if England were invaded by a Catholic prince; the answer was often a plain statement that the accused person would aid such an invasion; such an answer was necessarily treasonous. Yet many Catholic families were never molested and many priests were merely confined, without any particular severity, in Wisbech Castle. The chronological table of executions shows how entirely the executions were acts of war, counter-measures to the threat of invasion. There were two executions in 1583, fifteen in 1584 and thirty-four in 1588; there were nine in 1589, eleven in 1590, fifteen in 1591 and thereafter not more than ten in any one year.[1]

The moderated rigour of the queen was far from satisfying England's parliamentary classes. Leicester, as always, tried to advertise his agreement with the dominant feeling of the day. In 1582 he did

---

[1] Quoted in Rowse, p. 445.

so in the following terms: 'Nothing in the world grieveth me more than to see her Majesty believes that this increase of Papists in her realm can be no danger to her'.[1] Back in 1572 men had asked for the execution of Mary Queen of Scots. Again in the 1580s men demanded her execution because these many attempts to assassinate Elizabeth were organised for the benefit of Mary and with the encouragement of Mary's personal agents such as Thomas Morgan.[2] The motive for assassination was the desire to make Mary queen; men believed therefore that assassination could be discouraged by removing all chance that the motive could be fulfilled, and this could only be achieved by destroying Mary herself. Burghley and Walsingham tried to find some less drastic means of depriving Catholic assassins of their motive; to this end they drafted in October 1584 a formal pledge which came to be known as the 'Bond of Association'. The Bond was a solemn pledge, undertaken by as many as signed it, to prevent the succession to the throne of anyone by whom, or in whose interest, an assassination should be attempted and to pursue those persons to the death, together with 'any that may any way claim by or from' those persons. Elizabeth valued the enthusiasm of her loyal subjects, but her regal spirit heartily disapproved of popular lynch-law and she saw diplomatic folly in a decision which would destroy James's hopes of succession as well as those of his mother.

In the following parliament (December 1584 to February 1585), she responded warmly to her people's loyalty, but skilfully moderated the Bond into a statute which removed any danger to James unless he should be 'assenting and privy', and provided that Mary, though pursued to death, would be so pursued via a trial in a proper law court.

But the Bond of Association did not deter Anthony Babington and Mary Queen of Scots from the conspiracy of 1586. The safety of the realm, not to mention the letter of the new statute, therefore required the death of Mary. Elizabeth was perhaps truly and deeply reluctant to bring her cousin to execution; it was certainly an act of diplomatic tact that she should display her reluctance before

[1] Quoted in Neale (b).
[2] Not to be confused with Thomas Morgan, 'the old warrior', see p. 22.

the courts of Europe. In Paris, Edinburgh and Madrid, Elizabeth was described by her ambassadors as driven by irresistible forces of public opinion to accept a verdict which she utterly hated. Her hatred of the verdict and her recognition of its need were equally genuine. She wanted Parliament to take responsibility, but equally she did not want Parliament to meet. 'We stick upon Parliament' said Burghley, 'which her Majesty mislikes to have, but we all persist.' Under Parliament's pressure, the verdict was proclaimed (December 1586). Elizabeth's next gambit was to advise Amyas Paulet, governor of Fotheringay, to execute Mary out of hand without warrant, so that the queen could hold her own conscience clear of it. Principal Secretary William Davison who conferred with the queen in February 1587 found that the queen had finally (or was it impulsively?) signed the warrant. He sent the warrant to Fotheringay with such promptness that Elizabeth did, in fact, denounce his action in all the courts of Europe and lodged him in the Tower for eighteen months.

The execution of Mary was consonant with Elizabeth's general policy of treating rigorously all the active enemies of the realm: Jesuits, active conspirators, Mary herself. This rigorous policy had its counterpart in her lax, accommodating attitude to Catholics who were loyal to her regime and quietist in their religion. Such Catholics remained numerous in Lancashire, Yorkshire, Hampshire, Sussex and London. Her double-sided policy must be counted a success. Catholic conspiracy was crippled, but on the other hand Elizabeth retained the loyalty of the majority of English Catholics; they did not betray her: 'Mary Queen of Scots had been executed; the Armada was defeated. Yet, at two such delicate moments for English security, nowhere in the country had a single Catholic done anything to hinder the government in its defence precautions.'[1] Of course, Elizabeth's rigour—in particular the execution of Mary—together with the defeat of the Armada did weaken and waste the motive-power of the Catholic zealots. They ceased to plot assassination and waited for times to change, after her death and under her successor.

The queen, in her old age, could not bring herself to deal openly

[1] Hurstfield.

with the co-religionists of a Pope who had for so long proclaimed her to be illegitimate and a usurper. But she allowed her Robert Cecil to discover, even among the Catholic priesthood, a body of reconcilables with whom he was able to negotiate. With these he drew up a statement of allegiance which thirteen priests accepted in January 1603. The statement was, of course, unacceptable at the time to very many priests, to the Jesuits and to the Pope himself, but it was the beginning of a relationship under which Catholics would become once more an important community with positive influence in England.

This twenty-year threat of Catholicism to realm and monarch after 1580 was increased by events in Scotland and Ireland at this time. The regent Morton barely defeated an attempt to oust him in 1578. The intrigues by which he did so included a recognition that James, thirteen years old in April 1579, was of age and was the sovereign ruler of Scotland. But James hated his dour-spirited regent and soon used his new sovereignty with unexpected independence. James welcomed back to Scotland his second cousin, Esmé Stuart, who arrived from France in October 1579. Esmé Stuart was the emissary of the Guises; he was commissioned to work for the restoration of Mary Queen of Scots to her throne and of Catholicism to Scotland. French influence was to be restored in Scotland; England's 'postern gate' was to be reopened. Esmé Stuart had favourable prospects in Scotland. Catholicism was still strong in important border areas of Scotland and in Aberdeen, Moray and Inverness.

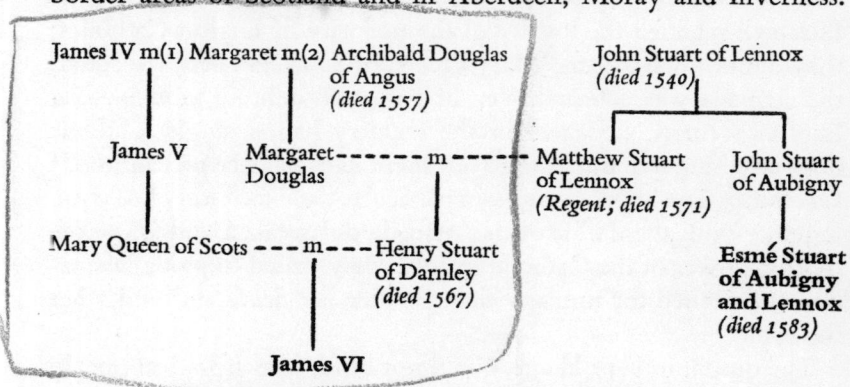

Genealogy 12. Esmé Stuart and his cousin James VI

James welcomed his gay cousin with enthusiastic relief; the regent was unpopular with many of the nobility as well as with James. Only the ministers of the Scottish Church and the citizens of Glasgow and Edinburgh could be relied upon to resist the schemes of Esmé Stuart.

By June 1581, Elizabeth faced a Scotland in which the regent Morton had been executed for having been a party to Darnley's murder back in 1567, Esmé Stuart (promoted to be Earl of Lennox) was chief influence in Scotland's government and the king was interesting himself in Catholicism. Agents representing Philip of Spain and the Guises were soon in Edinburgh, planning the great 'Enterprise' whereby England was to be overrun by simultaneous invasions from north and south. By February 1582 this became a formal undertaking that Esmé Stuart would take Scotland over to Catholicism in the autumn, on the arrival of 20,000 troops from Spain or France. Luckily opposition to Esmé Stuart began to develop among Scottish nobles, who feared his ascendancy as much as they had disliked Morton's regency. English agents got to work among them. A group were convinced that Esmé would arrest them for the murder of Rizzio. Burghley, through Archibald Douglas, Earl of Angus, and an exile in England, encouraged them to kidnap James while he was on a hunting expedition, and thus to anticipate their own arrest. This was the Ruthven raid of August 1582. The kidnappers, with the king in their power, ordered Esmé Stuart out of Scotland in the king's name. A head-on battle-of-arms between the two factions seemed certain, but Esmé lost his nerve, retired to Dumbarton Castle and thence to France (December 1582). A Scottish ambassador was sent to London to restore collaboration between Scotland and England.

But six months later, Elizabeth found that all her anxieties were restored. James, now eighteen years old, gave his guardians the slip and took refuge with the Catholic Earl of Huntly (June 1583). Not long afterwards the Ruthven lords fled to England. James renewed correspondence with the Guises and opened it with the Pope; he emphasised the likelihood of his own conversion to Catholicism 'especially if I am aided in my great need by your Holiness'. Walsingham was sent to Edinburgh to restore James to a proper sense of his best interests, but withdrew after a week. James's favourite and familiar was Captain James Stuart, an adventurer who had been advanced at court by Esmé Stuart and was created Earl of Arran. No one could regard this Arran as a reliable influence, but at least he reckoned that his own interests were to be advanced rather by Elizabeth than by the Guises. He prevailed on James to reopen negotiations at Berwick-on-Tweed in August 1584, and before long James accepted a present of £5,000 from the English ambassador and the prospect of military alliance with England. Meanwhile, the English negotiators found that Arran's own emissary, Patrick, Master of Gray, was willing to double-cross his chief for his personal profit. Patrick of Gray arranged with his English colleagues that the Ruthven lords should return to Scotland, armed by Elizabeth to overthrow Arran—and this they achieved in October and November 1585. A formal treaty of Berwick (July 1586) created a defensive and offensive alliance between the countries and provided a pension of £4,000 a year for James. If the execution of Mary Queen of Scots stirred Scottish public opinion against Elizabeth and England, James himself was certainly not distressed by the event. The Master of Gray, James's ambassador in London, was entirely cynical about it: 'mortui non mordent' said he. By the time that the Armada sailed into the English Channel, the Scottish crisis was over and James was sure that his chance of becoming King of England depended on an English victory over Spanish invaders. Elizabeth took his self-interest as sufficient guarantee that he would not willingly allow the Spaniards to take shelter in Scottish ports. There was however a danger that the Catholic earls of northern Scotland would welcome the Spaniards; in 1589 Elizabeth intercepted correspondence between them and Philip. But James confirmed his own commitment to the protestant cause by marrying Anne of Denmark in August 1589, and he settled down to rule Scotland under the advice of Sir John Maitland, 'the wisest man in Scotland' as Burghley thought. Catholic earls continued to correspond with Philip and to hope for Spanish intervention, but in spite of occasional forays on the border, England and Scotland remained true to the alliance of Berwick and the 'postern' remained closed.

While Elizabeth and Burghley were thus, in the years after 1579,

Defence of monarch and realm from Rome and Spain

harassed by events in Scotland, they had to face events in Ireland which were equally dangerous.[1] Esmé Stuart's arrival at Leith in 1579 coincided with the return of Fitzmaurice Fitzgerald to Munster from Europe. He returned to proclaim that European Catholicism of the counter-reformation was the unifying creed in whose cause Irishmen could fight the Tudors and could count on European support. Fitzmaurice Fitzgerald came to Ireland from Rome by way of Lisbon and brought a volunteer force of Spaniards, Portuguese and Italians, with Nicholas Saunders as papal legate to the Irish people. Ireland was intended to be a launching base for a Spanish and Catholic reconquest of England. But Fitzmaurice Fitzgerald and his companions got little support in Ireland, except from the Fitzgeralds in Munster and from Viscount Baltinglass, a devout Catholic landlord of the Pale. Before long, news reached London that Baltinglass had destroyed a government force in Wicklow and that Philip had sent in an army of seven hundred Spaniards to support the rebellion (October 1580). The Spaniards established themselves at Smerwick, but the reaction of the deputy lieutenant in Dublin was prompt. He was vigorously supported by the English-born landlords of Munster and by some Irish clans who traditionally opposed the Fitzgeralds. Smerwick was captured and the Spanish garrison massacred as pirates in November 1580. Fitzmaurice Fitzgerald was killed in battle, and the fortresses of Munster were, one by one, captured and destroyed between 1580 and 1583. During this time, Desmond (head of the Fitzgeralds) was executed, Saunders died of exposure, and Munster was devastated, bringing terrible loss of life to the native Irish. But Elizabeth had spent £500,000 in four years, an inescapable expenditure, as she judged it to be, necessary to prevent Ireland from falling into Spanish control. To avoid a repetition of this danger to England's home defence, 200,000 acres of Munster were confiscated and granted to English 'undertakers' who agreed to bring in English settlers. Sir Walter Raleigh received 40,000 acres.

As a consequence of this harsh policy, England's defence was not jeopardised by any events in Ireland during the critical year of 1588, but Ireland remained an anxiety, because many Irishmen came to

[1] See map 12 on p. 156.

feel the sort of romantic sympathy for all things Spanish that, one hundred and fifty years later, had the Scottish Highlanders marching at the call of Stuart Pretenders. Many Irishmen looked to Philip as the natural leader of Europe and to Spain as their spiritual home—even perhaps as the mother-country from which they believed their ancestors to have emigrated. But the Armada was defeated and ship-wrecked Spaniards who came ashore in Ireland were robbed and murdered unless they were lucky enough to find themselves in Ulster. In that province, Hugh O'Neill, Baron of Dungannon and Earl of Tyrone, was a great Gaelic chieftain, somewhat Anglicised by six years' residence in the Earl of Leicester's household (1562 to 1568) and by occasional visits to Elizabeth's court thereafter. He learnt from his hosts to value the sophisticated nationalism of Elizabethan England and to develop a personal Irish nationalism, expressing the fierce Gaelic clan loyalty but in a greater national context. He also learnt to appreciate those skills in deception which were necessary to the art of politics. Thus he acquired the attributes of the first modern Irish political leader. Elizabeth and Burghley were aware that, in him, they faced a new phenomenon more potent than Fitzmaurice.

His patriotism was stung to indignation in the 1570s by attempts, made in the name of Queen Elizabeth, to dispossess established Irish landowners and to transfer their land to Walter Devereux, Earl of Essex, but he held his peace and slowly, in the course of the 1580s, created a small well-equipped personal army. On the retirement of his cousin, Turloch O'Neill, in 1593, Hugh took to himself the title of 'The O'Neill', a formal claim to be the all-powerful, independent King of Ulster. The other chieftains of Ulster accepted his leadership. Thus Elizabeth's government had to face this second great Irish defiance, again at a time when Spanish Armadas were often expected to threaten the English coast. The O'Neill was in correspondence with the Pope and with Philip; he defeated all attempts to dislodge him from Ulster so that Elizabeth was grateful to accept a truce in 1596. In 1597 and 1598 major plans for the invasion of Ulster were put in hand. Once again the English suffered a series of defeats culminating in the destruction of Sir Henry Bagenal's army at Yellow Ford in August 1598.

At this the province of Munster rose to arms and Philip III, the new King of Spain, promised the help without which O'Neill could not take Dublin. Elizabeth's government faced a major crisis which Robert Devereux, second Earl of Essex rashly offered to tackle. He accepted the post of Lord Lieutenant of Ireland and arrived in Dublin with an army of 18,000 (April 1599). Difficulties with the Irish terrain, disease among his own troops, and lack of reinforcements from England quickly discouraged Essex. Elizabeth denounced his dilatory proceedings and required him 'not to come out of that kingdom by virtue of any former licence whatever until the Northern action be tried'. But Essex opened negotiations with the O'Neill and made his own truce, to last until May 1600 but always terminable at fourteen days' notice. Essex thereupon returned to London contrary to orders.

Charles Blount, Lord Mountjoy, a cautious, calculating commander, was sent out in his place with an army of 20,000 in February 1600. He destroyed all rebel positions in Munster in the course of the year 1600 and at last turned to the systematic destruction of O'Neill in 1601. But in September a Spanish expeditionary force of 4,000 occupied Kinsale harbour on the south Irish coast. Mountjoy immediately moved south to besiege the Spaniards. The O'Neill followed with 12,000 men who soon had Mountjoy's army hemmed up against the Spaniards (December 1601). The English might well have been destroyed by a double attack (as the French had been at Pavia), but the problem of co-ordinating Irish and Spanish armies was too much for the commanders. The English routed their outer and inner enemies in detail and Mountjoy promptly accepted the Spaniard's offer to leave Ireland (December 1601). Thereafter, Ulster was subdued, stronghold by stronghold, until the O'Neill capitulated in March 1603. Unaware that Elizabeth was already dead, he renounced this proud title and accepted the status of landowner under the English crown. The war cost Elizabeth £1,200,000 in five years, but no more in Ireland than in Scotland or on the English home-front did the Spanish government ever manage to mobilise essential help to reinforce a major Spanish invasion of England.

21 Elizabeth: England and the North Netherlands, defence indivisible

In the context of multiple struggles on three other fronts—in Ireland, in Scotland and on the home-front—Elizabeth's government fought out its direct conflict with Spain. While Spanish strategy attempted to strengthen Spain's allies on these three fronts in preparation for the main assault, England's central strategy was still the unremitting effort to get the Spanish armies out of the Netherlands (while yet preserving Spain's political presence, in order to keep out the French). But as in 1570, so also in 1580, the struggle to weaken Spain in Europe had a global character and the Anglo-Spanish war of the 1580s may be said to have begun where the rehearsal of 1570 finished—namely with a long-range 'silver blockade', which sought to bring Philip's military operations to a standstill by depriving him of the means to pay his troops and buy his war supplies.

In December 1577, Don John began to reassert himself in the Netherlands and Philip ordered Spanish troops to move back to the Netherlands. The course of events turned against England's interest. Events, which since the Pacification of Ghent had moved in a direction favourable to Elizabethan policy, were reversed. In this same December Drake sailed for the Pacific. He and his sponsors probably had many objects in mind for this expedition. Included among these plans, perhaps at the last minute with the connivance of the queen, was the possibility of attacking Spanish bullion-ships in the Pacific between Lima and Panama. Beyond a single attack, there may have been the further possibility that Drake would join forces with John Oxenham who was thought to have established a stronghold somewhere in Darien on the isthmus of Panama; Drake and Oxenham together might establish a permanent land base from which a sea-blockade could be maintained continuously.[1] Such a scheme might seem far-fetched; evidence for it is slight and circumstantial,[2] yet it accords with much subsequent thinking.[3]

Tudor and Stuart strategists knew that a blockade was difficult to maintain without a base nearby; usually, therefore, they thought in terms of setting up a local stronghold—on the American coast, in the Azores, or on the coast of Spain—and of using the stronghold as an operational base for the ships of their blockading fleet (one hundred and twenty years later such a stronghold was permanently established at Gibraltar). But Oxenham was captured and his force destroyed long before Drake reached the Pacific, in fact before he had left Plymouth. Drake's aggression in the Pacific was therefore limited to the capture of one treasure ship, the *Cacafuego*, carrying about a third of the annual output of the mines. In foreign affairs the episode had a double significance: in itself it demonstrated that English and allied sea-power might be sufficient to cut the flow of bullion to Spain, that is to cripple Spain's European war effort by destroying the financial credit of the Spanish government, in particular to hamstring Parma's Dutch offensive by operations in the Caribbean. In the use which Elizabeth made of the episode—her visit to the *Golden Hind* at Deptford, and her bestowal of knighthood on Drake (April 1581)—she seemed to declare that the damage inflicted on Spain was intended and approved by her government and would be repeated until Spain's policy (particularly in the Netherlands) was consistent with England's security.

Elizabeth, a few weeks after the return of the *Golden Hind*, authorised Drake to occupy the Azores in collaboration with Don Antonio, claimant to the Portuguese throne and a refugee in England. These islands would be a splendid base from which to prevent the transport

[1] See map 2 on p. 25.
[2] See Wernham (a), p. 350–52.
[3] See Oliver Cromwell's letter 'To Generals Blake and Montague, at Sea': . . . 'Whether any other place be attemptable; especially that of the Town and Castle of Gibraltar—which if possessed and made tenable by us would . . . enable us . . . with six nimble frigates lodged there to do the Spaniard more harm than by a fleet and ease our own charge?' (April 1656.)

of both bullion to Spain and spices to Portugal, but, before Drake sailed, Elizabeth reconsidered the hazards and withdrew her permission.

However, the situation in Europe worsened; the power of Spain in the Netherlands and even in France grew more ominous. In May 1585, Philip ordered the seizure of English ships in Spanish ports. The response of Elizabeth's government was to authorise Drake, at the expense of private shareholders and for their profit, to intercept bullion ships off the coast of Spain or in the Caribbean. He plundered Vigo (September 1585), made his way to the Canaries and then crossed the Atlantic to the West Indies. There his plunder was enormous. More important, his presence delayed the sailing of Spain's bullion fleet for about six months and temporarily destroyed Philip's credit with European bankers. This held up Parma's operations in the Netherlands and Philip's ship-building in Spanish and Portuguese shipyards. While Drake imposed this short-term blockade on the Caribbean, Sir Richard Grenville tried to establish an English colony on Roanoke Island (1585-86) to serve as a permanent base for continuous Caribbean blockades. Drake inspected this colony on his homeward voyage (June 1586), but found the settlers to be starving and brought them back to England. A second attempt to colonise Roanoke Island (made in 1587) also failed.

By the time that Drake had returned from this expedition, his government was well aware that ships were gathering in Lisbon and Cadiz which were probably intended for an invasion of England. During the winter, Drake was again authorised to collect a fleet of privately-owned fighting ships and to intercept Spanish shipping for the profit of his syndicate. He was also 'to impeach the purpose of the Spanish fleet and stop their meeting at Lisbon ... distressing their ships within their havens'. The queen joined the syndicate with a contribution of six ships. He sailed in April 1587 and promptly destroyed over thirty ships in Cadiz harbour, many of them with cargoes for the fleet in Lisbon. More important, Drake made a landing at Sagres, captured the castle and established his fleet in a harbour from which he could sally forth to capture individual ships coming out of the Mediterranean or converging on to

England and the North Netherlands, defence indivisible

Spain from America or the East Indies. He maintained this base during the month of May, forced all coastal shipping to stay in harbour and thus brought war preparations in Lisbon to a halt for lack of supplies. In June he left Sagres, perhaps in the knowledge that a large Portuguese merchantman was moving up the African coast. This prize, the *San Felipe* with its cargo of £114,000, he captured and brought back to London to pay the expenses of the expedition. Drake's campaign had seriously interrupted preparations in Lisbon so that the sailing of the Armada had to be postponed until 1588. Philip intended that it should leave in January, lest Drake should contrive to inflict another postponement. But by January 1588, Santa Cruz, the veteran commander of the Armada, was dying and was replaced by Medina Sidonia, who himself claimed to possess 'neither aptitude, ability, health nor fortune for the expedition'.

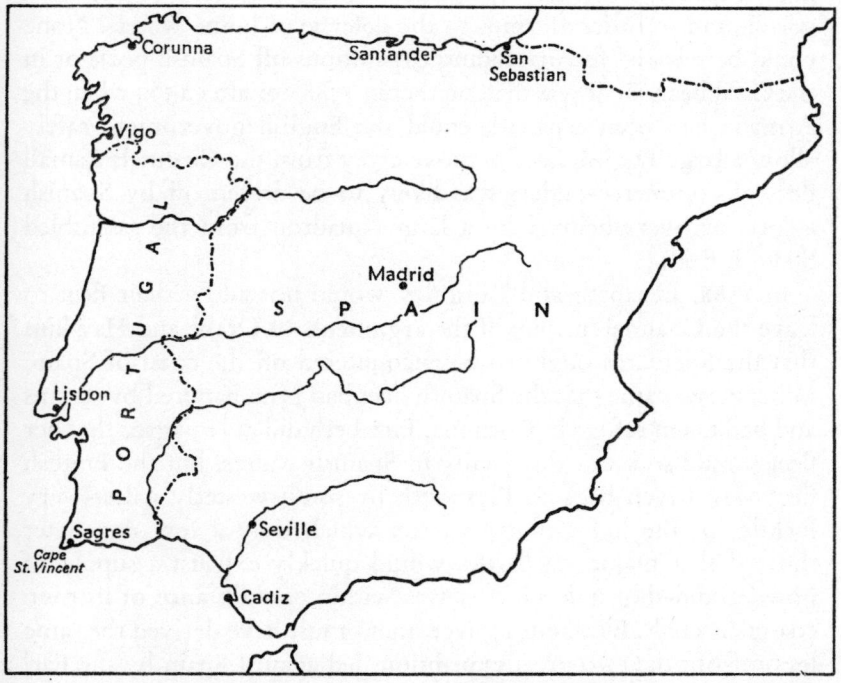

Map 14. Spanish naval bases, 1585–1600: English objectives in Spain

The English government knew that the Armada was ready to sail by the end of 1587 and expected it month by month from January 1588. Because of this danger, the government ordered English ships to remain in the Channel on the defensive. Thus, the existence of a powerful Spanish fleet-in-being revealed, both in 1588 and often in the 1590s, the frailty of the 'silver blockade' if it was ever intended as the master-strategy of Elizabeth's foreign policy—the policy of forcing Spain to acknowledge her weakness and withdraw her troops from the Netherlands. If English ships could have maintained a continuous blockade, then doubtless Spain's military efforts would have been crippled for lack of bullion to pay the troops and buy supplies. But as long as the blockade was intermittent, bullion ships would get into Spanish ports; moreover, once the Spaniards had a fleet-in-being, mobilised in Lisbon or Santander, not even an intermittent blockade could be attempted. A Spanish fleet in Lisbon was a threat so imminent that England's government was bound to order all ships to the defence of home waters. None could be released for marauding expeditions off Spanish ports or in the Caribbean. So it was that, neither in 1588 nor after 1590 when the Armada had been repaired, could the English government safely allow a large English fleet to move away from the Channel; a small fleet of commerce-raiders was likely to be driven off by Spanish escorts or overwhelmed by a large squadron from the assembled Spanish fleet.

In 1588, Elizabeth and Burghley would not allow their fleet to leave the Channel in spite of the arguments of Drake and Hawkins that the Spaniards ought to be encountered off the coast of Spain. When news came that the Spanish fleet had been battered by storms and had taken refuge in Corunna, Elizabeth did at last agree that her fleet should seek out the enemy in Spanish waters, but the English fleet was driven back to Plymouth by south-westerly gales—very luckily, in the light of experience, which only a few days later showed that major sea battles would quickly exhaust a supply of powder-and-shot unless a fleet was within easy distance of its own coastal arsenals. Elizabeth's government must have derived the same lesson from the two great expeditions led against Spain by the Earl of Essex (1596 and 1597). Both of these expeditions put England's own defence at risk. In 1596, Essex brilliantly captured Cadiz and did much damage to Spain's war effort, but the effects were temporary and, when a Spanish Armada approached the Channel, England had no fleet with which to withstand it and was lucky that gales dispersed the Spaniards. Similarly, in 1597 Essex led a large but ineffective fleet of commerce-raiders to the Azores. The Spaniards took his absence to be an opportunity to capture Falmouth and the Scilly Isles. Again they were prevented only by gales.

Hawkins believed that relays of six or eight commerce-raiders could maintain a permanent blockade of Spanish trade-routes without reducing England's main Channel fleet, but of the minor expeditions which went out in accordance with this strategy, Thomas Howard's was in 1591 driven off station with the loss of the *Revenge* by twenty Spanish fighting ships; much the same occurred in 1592; in 1596 the great Drake–Hawkins expedition to the West Indies was kept at bay by Spanish fighting ships that escorted their merchantmen. Only in 1590, when the Armada was not sufficiently repaired, did Hawkins' expedition to the Azores cause Philip to cancel the sailing of his annual treasure fleet from America.

An effective 'silver blockade' depended first of all on the destruction of the main Spanish battle fleet. When the Armada lay at anchor, crippled, in 1589, there was a chance of destroying it. This was Elizabeth's intention for the Drake–Norris expedition of 143 ships and 19,000 men in 1589. But instead of attacking Santander and San Sebastian where the Armada was at anchor, Drake attacked Corunna without success and then moved south to test the defences of Lisbon.

Perhaps the only way to establish a blockade after 1589 was Essex's master-plan for a combined operation.[1] He wanted a small, highly-trained army, which would be landed in Spain to capture and retain a major port. It would destroy such part of the Spanish fleet as was in the local harbour and would thereafter succour a small permanent English fleet of commerce-raiders which would harass Spanish shipping as it brought in bullion from the west and ships' stores from the Baltic. His strategy has much in common with

[1] See Henry.

that which led to the capture and retention of Gibraltar. In 1597 he was given about a hundred ships and 10,000 troops to attempt this, but the troops were raw and he preferred to move to the Azores for another attempt at old-style commerce-raiding. After 1597 no troops could be spared from urgent campaigns in Ireland.

The 'silver blockade' manifestly failed to achieve its ambitious purpose: it did not, of itself, force Spain to moderate her aims, to remove her armies from the Netherlands and accept political suzerainty there without military presence. The 'silver blockade' failed also to achieve its second purpose: it did not take away Spain's ability to mobilise an Armada and send it against England; it did not so impress Spain with England's fighting qualities that she thought better of the attempt. In the end, it provided no alternative to years of slogging warfare in the Netherlands and to meeting the Spanish invasion head-on in the Channel. But as the allied bomber offensive, 1940–44, did not achieve its purpose and yet made the contribution without which D-day could have been a disaster, so the 'silver blockade', which failed of its main ambitions yet made the contribution without which Spanish armies would have occupied England and the north Netherlands, as they occupied Portugal and

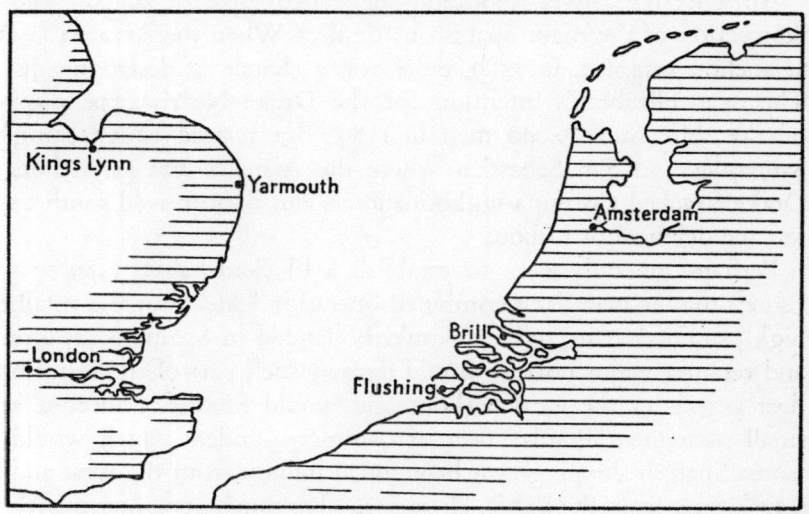

Map 15. The 'Low Countries' of north-west Europe

Italy. English blockading caused the failure of Philip's financial credit in 1575 and 1586 and in the 1590s; these financial failures were vital to the survival of the Dutch and made for their ultimate success. Drake's blockading in 1587 imposed delays on Santa Cruz, contributed to the defeat of the Armada and thus closed the Channel to Spanish shipping: this also was vital to the survival of the Dutch. The blockading was of critical importance, but the main direct war had also to be fought once Spain had returned to her conquest of the Netherlands, especially as the 'Low Countries', in the mind of Philip, became a more comprehensive entity than previously they had been.

In the early years of the new conflict in the Netherlands, England made only a minor and cautious contribution to the joint defence of these Anglo-Dutch lowlands of north-west Europe. The English government had restocked its own arsenals during the 1570s, but although the government possessed a better armament by 1580, its foreign policy refrained from any manifest use of these weapons against Spanish armies in the Netherlands. The new armament was brought to bear on Spanish troops only by English volunteers who entered Dutch service after July 1577 under leaders such as Norris and Morgan, or by the Dutch themselves who were able to buy English arms with loans guaranteed by the English government. For Elizabeth utterly refused to accept sovereignty over Dutch affairs, or to enter their war as an open combatant until the Dutch cause was *in extremis*. She hated having to help the Dutch; she disliked their commissioners and she exasperated them with her changing moods, blowing hot and cold on the Dutchmen's hopes from one day to the next. Burghley wrote to Walsingham, whose sympathies were all with the Dutch, 'I can but wish you patience for I know that the tentation [strain] of this time in service is great, to serve so well ... and to find so small fruits by good answers from hence';[1] and again 'though her Majesty showeth no reasons to move her to persist in her former direction, but that so (she says) she will have it ... yet I think as soon as she shall hear from you that the States [of the Netherlands] cannot and will not accept the conditions she will be brought to qualify the same'. In principle, this was the nature

[1] Quoted in Read (a), p. 200.

of Elizabeth's dealings with the Dutch from 1578 until 1585: she helped them as little as she dared, imposing impossible conditions until satisfied that 'the States cannot and will not' accept them. In these six years the practical help received by the Dutch was considerable; its cost to Elizabeth was considerable, but very little went directly to the Dutch armies. Elizabeth preferred to help them indirectly, as in 1578 when loans, raised on her security, were used to cover the cost of Norris's expedition and to hire mercenaries from John Casimir for Dutch service. Similarly she evaded direct assistance to the Dutch but helped them enormously by financing the military diversions which Anjou stage-managed on the southern frontiers of Parma's Netherlands.

For all her caution, Elizabeth was brought to a crisis in 1584, when Parma's careful preparations began to yield devastating progress. Ypres fell to his armies in April, Bruges in May, Dendermonde in August, Ghent in September. The siege of Brussels, Ostend and Antwerp was in preparation by late summer 1584.[1] The effect of these disasters was reinforced by the assassination of William of Orange (July 1584).

Elizabeth and her council were brought to a crisis of commitment. Either their policy must be based on a withdrawal from the Netherlands, in which case they would have to organise England's defence as a self-contained operation, dependent wholly on English ships, ports and land forces. Alternatively, policy must be based on the assumption that England's defence could not be a self-contained operation, since England was not defensible against an invasion based on the Netherlands. Queen and council were sure that an invasion was intended because they knew that ship-building for just such a purpose had been going ahead in Philip's ports ever since he had annexed Portugal (1580-81). Moreover, Philip's agreement with the papacy acknowledged such a project and the Pope was to support it with a million ducats once a Spanish army had landed in England.

Elizabeth's choice was either to concentrate England's forces in England for home-defence, or to commit a large expeditionary force to the defence of Holland and Zeeland. The council urgently

[1] See map 17 on p. 228.

debated this choice during the last months of 1584; 'it was concluded to advise her Majesty rather to seek the avoiding and diverting of the great peril than . . . to suffer the King of Spain to grow to the full height of his designs'. The council was probably correct in its judgement that the naval defence of England was inseparable from the military defence of Holland and Zeeland. Experience a hundred years later demonstrated that quite a feeble expedition like that of Monmouth (1685) or of William of Orange (1688) could easily invade England from the Netherlands in spite of the large Royal Navy, provided that the invader was willing to wait for what men then called a 'protestant wind'; this was simply because the windward position gave them full choice of manoeuvre. The Armada on the other hand was disastrously handicapped since it had no safe deep-water anchorage in which to wait, either in the Netherlands or even on the north coast of France (see chapter 18, p. 185).

During the first months of 1585, Elizabeth slowly and reluctantly agreed to large-scale intervention in the Dutch wars. As the Spanish siege of Antwerp pressed gradually closer, so English intervention seemed more urgent, for Antwerp was precisely the port from which an invasion fleet might sail against England (except that the Island of Walcheren, still in Dutch hands, controlled the route from Antwerp to the open sea). Dutch commissioners reached England in June 1585 and again offered Elizabeth the sovereignty of the Netherlands. Her attitude to this was as decisive as ever: she refused to take political responsibility for the Netherlands because she always wanted to preserve Spain's political involvement there. But she accepted a general treaty of assistance, whereby England was to provide an army of over 5,000 men and was to garrison Brill and Flushing as security that England's expenses would, in the end, be repaid by the Dutch. Elizabeth agreed to commit to the Dutch wars over £125,000 a year, almost half—about forty-two per cent—of her revenue from all sources. The Dutch on their side agreed to help England against any enemy in the narrow seas. Norris, who had returned to England back in March 1584 to plead the case for Dutch aid, was made commander of an expeditionary force. Twelve days later (24th August 1585) his force left England. But Antwerp had fallen to Parma on the 17th. Soon afterwards the Earl of Leicester was appointed commander in chief of English forces in the Netherlands; his close association with the queen and his eminence in the council proclaimed to the diplomats of Europe that this defence of the Netherlands was central to English policy. He reached the Netherlands in December 1585. In January 1586, Philip commissioned Santa Cruz to command the invasion of England: 'the Catholic King was planning his just revenge on the queen of England', as Antonio de Herrera put it, writing in 1606.[1] The twenty-four months of 1586 and 1587 were occupied with fighting in the Netherlands, defence preparations in England and various indirect communications with Spain and with Parma—Portuguese businessmen were the usual intermediaries—to see whether a peaceful settlement was possible after all. These negotiations with Spain, however secret, led the Dutch to fear that they would be betrayed, but the negotiations were necessary to convince Elizabeth that Spain could not be brought to bargain for suitable peace terms.

Defence preparations in England included an expansion of shipbuilding in the royal dockyards; there, Hawkins was no longer content to replace existing ships or maintain them in top condition; from 1586 he was building ships that were specifically additional to previous strength. Since 1573 every county had been expected to arm three or four hundred of its militiamen with modern weapons (musket and pike) and to have them trained for a week or a fortnight a year. These duties had been neglected, but from 1586 the 'trained bands' tried hard to become soldiers, especially the Londoners, who drilled regularly three times a week at Mile End. Cannon were cast; manufacturers of gunpowder were licensed to dig for salt petre in dovecots, barns, stables, stalls and outhouses anywhere outside London.[2] The queen's seamen had their wages raised by fifty per cent. The fundamental problem of re-armament for a small nation is always the problem of timing. The effort of re-armament cannot be kept up indefinitely; if it starts too late, then the nation is unprepared when the enemy attacks; if it starts too soon, impetus will have been lost before the attack comes— militiamen will have dispersed to sow the season's crops or to gather

[1] See Thompson.
[2] See Cruickshank, p. 68.

in a harvest, beacons will have become sodden and won't ignite, military stores of food will have gone rotten.

One cannot say that Elizabeth's military and naval preparations in 1586 or 1587 or 1588 were ever fully satisfactory; one can say that in all those years she and Parliament imposed extraordinary taxation on the nation and that she greatly overspent her revenue. These two facts together imply that war preparations imposed as heavy a burden as the economy of the nation could bear 'for the long haul'—for the five or fifteen years of danger which Elizabeth expected and which were actually endured. If the nation had been a hundred per cent alert and ready in 1586, it would probably have been less than ready in 1587 and 1588. If its fighting resources had been continuously mobilised from January 1588, its fighting power would have been much reduced by July 1588. Even as things were, the sixteen weeks spent by the fleet at Plymouth consumed all the local stocks of food, and the west winds, which brought the Armada, prevented new supplies from reaching Plymouth from further up the Channel. England's preparations in July 1588 were incomplete; they were also over-complete and going stale; the fleet was eating itself to extinction and Burghley observed with growing anxiety 'a man could wish, if peace cannot be had, that the enemy would no longer delay but prove (as I trust) his evil fortune'. When the Armada appeared, the fleet was sufficiently ready, large contingents of land forces did mobilise (and did also manage to disperse in time for the harvest), the beacons did ignite ('and the red glare of Skiddaw roused the burghers of Carlisle', if Macaulay was correct). Rearmament was well judged, within the coarse limits of what is possible for a small nation—'a damned nice thing' Wellington would have said—and this degree of armament could be maintained, after the first Armada had come and gone, for another sixteen years of war. A nation which is faced with the long haul dare not be whole-hearted in its effort.

During 1586 and 1587 the Netherlands provided the battle zone for direct warfare between English and Spanish armies. The English campaigns were inglorious as military operations, but they achieved their main strategic purpose: Parma was prevented from overrunning Holland and Zeeland; he did not capture a single deep-water port in which the Armada could anchor and take his army on board.

England's military effort was handicapped by the inexperience of both officers and men, but above all by Leicester's weakness as a politician. From the first he cherished political ambitions which diverted his mind from his limited military task. In January 1586 he accepted from the Dutch the title of governor-general of the

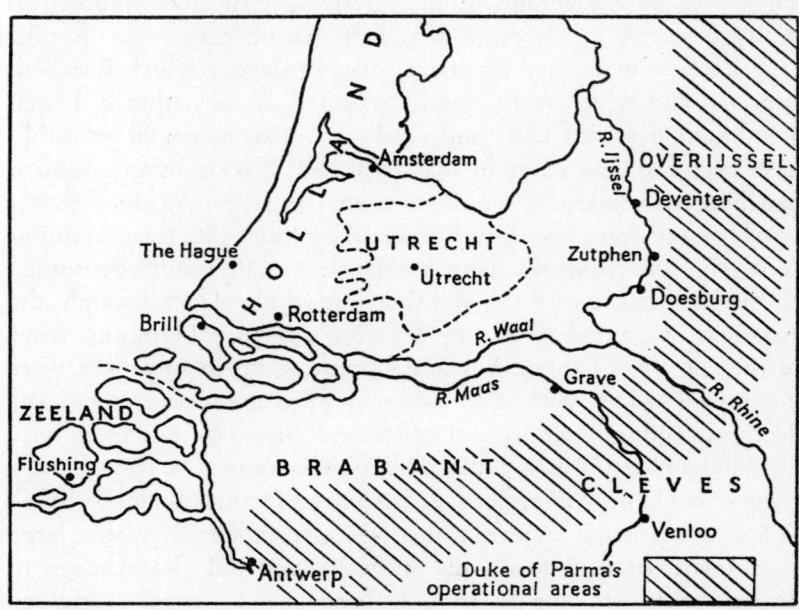

Map 16. Zeeland, Holland and Utrecht under pressure: the operational areas of the armies of the duke of Parma, 1587

states-general; by accepting this office from the Dutch, Leicester pretended to recognise that the Dutch were wholly independent of Philip and to flout Elizabeth's fixed intention of preserving Philip's political authority in the Netherlands. Still dissatisfied with his authority, Leicester intrigued with disaffected Dutch politicians in an attempt to overthrow the dominant republican burghers of Holland. But in spite of sowing great discord between the queen, himself and his Dutch allies, Leicester did contribute to Dutch defence by regaining control of the river Ijssel in August 1586.

England and the North Netherlands, defence indivisible

Parma controlled the bridges over the Maas at Grave and Venloo; consequently he could freely move his armies between Overijssel in the north and Cleves or Brabant in the south. He had also captured the crossings of the Ijssel at Zutphen and Doesburg; consequently, his armies were well placed for an invasion of Holland itself with the prospect of capturing Amsterdam, the Hague, Rotterdam and even Brill. This was the desperate danger which Leicester removed when he recaptured the forts at Zutphen and Doesburg (August 1586).

But the experience of 1586 demonstrated that neither the Dutch nor the English could keep big armies on a war-footing under the conditions that prevailed in the Netherlands at this time. The problems of supply and of financial control soon overwhelmed the best intentions of officers and civil administrators. In fact the best officers were likely to give up in despair, whereupon corrupt officers took their places. Elizabeth saw quite correctly that armies must be kept small, because large ones would, in any case, soon become small by desertion for lack of pay and supplies. The armies of 1586 had cost, not 42 per cent of her revenue, but over 53 per cent. The Netherlands must indeed be defended by English troops, but the effort must be limited to well-defined defensive operations. Otherwise warfare in the Netherlands 'is a sieve that spends as it receives to little purpose';[1] such was Elizabeth's conclusion. Leicester was recalled in November 1586, because he was not trusted to stick to this strategy of limited action.

Leicester's incompetence still influenced events after his departure and the strategy of defence suffered a serious set-back. Stanley and Yorke, commanding the English garrisons in Deventer and Zutphen, were both Roman Catholics, appointed, in spite of Dutch protests, by Leicester who staked his reputation on the loyalty of his officers. In Janaury 1587 they both handed over their forts to Parma's troops. Parma, however, did not exploit the opportunity of an advance into Holland, perhaps because he was already under orders from Philip to make other preparations for a rendezvous with the Armada; his objectives for 1587 seem to have been Sluys and Flushing. Elizabeth was immediately alarmed. Leicester returned with 5,000 men in an attempt to hold Sluys and Flushing (June 1587).

[1] Quoted in Neale (c), p. 189.

The first he lost in July, but Flushing he retained—and, of the two, Flushing was all important for it had a deep-water anchorage, which Sluys had not.

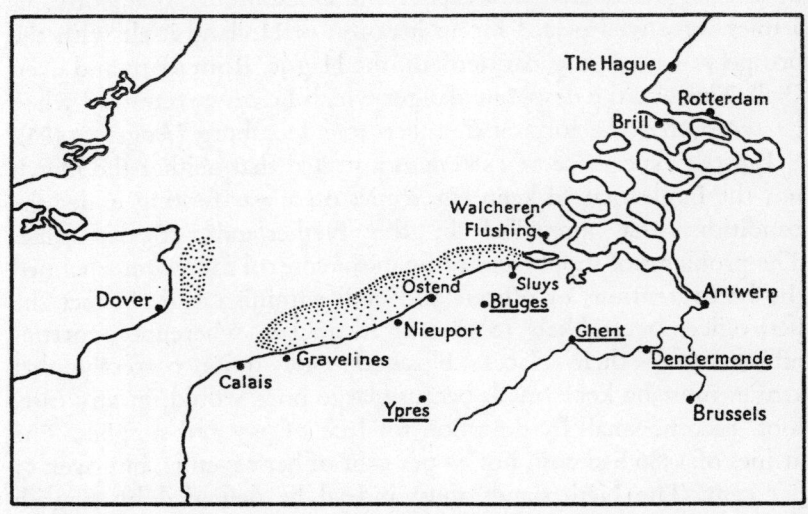

Map 17. Spanish gains, 1584 (underlined), and Flushing, Sluys and the shallow seas, 1588

From June 1587 until July 1588, Parma held his army ready for a rendezvous with the Armada. He made no attempt to capture Flushing. On the contrary, he held long peace negotiations with England's representatives at Bourbourg (near Dunkirk). In 1586, his despatches to Philip had argued for the conquest of England by means of a surprise attack: 30,000 men would make the short crossing from Flanders to Dover in flat-bottomed barges; since both the soldiers and the canal craft were in Flanders already, no special mobilisation would bring England to the alert. But by 1588 the Armada project was so widely known that Parma despaired of surprise and therefore of victory. One must assume that he did not try to capture Flushing because he believed that the Armada could not in any case carry his army across to England. But without deep-water anchorage, he could use only shallow-draft barges for his troops; he had no shallow fighting craft which could defend his troops' transports while they were getting out to deep water where the Armada might be waiting for them. For whatever reason, Flushing remained in English hands and Leicester went home to organise England's land forces there. As for the negotiations at Bourbourg, perhaps they served Spain's purposes by sowing a belief among the Dutch that England intended to betray them. For this reason the Dutch main fleet did not work with the English (as had been agreed by the terms of the treaty of 1585) when the Armada entered the Channel; the Dutch could not afford to let their fleet go so far off-shore since there seemed to be a chance that Elizabeth would suddenly make peace with Philip and betray the Dutch fleet to destruction by the Armada. But the Dutch fly-boats, shallow-draft fighting-ships commanded by Justin of Nassau, kept patrol along the Flanders coast and made sure that Parma's army remained on shore.[1]

The Armada sailed from Corunna to the English Channel during the last week of July 1588. It was, in itself, a combined, amphibious force of 130 ships, manned by 10,000 sailors and galley slaves and carrying 20,000 soldiers. Back in December English coastal counties had mobilised their militia at a rumour that the Armada was at sea and some of the royal ships had been commissioned for service. But these men were disbanded as soon as the rumour passed. Since April the queen's ships had been kept in full commission and had thereafter been stocked with provisions for one month at a time. The aim of the queen's council and of her naval commanders was to prevent the Armada from achieving either of its two possible objects: from establishing a Spanish stronghold anywhere on the coast of Ireland or England and from escorting Parma's army from Flanders to Kent or Essex.

The council accepted the general principle that England's main defence force ought to be based as far to the west as was consistent with keeping it supplied; consequently, in May, Lord Admiral Charles Howard with most of the queen's ships moved from the Medway to join Drake's fleet at Plymouth. Howard's job was to keep watch on the approaches to Ireland, the Bristol Channel and the English Channel. This was an enormous task; there were not

[1] See Mattingly (a), pp. 332, 336 and 339.

enough reconnaissance craft to do it reliably. Moreover, no port west of Plymouth could provide for his main fleet. Based on Plymouth he could hardly have intercepted any Spanish fleet that had been ordered to establish a stronghold somewhere up the Bristol Channel—a Spanish equivalent to Gibraltar on the south coast of Wales. Doubtless these anxieties brought the council to a momentary agreement with Drake's offensive strategy and so they ordered Howard and Drake to seek the enemy in Spanish waters. But the English fleet was driven back from the Bay of Biscay by the southwesterly winds which brought the Armada to the Channel.

Once action was joined (30th July 1588) with the English to the windward and the Armada making its way up-Channel, Howard's aim was to keep in such close attendance on the Armada that its commanders would not dare to break their formation sufficiently to be able to attack and capture any English port. Howard wanted to shepherd the Armada up the Channel; his work was made easy by Philip who had ordered the Armada to sail directly to its rendezvous with Parma off Margate. Howard's achievement in the Channel was to force the Armada to spend a tremendous quantity of powder and shot during its voyage. By the time that it reached Calais it needed new supplies before it could reasonably go into action again. Howard's own supplies were replenished from the south-coast ports of England. He redoubled his advantage over the enemy when he broke up their formation with his fire-ships and then inflicted terrible casualties on Spanish troops and sailors. After the battle of Gravelines, the Armada no longer possessed the fighting resources to win a foothold anywhere in the British Isles. But they had lost only seven ships; they were a force in prospect, but not for the moment a force in being; they would have recovered their power quickly enough if they had been able to refit somewhere in the Netherlands or in Scotland. English naval commanders were certain that a renewed Armada would return to the attack in a year or two.[1]

[1] The Channel battle was of a size and type unprecedented in naval warfare. Such a confrontation is awe-inspiring and bewildering to victor and to vanquished. For a comparison, see Winston Churchill's account of the Battle of Midway Island in Vol. IV, Book I, Chapter XIV of *The Second World War*.

Meanwhile the trained bands of western counties had mobilised in the hinterland of Plymouth—20,000 of them; another force of 14,000 was near Poole, and one of 16,000 near Portsmouth;[1] each local army group dispersed to the harvest once the Armada had disappeared up-Channel. The main national army came together at Tilbury about a week later under the command of Leicester for the defence of London. By 10th August most of these 20,000 men had been dispersed in order to save the harvest and the queen's exchequer. For the short-term (that is for the campaigning season of 1588), queen and council had three aims: to prevent Parma's embarkation, to shepherd the Armada past all vulnerable harbours, and to conserve England's resources for long years of war ahead. Like their successors of 1914 and 1940, they survived this first onslaught with sufficient resources for the long haul.

Other armadas were of course to be expected and therefore counter-measures had to be maintained after 1588 as before. But, in these later years, developments in France altered the balance of forces. Parma was often ordered to open an offensive in France; that is to say his military strength was diverted from the Netherlands. With Spanish troops operating in France, England was also compelled to move troops from the Netherlands to garrison French ports which would otherwise fall into the hands of Spain and the Guises. To garrison French ports as well as Dutch ports put a heavy strain on English manpower; every year 5,000 recruits had to be sent to English units in Europe in order to keep their total strength to about 10,000 men. The financial strain was also severe. Parliamentary grants in the middle 1590s were twice as large as in the Armada years (about £135,000 a year in comparison with £72,000 a year); the cost of defence to the queen was approximately £200,000 a year. Poverty, inflation and discharged soldiers were characteristic of Shakespeare's England; such miseries were the price of defence. Of course, Elizabeth tried to minimise England's commitments. Only a very small field force served with Maurice of Nassau as year by year he drove the Spaniards out of the towns of the north Dutch provinces. Elizabeth accepted a formal alliance with Henry IV and the Dutch in 1596, but in 1598 she ended her financial com-

[1] See Wernham (a), p. 400.

mitment in the Netherlands; English units continued to fight and were still kept up to strength, but all payments were made by the Dutch. In the brilliant siege and capture of Nieuport (July 1600), Sir Francis de Vere's 1,600 men suffered eight hundred casualties. As the Dutch consolidated their position in the northern Netherlands, so did the Spaniards consolidate theirs in the south. Ostend was bitterly besieged by the Spaniards for three years; this fishing village fell to Spinola in September 1604; new contingents were still leaving England for Ostend when the old queen died in March 1603. Of the utmost gravity for England's defence, one might suppose, was the capture of Calais by the Archduke Albert in 1596— only to have it returned to France in the peace-treaty of Vervins (1598).

But Philip II had long ago recast his plans for the subjugation of England. The armadas of 1596 and 1597 aimed not at Kent and London, but at Falmouth, the Scilly Isles and Ireland (a Spanish expedition landed at Kinsale in September 1601). Spain's plans of invasion were based not on the Netherlands but on Brittany or the estuary of the Seine, and that was where Spain and her allies had to be fought. Essex had 7,000 men fighting to capture Rouen for Henry IV in 1591. 4,000, under Norris, were in Brittany from 1591, fighting to hold St Malo and Brest against a Spanish invading army; it cost another 7,000 men to keep this contingent up to strength for four years. The drama of Tudor defence ended, under Elizabeth, where it had begun under Henry VII, namely with men's minds focused chiefly on Brittany. This province which in 1490 seemed to be 'situate so opportunely to annoy England either for coast or trade'[1] was in 1595 the base from which Spanish invasion was most to be feared. By 1603 dramatic symmetry mirrored the situation of 1490 at also a deeper level. In 1600 as in 1490, the ports of the Netherlands were securely controlled by a people whose defence aligned them with England; Philip III, the Archduke Albert and Maurice of Nassau were reminiscent of Ferdinand, Maximilian and the Archduke Philip rather than of Philip II and Alva. France, however, had become once more the nation and the threat which she had been before 1494 and from 1548 until 1560.

[1] Francis Bacon quoted in Wernham (a), p. 34.

England's survival had involved a struggle for twenty-five years with the military and diplomatic forces of Spain in America, France and the Low Countries, in Ireland and Scotland, and also in Spain itself and on the home front. The underlying condition of survival was always conservation of resources, choice of priorities, co-ordination of effort. The chief architect of survival, beside the queen herself, died in 1598. Lord Treasurer Burghley had a comprehensive mind and a ubiquitous influence on government—'making decisions in any one sphere against the background of equal responsibility for all others'.[1]

[1] Gould, p. 222.

PART III
Economic Objectives of Tudor Foreign Policy

PART III

22 Wool, cloth and the Netherlands

'Henry VII repeatedly subordinated and sometimes even sacrificed the encouragement of trade and navigation to more pressing dynastic and strategic interests',[1] and so did all of the Tudor monarchs—rightly so, because the first function and duty of government has always been to preserve the life of its community together with the right of self-determination against alien forces; only when that has been fairly secure has a government been able to apply its resources to a struggle for economic advantage. But in the famous phrase of Francis Bacon, Henry VII equally 'could not endure to have trade sick'. Nor, in terms of practical statecraft, could either of the other two great Tudor monarchs.

For England's economy by 1500 was by no means the simple economy of an underdeveloped country. Perhaps in the early middle ages the national economy had been just that: namely a subsistence agriculture to employ and feed most of the population, supported by a lesser cash-crop for export to the industrialised and richer provinces of Europe. This cash-crop was a typical primary product (raw wool) which foreign traders collected and exported in exchange for luxury imports—wine, silk, soap—and also for salt. By 1500 the demand for English wool had grown so great as to alter the organisation of English farming and trading. Wool production was no longer a sideline of the agricultural economy; much agriculture was strictly geared to the wool trade. The handling of the wool was no longer chiefly the business of alien traders; along the whole length of the route, from producer to foreign market,

[1] Wernham (a), p. 62.

the wool was largely and increasingly handled by English clothiers and exporters. Moreover, for the previous 150 years, less and less wool had been exported as a primary product, more and more as a finished or semi-finished article, namely cloth. In 1350, 30,000 sacks of wool were exported with 5,000 cloths; in 1500, 5,000 sacks with 80,000 cloths. This was a development which Tudor Englishmen wanted to carry forward with the same motives as inspire a twentieth-century oil-nation of the Middle East which wants to complete the industrial process within its own territory and export petrol etc rather than crude oil. By 1500, 'trade'—that is the export of English wool and wool products—was very important to the livelihood of large sections of the population. Prosperity and therefore public order were related to trade; royal revenues from royal estates and from customs duties were related to trade. Any monarch who ruled long enough to become aware of his circumstances 'could not endure to have trade sick'.

The first economic aim of Tudor foreign policy was to maintain this traditional export trade, endeavouring at the same time to increase the proportion of the trade which was in cloth rather than in fleece or unwoven thread. The traditional markets for these exports were in the Netherlands. Though west of England traders did take small quantities to France, to Seville and even to the Canaries, the bulk was taken to the Netherlands by the two great groups of London merchants, the Merchants of the Staple who generally carried the wool and the Merchant Adventurers who generally carried the cloth. Each of these was a 'regulated company'; that is, it was a society of merchants who traded independently but who had to be members of the company, observe its regulations and pay its fees as a condition of being permitted to trade in particular goods and markets. The Merchants of the Staple were wool-suppliers to the greatest weaving industries of Europe, those of the southern Netherlands, 'of Yprës and of Gaunt'. Usually they sold only in one market and, more often than not, this market was in Calais. The Merchant Adventurers sold their cloth, in various stages of manufacture, in many towns in the southern Netherlands, but increasingly at Antwerp. Antwerp was a fine port unless silt or hostile fighting ships blocked the approach; neither of these was an obstacle in the second half of the fifteenth century. Moreover, Antwerp gave access to the Rhine as well as to the southern Netherlands; this meant that much of Germany was added to the market of merchants who brought their goods to Antwerp, while Germany was also a source of supply to Antwerp, of copper and silver for example. For this reason, Portuguese traders established themselves at Antwerp and, after 1501, Antwerp became the market in which European traders, including Merchant Adventurers, bought eastern spices for shipment to their respective countries.

The traditional trade which Tudor monarchs wanted to perpetuate and improve was the wool or cloth trade with the southern Netherlands and with Antwerp. The aim of Henry VII was to see that his subjects who traded with the Netherlands were not subjected to tolls and taxes in excess of those paid by others, or to persecution in local law courts. At the beginning of his reign, Henry did nothing to help his traders; on the contrary, in 1493 he restricted their trade with the Netherlands in order to compel the rulers of the Netherlands to withdraw support from Perkin Warbeck. The Merchant Adventurers were ordered, to their evident disadvantage, to trade only in Calais. But these dynastic affairs were settled by treaty in February 1496 and this included a trade agreement, known as 'Intercursus Magnus', between Henry VII and the Archduke Philip. In this Henry showed his concern for his traders. He got for them exact guarantees of fair treatment in the archduke's courts, they were guaranteed that customs duties etc would not be raised above the highest level of the previous fifty years, and they were allowed to sell their goods wholesale anywhere in the archduke's territory. Within the next two years the archduke imposed an excessive duty and ordered the Merchant Adventurers to limit their trading to Antwerp; Henry replied to the archduke with goad and carrot; he limited the Adventurers' trade once more to Calais but he also offered to lower the export duty on wool sold in Calais. The archduke replied by withdrawing his two offensive orders. In all of these commercial exchanges, Henry exploited to the full the influence of his ally, Ferdinand of Spain, who was also the archduke's father-in-law.

The events of the years 1493 to 1496 repeated themselves between

1504 and 1507. The archduke gave protection to Edmund de la Pole, Earl of Suffolk, who was a senior Yorkist claimant to the throne; Henry ordered his traders to limit their exports to Calais; then, when circumstances permitted, Henry extracted from the archduke the 'Intercursus Malus' which restored the 'Intercursus Magnus' together with the privilege of self-government for Merchant Adventurers within the archduke's dominions (that is to say, they could have their own law-court in order to try members of their company according to English law) and the privilege of selling goods retail (but this was withdrawn in 1507).

Meanwhile Henry imposed two minor regulations which were calculated to increase the proportion of fully manufactured cloth in the total of woollen exports: in 1486 he forbad the foreign Hanseatic merchants from exporting 'undressed cloth'; in 1487 the export of unfinished cloth was forbidden below a fixed minimum price.

In 1497 he gave the Merchant Adventurers Company a monopoly of cloth exporting to the Netherlands, but he required membership of the company to be available on such easy terms, and with such a low fee, that for all practical purposes free-trade was established in this commercial sector. Since the Merchant Adventurers were exporters of cloth rather than wool, this freedom contributed to the healthy growth of England's cloth export. The growth of this trade is illustrated by these approximate figures for the export from London of 'short-cloths', which were about the most important of all exports. The approximate numbers of these cloths that were likely to have been exported from London were:

1500	49,000
1510	58,000
1520	66,000
1529	75,000
1535	83,000
1540	103,000[1]

The Merchant Adventurers, as thus organised, were a recognised society with recognised officers, too weak to restrict the growth of

[1] See Fisher.

trade but useful to the government, because they could speak on behalf of their fellow-traders when taxes or minor regulations were under consideration; for example, in 1505 standards of quality were specified for exported cloth. In the second half of the century the government was able to use this loose organisation as the basis for a much tighter monopoly which European conditions made necessary in the 1560s.

All in all there was a big expansion in the export of cloth to the Netherlands during the reign of Henry VII. It had been brought about by men and by forces which Henry did not create. His policy was to aid, protect and encourage.

This great sector of English trade enjoyed robust development during the next forty years; all events conspired to this end without any aid from the governments of Henry VIII, which did, in fact, give negligible attention to the needs of these exporters. Antwerp grew steadily as a market for English wool and cloth because more and more traders, who needed this cloth, could offer in exchange an increasing variety of goods from the far east, from Germany and from the Baltic. The long wars in Italy had an economic influence throughout Europe; they created inflationary conditions in which cloth sold well. But Italian wars were not physically destructive in the trading area of Antwerp and its hinterland; they did nothing to restrict business there. The draining away of manpower from Castile began the long decline in Spanish agriculture and so reduced competition against England's products. The Antwerp market was profitable and all-sufficient; English traders could not be tempted in these years to seek markets elsewhere. They felt so sure of themselves that when Wolsey imitated Henry VII and ordered them to trade only with Calais (1528), they disregarded the order. Henry VIII, on his side, felt so sure of the trade that, at the height of his diplomatic crisis in 1533, he banned it and successfully revealed to Charles V how dependent Netherland prosperity was on supplies from England. Finally, in the years from 1540 to 1550, the severe debasement of England's coinage caused the pound sterling to fall in value from twenty-seven Flemish shillings to fifteen. English prices rose but by a much smaller amount, and so, in terms of Flemish shillings, English cloth became very cheap; the demand for it in Antwerp rose proportionately: annual exports from England increased by fifty per cent in the years 1540–50. Indeed the Duke of Somerset's chief concern with this trade was to reduce it, in order to limit the social dislocation caused in England by so much sheep-breeding. His government imposed a poll-tax on sheep (March 1549). 'This Act . . . marks the climax of the attempt to hold back agrarian change by legislation. It failed.'[1]

But the dealers in Antwerp who bought heavily when the price of English cloth seemed unbelievably low suddenly found that they had more on their hands than they could sell at any profit. The demand for English cloth fell abruptly during the last months of 1550. In 1552, even though the Merchant Adventurers had lowered their prices, the volume of exports from London was only two-thirds of the amount for 1550; customs receipts fell by forty per cent; spinners and weavers and all those concerned with raising sheep received less for their work; many became unemployed or bankrupt. The approximate figures for exports of short-cloths through London tell the tale. These were:

1540	103,000
1547	119,000
1550	133,000
1552	85,000
1560	94,000

Northumberland's hostility to Charles V disqualified him from seeking any help from the government of the Netherlands in any attempt to boost England's sales there. He did however suspend the privileges of the Hanse traders in order to give English merchants a bigger share of the reduced volume of exports (1552). He imposed on the Hanse the same import and export duties as were paid by other alien traders. But Mary Tudor renewed the Hanse privileges in 1556 out of deference to Philip, who wanted the Netherlands to benefit from the cheapest possible supply of unfinished English cloth. Mary took this action in face of the opposition of her council. Exports to the Netherlands were also handicapped by higher export dues on unfinished cloth which were imposed in 1558, but this

[1] Lockyer, p. 137.

Wool, cloth and the Netherlands

brought some benefit to those English craftsmen who were rivals of Netherlanders in the finishing trades. Similarly, the loss of Calais in 1558 was a crippling blow to Merchants of the Staple who had always sold English wool there; they never found an alternative market that was satisfactory, but these misfortunes of English wool-exporters usually turned in the end to the advantage of the English cloth industry.

In the 1550s the focus of European warfare shifted from Italy to the middle Rhine, Flanders and the Netherlands. In 1559 Cardinal Granvelle began to dominate the government of the Netherlands and so began also that long period of turbulence which, in about fifteen years, destroyed the prosperity of the southern Netherlands and the assets which had made Antwerp the chief centre of European trade. In these conditions, the old Tudor policy of maintaining the greatest possible trade with the Netherlands could hardly bring prosperity to Queen Elizabeth's subjects. Indeed in 1563 Cardinal Granvelle banned the import of English cloth in retaliation for England's hospitality to Netherland refugees and aid to Huguenot rebels. (English merchants in the Netherlands had also abetted local resistance to his persecution of heretics.) Elizabeth replied by forbidding imports from the Netherlands so that trade was reduced to a trickle carried in neutral ships. There was only a partial resumption of trade after the departure of Granvelle in 1564, and this came to an end when Elizabeth quarrelled with Alva in 1568. She made peace with Governor de Requesens in 1574 and, by the agreement of Bristol, trade was to be reopened, but the Dutch sea-beggars were able to prevent any access to Antwerp, which was in any case destroyed by mutinous Spanish troops in November 1576. Any remaining trade to the Netherlands was ended by Parma's victories in 1585, which closed Brussels and Ghent and cut the routes through the Netherlands to the Rhine. Refugees, escaping from war and persecution in the Netherlands, were welcomed by Elizabeth's government. The refugees established themselves in East Anglia and Kent; they taught English weavers how to make and export cloth which was equal to the finest in Europe. These were the 'new draperies' of English industry which, taken with already established types of English cloth, gave our exporters a competitive pre-eminence in Europe. Not surprisingly, the Merchants of the Staple, who had exported 3,000 sacks of wool in 1565, exported only two hundred in 1585.

23 Diversifying into other markets

GERMANY AND THE BALTIC

Economic salvation had, in Elizabeth's reign, to be sought in the export of cloth elsewhere than to the Netherlands. It was sought and found along two lines of diversification, each well established in the sense that previous Tudor governments had encouraged their subjects to pursue them. But what had been minor interests to Henry VII and Henry VIII became a major concern of Elizabethan economics in relation to foreign countries. The two lines of enterprise to which Henry VII and his successors had given minor encouragement were that merchants should multiply the areas of the world with which they traded (instead of restricting themselves to the Netherlands) and that they should diversify the products in which they traded rather than restrict themselves to cloth and wool.

North Germany and the Baltic were the most important areas beyond the Netherlands to which traders sought access. Baltic cities of the Hanseatic League opposed the house of Lancaster after 1449 and excluded English merchants from the Baltic in retaliation for a piratical attack on their convoy on its voyage from Brittany to the Baltic. They supported Edward IV who gave them generous privileges in the treaty of Utrecht 1473. But this treaty did not give English merchants any reciprocal rights of entry to the Baltic. Indeed England's successful return to the trading areas of north Germany and the Baltic was only achieved eighty years after Henry VII first attempted to pare away the privileges of the Hanseatic League. He brought the Hanse to negotiate and even to agree that English ships should enter the Baltic, but he could not overcome the

245

local boycott which Baltic wholesalers imposed on English traders whether the Englishmen came to sell cloth or to buy the ships' stores (masts, pitch etc) of which Baltic countries were the chief suppliers.

Henry confirmed all Hanseatic privileges in London in 1486 (to live where they liked; to sell wholesale and retail), but thereafter he put pressure on them by forbidding their export of undressed cloth (1486) and of bullion (1489); he redefined Hanseatic goods

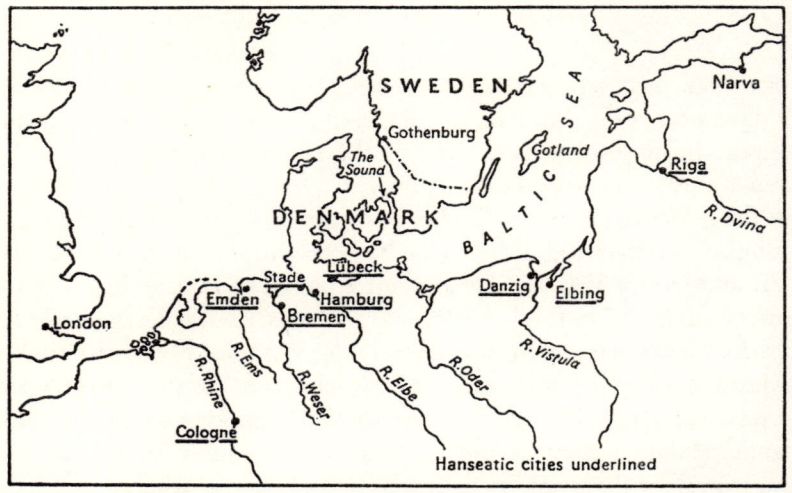

Map 18. The Hanseatic League and the Baltic Sea

(which paid a lower import duty) as goods which were made in Hanseatic towns. By exercising this sort of pressure Henry extorted agreements that the English should be permitted to trade with Danzig (1491) and Riga (1499), but in both cases the treaties were ineffective for the reason given.

English exports to these areas were still controlled by the Hanseatic League when the collapse of the Antwerp market in 1550 made English traders look desperately to North Germany for an alternative market.

Preoccupied with urgent affairs at home, Northumberland did little and Mary did nothing to help them find a market in the Baltic.

Diversifying into other markets

But the Merchant Adventurers, still responsible for about half of England's exports, did get powerful encouragement a few years later from Elizabeth's privy council. The Adventurers were re-organised under a strong charter which created a smaller, more monopolistic group. Thus reinvigorated, they temporarily established their cloth market at Emden in 1564, and then, on the initiative of William Cecil, at Hamburg on a ten years' agreement which the other Hanse towns could not prevent (1568-78). Hamburg was tempted to make this agreement because English cloth was a commodity which drew all sorts of traders to the city. The Hanse cities could not prevent the agreement because they had been weakened by the rise of other Baltic states—Denmark, Sweden, and even Russia which took Narva in 1558 and held it for half a century. The Hanse cities suffered heavy losses during a war with Denmark in 1536 and again as Denmark's ally in a long war with Sweden (1563-70). Besides, they were concerned at the news of English ships in the White Sea and feared that all Baltic exports to England might cease if English traders found alternative supplies by way of the White Sea. In any case, the English privy council negotiated agreements with Denmark and Sweden which opened other Baltic markets to English traders, but this was only on the payment of dues which the Danes, for another eighty years, were able to demand from ships passing through their Sound.

During Alva's bitter conflict with Elizabeth (1568-73), he undertook to capture English shipping en route for Hamburg, but Queen and council were intensely concerned for the success of this trade; two protected convoys were organised by the government and sent under command of Admiral Sir William Wynter (1569). In this decade, trade, by way of the Baltic, was also being developed by the Muscovy Company (chartered 1553, 1555 and 1566) and by the Eastland Company (chartered in 1579 to trade chiefly with Elbing). When Hamburg failed to renew its agreement in 1578, the Merchant Adventurers moved first to Emden and then to Stade. Meanwhile they had captured from the Hanse the whole business of exporting English cloth to the Baltic and much of the trade in Baltic products for England. In 1598, the Hanseatic agency at the Steelyard in London was closed down. But by this date Dutch rivalry in the Baltic was beginning to gather momentum; England's Baltic trade had many new difficulties to overcome in competition with these new rivals.

In the twenty years, 1550 to 1570, Antwerp had first declined and then disappeared as the major market for England's only great exporting industry. This faced English traders with a critical problem and threatened the people of England with a severe decline in economic prosperity. The economic corner had been turned by traders and government in an energetic alliance, which shifted trade eastwards to areas which had been probed by Henry VII eighty years before. By this policy, England's level of exports was maintained, as is suggested by the following approximate figures for London's export of short-cloths, which were:

1560	94,000
1566	95,000
1570	93,000
1575	100,000
1585	101,000
1593	102,000
1600	103,000

(The shift of trade to German and Baltic ports increased the traffic through Hull and Newcastle, so that these figures for London may bear a smaller and smaller proportion to England's total export.)

There was one more crisis for the cloth industry; that was when war-conditions in the 1580s interrupted trade routes or diverted ships to war service. (London's short-cloth exports in 1588 fell to about 95,000.) As a desperate expedient the government ended monopoly control of cloth exports for twelve months (May 1587) and opened it to all English merchants; the experiment in free trade was not continued beyond the twelve months.

THE MEDITERRANEAN AND THE INDIES

Henry VII tried to bring many areas, besides Germany and the Baltic, within range of English exporters. The variety of areas to which he gave attention is testimony to his interest; the number of treaties negotiated, and the number of enterprises which he chartered, is testimony to his energy. He was interested in the markets of

Diversifying into other markets

France, Spain, Portugal, the Mediterranean, the far east (as one can say in the light of instructions given in 1496 for John Cabot's first voyage) and America itself (in the light of the patent issued in 1502 to the Company of Adventurers to the New Found Lands).[1]

Treaties with France in 1486, 1492, 1495 and 1497 all sought in one way or another to protect the interests and personal safety of English traders. With Spain, the famous treaty of Medina del Campo (1489) gave English merchants in Spain the rights of Spaniards and Spanish merchants in England the rights of Englishmen; customs duties were fixed as in 1459. With Portugal a treaty of 1489 gave English traders the rights enjoyed under the treaty of 1378.[2] To gain access to Mediterranean ports on behalf of English traders, Henry waged a tariff war against Venice who wanted to exclude competitors. He negotiated an agreement with Florence for the export of English wool to their port of Pisa, from which wine would be imported to England. Venice tried to disrupt this agreement by preventing the accumulation of sufficient stocks of wine at Pisa; Henry therefore imposed penal customs duties on all wine brought to England by Venetians (1492). As soon as the Italian wars began in 1494, Venice came to terms and accepted the presence of English traders in the Mediterranean.

In 1496 Henry conferred on John Cabot and his associates all trading rights in any new lands which they might discover. Cabot sailed and returned in 1497, reporting that he had found the mainland of Asia, 'the territory of the Grand Khan'. By 1502 Henry and his advisers had probably realised that John Cabot had discovered a coast line which was not Asia, for he began to charter groups, and grant rewards, for the exploration of the 'new found lands' and for the discovery of a passage around them to the north-west.

The kings of Spain and Portugal had already established sovereign rights in these distant worlds. Henry's policy towards the claims

---

[1] See Williamson (b), p. 22.
[2] England's commercial connection with Portugal in the fourteenth century was slight; England imported small quantities of Portuguese dye. Nor was the connection popular in England. The 1378 treaty was an expression of hope, which reflected John of Gaunt's political connection with Portugal; it was not a portent of any real growth in commerce.

of his brother-monarchs is evident from the patents which he granted to his own explorers. From the first, he rejected the Pope's treaty of Tordesillas (1494), whereby Spain and Portugal monopolised all newly-discovered sea-routes and land masses; Henry would not accept the exclusion of his subjects from these areas, in spite of the protests of the King of Spain (1496). Nevertheless, Henry did, at first, accept the right of discovery; he granted monopoly trading rights to his explorers only if they should discover lands which were previously unknown to Christians, and he put into the Tower a renegade from Portugal who offered to reveal the route to India. But in and after 1502, Henry's patents ceased to accept the right of discovery; he then recognised only the right of effective occupation; his explorers were free to assert claims in any lands except those which were effectively controlled by foreign friendly rulers. Recognition of the right of effective occupation, and refusal to recognise the right of discovery, continued to be the twin principles of royal policy throughout the Tudor period and beyond it, except during the reign of Mary Tudor.

The chance of commercial expansion into the new world of America aroused the active interest of the governments of Henry VIII. Wolsey and Thomas More are believed to have inspired John Rastell and others to plan the expedition of 1517 which was intended to discover land in America for colonisation and to explore coastal waters for fishing.[1] Henry VIII provided the expedition with royal letters of commendation, but the crew refused to sail west beyond Waterford. In 1521 Wolsey, with the enthusiastic support of Henry, planned a major expedition, to be led by Sebastian Cabot through the north-west passage to the richer parts of China. But Cabot rejected the invitation to return to English service. Wolsey therefore turned to the merchants of London, but, though 'his grace would have no nay therein, but spake sharply to the mayor to see it put in execution',[2] the Londoners were wholly preoccupied with profitable trade to Antwerp and did not want to hazard their good relations with Charles V. Henry's interest was momentarily roused by the Robert Thorne project of a direct passage to the Pacific across the

[1] See Scarisbrick, p. 123.
[2] Quoted in Scarisbrick, p. 124.

Diversifying into other markets 251

polar seas (1526), but he rejected Sebastian Cabot's offer to serve him in 1537. During Henry's reign, north-western exploration and American enterprise were remembered as activities to which Englishmen might one day return. For practical purposes, government interest in this enterprise receded, to become a mere dream which ceased to concern practical polititicians.

As the failure of the cloth sales in Antwerp in 1550 led in the end to the exploitation of north German markets, so also it led merchants to turn with some desperation towards all other possible markets—in France, Spain, Portugal, the Mediterranean, and even in such unknown areas as Morocco and Guinea. But the government of Northumberland was preoccupied and could do little but expound visionary schemes for developing trade. Northumberland did himself have a real belief in these schemes and found time to bring the government into one particular project for the expansion of trade. This was the project of John Dee, tutor to Northumberland's family, who believed that the north-eastern coast of Asia ran in a south-easterly direction from the northernmost cape of Scandinavia, until it reached tropical China. By following this coast, explorers could expect to find their north-east route to China. They could also expect to find ports all along the coast-lands of these cold latitudes whose citizens would want to buy the warm English cloth that could not be sold in Antwerp. Sebastian Cabot returned to England in 1548 and his advice was available in exchange for a privy council pension. His experience of the ice-bound seas of the north-west was added to John Dee's theoretical picture of the north-east coast of Asia. A company was formed with Cabot as its governor, Northumberland as its most distinguished patron and privy councillors among its shareholders. In May 1553 Sir Hugh Willoughby and Richard Chancellor sailed into the north-east, where Willoughby died, but Chancellor found the White Sea, Archangel and the way to Moscow. Since this enterprise led on to the foundation of the Muscovy Company and the Eastland Company, and to the development of important if minor trade with the Baltic, Russia and Persia, credit may well be given to Northumberland for his expansive aims, however little he himself achieved in his own time. His government also negotiated a trade treaty with the newly independent country of Sweden (1551). Besides this little that his government achieved, their activity created an atmosphere of national encouragement for private syndicates led by William Hawkins in Plymouth, Robert Reneger in Southampton and Thomas Wyndham from London, who were pushing English commerce into new waters.

Because of these minor achievements, Northumberland's government contrasted favourably with Mary Tudor's. Mary did indeed permit the continuation of exploration to the north-east; the Muscovy Company was chartered, with Philip's sanction, in 1555. But she did nothing to improve England's opportunities of worldwide trade; she imposed on England the burden of helping Spain against France but did nothing to get reciprocal concessions from Spain to England. In particular, she made no attempt to get for her own subjects the right to trade in Spanish America. This failure is the more surprising since the old treaty of Medina del Campo (1489) had permitted the citizens of England and Spain to trade in each other's country with the freedom of native citizens. Mary Tudor, however, was anxious only to meet her husband's requirements at every point; the policy that she imposed was hostile in detail, and discouraging in spirit, to England's commercial expansion. Expansion continued only because traders, and even privy councillors, disregarded the prohibiting decrees which Philip required them to issue (1555) in respect of English trade with Spanish territories and indeed with Portuguese territories also.

Perhaps the importance of Northumberland's enthusiasm for trade does not stand in the little that it achieved in his day, but in the experience which it gave to William Cecil, a young and rising councillor who carried into Elizabeth's reign a great capacity for using and abetting the enterprise of traders. Besides effecting the development of trade with north Germany when the Antwerp market collapsed, Elizabeth's government supported the efforts of John Hawkins to insinuate a practical trading connection with Spanish America and, when that failed, she connived at efforts to secure compensation by privateering. Similarly, Elizabeth supported the efforts of Drake to find Terra Australis Incognita and a connection with the Spice Islands. She supported Drake by becoming a shareholder in his syndicate, by lending royal ships for the voyage, and by knighting Drake at the end of his voyage on board his *Golden Hind*. She also supported Lancaster and others with letters of reprisal when they made their attempt to prove the Cape-route to India (1591). One of the last acts of her reign was to charter the East India Company (1601).

Unfortunately, the strictly political policies which were imposed on Elizabeth by events in Europe brought more and more difficulty on to the English merchants who traded directly with Spain. This important trade became impossible after May 1585 when Philip seized most of the English ships in Spanish ports (including grain ships under safe-conduct during a time of dearth in Spain). Thereafter Spanish trade ceased until 1604, except in so far as English traders sold to Germans, Frenchmen and Italians who resold in Spain.

Throughout the forty-five years of her reign, Elizabeth's government stood firmly to the policy of disregarding any territorial claims except those of effective occupation. She rejected Portuguese protests against the trading of John Hawkins on the west coast of Africa; for, if the Portuguese were in effective control, they could themselves prevent their subjects from trading with Hawkins. She, with Burghley, Walsingham and others subscribed to the funds raised by Sir Humphrey Gilbert and Michael Lok to send Frobisher in seach of the north-west passage (1576 to 1578). Expeditions led by Humphrey Gilbert and Sir Walter Raleigh for colonisation in North America similarly fulfilled government policy by respecting effective occupation, but denying a mere right of discovery. Mendoza twice protested against these plans for English settlements in America and was twice rebuffed by Elizabeth (1582 and 1583).

For the improvement of Mediterranean trade, Elizabeth's government chartered the Levant Company (1581) and the Venetian Company, thus supporting the merchants who had negotiated with the Sultan for trading privileges in Constantinople, Aleppo, Damascus, Alexandria, Tripoli and Tunis; she also accredited an English ambassador to the Sultan.

The policy of Elizabeth's government was to encourage the development of English trade in as many parts of the world as possible and so to maintain a steady level of exporting, even though political circumstances in Europe made trading more and more difficult in our traditional markets. It is in part to the credit of her government that exporting was maintained at a high level except in years of supreme crisis such as 1587 and 1588. By the end of her reign the country was well placed to build towards the great expansion which came in the second half of the seventeenth century.

24 Diversifying into other goods and services

Tudor governments were anxious that English merchants should trade in many parts of the world and should not depend entirely on Antwerp. Similarly, Tudor governments were concerned that English merchants should be able to offer a variety of goods and services and should not depend entirely on textiles. When these governments encouraged Englishmen to interest themselves in unfamiliar products their policy supported three complementary purposes: first, they intended that Englishmen should produce a greater variety of goods to export, for example the development of coal-mining added an important commodity to England's range of exports; secondly, they intended that the English population should rely less on imported foreign goods, for example the development of salt-mining reduced dependence on imports from France; thirdly, they intended that English importers and exporters should rely less on foreign ships to carry their freight between this country and any other. All three types of development had a purely economic justification for they were likely to make England's citizens more prosperous, but the second and third also had important military consequence; they were aspects of autarky (alias military economics) with which Tudor governments rightly concerned themselves, because Tudor England could not defend herself against an enemy country if she depended entirely on that country for a vital supply, particularly if the supply had a direct military application. An increase in English merchant shipping was seen to bring an increase in the size of England's fighting fleet and of her reserves of fighting seamen; the development of a metal industry was seen to provide a reliable supply of pikes, muskets, artillery and ammunition.

Henry VII was immediately concerned that England should have a bigger merchant fleet. During the first months of his reign he offered subsidies to citizens who built ships of over eighty tons. He himself invested in the *Regent* (six hundred tons) and the *Sovereign* (four hundred tons); he needed the ships chiefly as fighting ships but he also hired them out to English traders as cargo ships. Thus, he demonstrated that large ships could be profitable investments. To divert more business to English ship-owners he passed Navigation Acts through Parliament—in 1485 requiring that Gascon wine should come to England in English ships, in 1489 that Toulouse woad should do so. Similarly, Henry's conflict with the Hanseatic League for entry to the Baltic was intended to bring more freight to English ships, and so was his conflict with Venice for entry to the Mediterranean. In the long term his greatest service to English seamanship was his encouragement of John and Sebastian Cabot. The Newfoundland cod fisheries, which they discovered, became the annual objective of an English fishing-fleet; this fleet was the school in which the first generation of England's oceanic seamen learnt their craft.

During the next reign the various governments of Henry VIII did not exert themselves to bring about an enlargement of England's merchant fleet, except that they passed two ineffective Navigation Acts (1532 and 1540) in order to reduce England's use of foreign ships, nor did they interest themselves in the dramatic development of new industries which took place in the 1540s. Professor J. J. Scarisbrick's full account of the interests and anxieties of Henry VIII makes no reference to Professor J. U. Nef's description of industrial development in the 1540s. This silence is eloquent testimony to the indifference of Henry to those industries. But although Henry's governments cannot be credited with any policy in these matters, their actions in other fields stimulated the development of this new industrial diversity. Coal-mining, various metal industries, glass and brick industries were all stimulated by inflationary prices in expanding markets. It was Henry's debasement of the coinage in the 1540s that provided the inflation and his wars that in many respects provided the markets (see chapter 25).

The industrial development of the 1540s was interrupted but not

Diversifying into other goods and services

destroyed by the changing policies of Northumberland and Mary Tudor. Consequently, there existed at the beginning of Elizabeth's reign an embryonic but varied industry ready to expand under direct government stimulus. Government initiative was important in all phases of the new metallurgical industries. First, metal deposits had to be discovered; copper was found in Cumberland, calamine (for zinc and brass) in Somerset; both discoveries were made by German experts who had been brought to England by William Cecil in 1565. Secondly, the government recruited young English goldsmiths who were sent to work in German brass-foundries; there, by a species of industrial espionage, they discovered how to make brass and to use it in the manufacture of fire-arms. Finally, the government established full-scale production in England. The 'Mines Royal' was given a monopoly of copper-mining in the north; the 'Mineral and Battery Works' was given a monopoly of brass manufacture—both in 1568. Similarly, in the 1560s, the government issued licences for the manufacture of saltpetre and of sulphur. In 1565 George Evelyn received his patent of monopoly for the manufacture of gunpowder and he began to set up his powder mills near Dorking in Surrey.[1] The government, profoundly relieved to be no longer dependent on supplies from Antwerp, could arm its militia and its ships with fire-arms, pike, cannon, powder and shot which were made in England (1570); it could even permit some export of these commodities.

There were, however, two old-established areas of economic activity, both of first-rate military importance and both declining (as it seemed to the government) in 1560. The first of these was arable farming, which provided not only food for the population but also men for the county militia. Cecil was observing before 1560 that 'the tillage of the realm is notoriously decade . . . the realm is driven to be furnished with foreign corn'. This was a grave military weakness: 'the strength and flourishing estate of this kingdom hath been always, and is, greatly upheld and advanced by the maintenance of the plough and tillage being the occasion of the increase and multiplying of people both for service in the wars and in times of peace'. The government wanted to encourage the

[1] See Rowse, pp. 124 etc.

growing of corn, but it also wanted the corn which had been grown to be sold cheaply. Its measures to keep down the price (such as 'an act to restrain carrying corn victuals over the sea')[1] naturally discouraged corn production, however much other statutes for the maintenance of tillage were intended to encourage it.

The second area in which Elizabeth's government detected a decline was in long-distance sea-going commerce; this was the commerce that trained ocean-going seamen who could man the fleet in time of emergency. Statesmen observed particularly that Mediterranean and Levantine trade had been active in Henry VII's time, but had diminished to nothing by 1550. This was because Mediterranean goods could be more cheaply imported from Antwerp. However, trade with Antwerp did little to train ocean-going seamen: 'these two-day voyages twice a year, where every pedlar may practise, whereby there is scant either a good mariner or a good ship maintained.'[2]

Back in 1548, a protestant government made fish-eating compulsory on Fridays and Saturdays in order to increase the number of sea-going fishermen. Mary Tudor's government in 1558 passed a stricter Navigation Act with the hope of increasing England's shipping: 'the natives here have laid a plot to ruin the trade of all foreign merchants' was a foreign merchant's comment. William Cecil in 1563 turned again to the fishing industry as the best school of seamanship and set out his 'arguments to prove that it is necessary for the restoring of the Navy of England to have more fish eaten and therefore one day more in the week ordained to be a fish-day'. Therefore, in spite of Puritan protests, Wednesday was so ordained. On the other hand, the wine trade with France seemed to Cecil not an appropriate way of training sailors: 'it is not meet to seek the increase of the navy by increase of wine . . . it enricheth France whose power England ought not to increase' (Cecil to Parliament, January 1567).[3]

However feeble a remedy this fish Act may seem to have been, it did demonstrate the government's belief that strength in war

[1] From the preamble to the Statute of 1597.
[2] Quoted in Wernham, p. 423.
[3] Quoted in Read (b), pp. 371 and 372.

Diversifying into other goods and services

depended on economic policy. In the event, however, Hawkins' seamen in the west and the Muscovy Company's men in the north-east acquired their experience in their own way, with government encouragement but without government direction.

By one means or another England had become, by 1600, less dependent on foreigners for important commodities and for the services of merchant shipping. Her exports were more varied in kind and in destination. Her imports were more varied and, as a symptom of national prosperity, more luxurious, but they were a type of luxury which would soon be for the many rather than for the very few. The country was better able to provide its means of defence (in trained men and weapons) than it had been since the loss of northern France in 1453. These economic achievements had been aims in the mind's eye of Henry VII, and of Elizabeth; some of them had been occasionally in the mind of Henry VIII, some in the mind of Northumberland.

25 Debt and policy, coinage and commerce

The strictly financial decision to borrow from foreign lenders affected the independence of English governments in their dealings with foreign countries. So too a decision to debase England's currency, to revalue it, or to stabilise it, affected the dealings of English traders in foreign markets.

Henry VII preserved independence of action by spending less than his revenue and by borrowing, when he had to, from his own subjects. His own financial reserves could be used to give diplomatic leverage, as in the case of his loans of £138,000 to Archduke Philip of the Netherlands in 1505.

Henry VIII enjoyed similar freedom of action from 1509 until 1525, by which date his father's reserves had been spent and his subjects themselves refused to lend any more. Then again, in the 1530s, money from sales of monastic land gave him freedom of action. But in the 1540s he became dependent on Antwerp, not only because he had to buy arms there, but also because he had to borrow from Antwerp bankers, and that at fourteen per cent.

Financial dependence on Antwerp, for a debt of about £100,000 at fourteen per cent, continued under the governments of Somerset, Northumberland and Mary. This reduced all three governments to the necessity of following an inactive foreign policy or of following obediently in the wake of Charles V and Philip II. The price of active diplomatic independence was financial freedom from these foreign loans. This in turn required great economy on the part of the English government, together with the maintenance of a healthy sense of national unity, so that taxes and loans to the government

Debt and policy, coinage and commerce

would willingly be granted. Elizabeth's government stimulated the growth of armament industries in order to be independent of foreign suppliers; it practised the parsimony, and achieved the degree of national unity, that ended our dependence on foreign financiers. For ten years Elizabeth's foreign debt was slowly and painfully repaid. Thomas Gresham was her agent: 'come in as small debt as you can beyond seas' was always his text. To this end he urged his government to relax English laws against usury so that they could borrow freely from their own merchants. Meanwhile, Gresham himself was resident in Antwerp and brilliantly *persona grata* with all men of financial ability. He raised short-term loans at progressively lower rates of interest. Like a juggler with billiard-balls, he kept this succession of loans in the air in so far as old loans needed to be replaced when they expired.[1]

Gresham's policy, together with Elizabeth's insistent economy and the sale of a quarter of a million pounds' worth of crown land (and sometimes of episcopal land) ended her dependence on Antwerp in about ten years. Her need for money was still very great whenever military and naval forces had to be mobilised; she was happy to have the use of foreign loans when national independence was not thereby sacrificed. Or perhaps one should rather say that she pursued a very independent foreign policy and therefore financiers would not lend unless they welcomed her policy or were indifferent to it. She was very happy indeed to borrow £85,000, which had been intended for Alva, from the Genoese in 1568. By 1574 crown indebtedness had been repaid, and she could borrow at nine per cent. By 1584 a war-chest of £300,000 had been accumulated, but the needs of 1587 and 1588 swallowed it all, together with parliamentary subsidies and forced loans of £100,000. The expenses of war in the 1590s absorbed all her revenues. More crown lands had to be sold, and crown debts of £400,000 were accumulated and bequeathed to James I. But these debts were owed by the crown to its subjects; they did not involve dependence on foreign powers.

These expenses of war also had an inflationary effect (which aggravated an inflationary tendency created by the growth of population in this century). Even if a government did nothing to

[1] See Outhwaite.

increase the number of coins in its realm, nevertheless in wartime the existing coins moved more rapidly from hand to hand, from transaction to transaction. As soon as money came into the Treasury in the form of revenue it was spent again; there was no chance of holding it as a reserve. The recipient (perhaps a corn merchant supplying an army at Dover) spent as soon as he was paid (if not sooner, on credit) in order to replenish his supplies. Inflation is caused as much by the speed or 'velocity' with which money changes hands as by the amount of money which is put in circulation. Or, as economists have often expressed it, $MV = PT$. When M (the amount of money in the realm) is increased, or V (the velocity with which coins change hands) is increased, then P (the price of articles) is also increased, unless T (which represents goods coming up for sale) has increased proportionately.

This inflationary effect of war was strongly felt in England during the war years of the 1520s, the '40s, the '50s, the '80s, and above all the '90s. Prices in England rose in response to the increased velocity with which money was circulating. But the crown's income did not increase in proportion to prices; consequently its ability to buy munitions of war etc was reduced and its freedom of action in foreign affairs was limited. Elizabeth was conscious of this sequence: namely that an active foreign policy, involving warfare, tended to put up prices and to deprive a government of the ability to wage war effectively; in other words, that a government which fought a war today would not be able to fight one effectively tomorrow. This was a realistic justification for the extreme hesitation with which she approached all diplomatic decisions and the extreme reluctance with which she committed herself to military expeditions.

A short-term way in which a government could increase its freedom of action in foreign affairs was by altering the value of the coins of the realm, for each of these alterations brought it a large profit or windfall. Debasement began experimentally in 1542 and brought a profit of £14,000. The great debasement of the twenty-four months, May 1544 to May 1546, brought Henry VIII a profit of about £400,000, to which over £500,000 was added in the years 1547 to 1550 and over £100,000 in the first six months of 1551. The specific purpose of the operation was to help pay for his active foreign policy towards Scotland and France. Without the profits of debasement, these wars could not have been fought: the total cost of wars in the 1540s was about £3,500,000; the yield of taxes from the laity was £976,000; the rent and sale of crown lands brought in £1,048,000; this total of £2,024,000 was only brought within reach of the costs of warfare by the £1,000,000 derived from the manipulation of the mint, which Chancellor Wriothesely described with expressive gratitude as 'our holy anchor'.[1]

After 1550 the crown twice revalued the coinage in the reverse direction, that is by increasing the metal relative to the figure imprinted on the coin. In 1551 and again in 1560 these revaluations were carried through to the profit of the crown. When an old 'base' coin was handed in ('base', because its minted face value exceeded its metal content), a new sound coin was given in return having a face value that was about three-quarters as large as the face value of the base coin; but the base coin possessed a metal content of about four-fifths of its face value. Thus the crown made a gross profit in metal of four-fifths less three-quarters. The crown's profit in 1560 was about £45,000.[2]

The trade of English merchants in foreign markets was distorted both by wartime inflation and by official revaluations of the coinage. Wartime inflation with its tendency to put up the price of English goods would have made the export of English goods difficult, except that war and inflation was worse in other parts of Europe than in England, worse in Spain, Italy and Germany—and, as the century moved on, worse still in France and the southern Netherlands —so that, if inflation made English goods more expensive, yet, in comparison with rising prices elsewhere, they were becoming cheaper to foreign buyers. Of course, late sixteenth-century devastation in France and the southern Netherlands meant that these countries had a lot less to sell in exchange for English goods; they were consequently bad markets for English merchants however advantageous English selling prices might have been in those countries. This obstacle did not apply in the case of Germany, which became a good market. Spain, with its American gold,

[1] These approximations are based on figures given in Challis.
[2] See Read (c).

against a background of severe internal inflation, was a first-rate market for English cloth, and so was Portugal (annexed to Spain in 1580) whose spices were always a good exchange. Nor were English merchants wholly excluded from these markets after 1585, for they could sell their cloth to Germans or Italians who would resell to Spaniards or Portuguese.

Thus the difference between England's rate of war-inflation and that experienced in other parts of Europe gave English merchants an advantage and helped to account for their success in maintaining their level of exports in spite of the collapse of Antwerp as a market and the dislocation to trade which was caused by Elizabeth's wars. Inflation which was due to warfare distorted the flow of trade in the sense that enterprise received an unexpected but healthy stimulus. In contrast, inflation which was due to government debasements grossly distorted the pattern of trade and left an aftermath of economic dislocation. Some of the Tudor revaluations of the nation's coinage distorted foreign trade abruptly and seriously. A government, as has been said, inflated its national currency by lowering the metal content of the coins but not the value imprinted on them (or by imprinting a higher value on them without changing their metal content). Until the twentieth century currencies have been linked to each other by being made of similar metals. That is to say the change in the metal content of a coinage has altered its value in terms of foreign currencies almost to the full extent of the change and almost as soon as the change has become generally known. During the debasements of the 1540s the value of the pound fell rapidly in terms of foreign currencies. But the price of English goods responded only slowly to the fact that there was more money about; the price of goods rose slowly. Consequently English goods became cheap to foreign buyers and English exports boomed tremendously. But then, quite suddenly, consumers became satiated, whereupon the market collapsed (1550, 1551), and the selling price of English goods slumped and produced a commercial set-back which had grave consequences for the whole nation.

During Northumberland's half-hearted recoinage (1551) the government called in a proportion of the debased coins (which had been marked with a value considerably higher than the tradi-

Debt and policy, coinage and commerce

tional value of the metal in the coins). The debased coins were re-minted with a lower face-value, so that the new face-value was approximately equal to the traditional value of the metal in the coin. Persons who received back their coins with this lower value printed on them had had their nominal purchasing power reduced. These people were, in many cases, English exporters who bought heavily from English cloth-merchants, weavers etc. Their loss of purchasing power meant that they bought rather less cloth than previously and at rather lower prices. At the same time, the value of the pound rose substantially in terms of foreign currencies. Consequently the demand for English goods, which was slumping already because of market saturation, slumped further still and exporters could not easily sell the little which they had bought. Mary Tudor's governments did not tamper with the national coinage, but did borrow heavily abroad. This action probably distorted the balance of money and goods at home. Moreover, this balance was upset in any case by calamitous harvests in 1555 and 1556. The political uncertainties of her reign, together with these monetary fluctuations, were obstacles to a revival of England's exports. The notable Elizabethan re-coinage of 1560 gave England 'a stable and honest currency'. The deflationary character of this re-coinage must have tended to create difficulties for English exporters. But the difficulties applied only for a few months beyond the actual period of re-coinage. During the forty years of her reign taken as a whole, exporters enjoyed the benefit of a 'stable and honest currency'; they enjoyed also the healthy stimulus of unobtrusive European inflation which was induced by warfare, by population growth and by the inflow of American bullion. For England's exporters this was, on the whole, the best of both worlds—stimulus without gross distortion.

'A stable and honest currency' was also the best monetary base for an independent national foreign policy, particularly if the government was careful to borrow only from its own citizens and to avoid dependence on loans from foreign bankers and governments. Queen Elizabeth's temperament, Sir Thomas Gresham's technical grasp and Sir William Cecil's comprehensive understanding combined to make the most of—in some cases to create—the monetary conditions that were conducive to foreign trade and to independence in foreign affairs. In this, as in every department of government, William Cecil made his decisions against the background of equal responsibility for all others'.[1]

[1] Gould, p. 222.

Index

(Monarchs, their consorts and children are under Christian names)

Aberdeen, 179, 208
Adrian VI, Pope, 82, 87
Aigues-Mortes, meeting at, 115
Albany, Alexander Stuart, Duke of (d 1485), 76
Albany, John Stuart, Duke of (d 1536), 76, 78, 86, 122
Albert, Archduke, Governor of Netherlands, 23, 169, 190, 232
Alençon and Anjou, Francis Valois, Duke of, 167, 168, 183, 184, 222
Aleppo, 253
Alexandria, 253
Allen, Cardinal William, 22, 202
Alps, 87
Alva, Fernando Alvarez de Toledo, Duke of, 26, 167, 180, 183, 190, 192, 193, 194, 195, 197, 232, 243, 247, 261
Amboise, Tumult of, 178
America, 31, 135, 153, 217, 249, 252 f.
Amicable Grant, 15, 89, 90
Amsterdam, 227
Ancrum Moor, Battle of, 134
Andrews, K. R., 14 n., 29 n.

Anglo-French treaty (1551), 146 f.
Anglo-Imperial defence treaty (1543), 127, 154
Angoulême, Charles, Duke of (d 1545, 3rd son of Francis I), 113
Angus, Archibald Douglas, 5th Earl of (d 1514), 65
Angus, Archibald Douglas, 6th Earl of (d 1557), 73, 94, 131 f.
Angus, Archibald Douglas, 8th Earl of (d 1588), 209
Anjou, Francis Valois, Duke of Alençon and, 167, 168, 183, 184, 222
Anjou, Henry Valois, Duke of (Henry III), 167, 182, 184, 185
Anjou, Margaret of, 18, 47
Annates, Act for conditional restraint of, 100, 107, 108
Anne of Beaujeu, Regent, 49, 61 f.
Anne Boleyn, 15, 21, 38, 93, 95, 99, 101, 110, 113, 162
Anne of Britanny (wife of Charles VIII), 61 f.
Anne of Cleves, 117
Anne of Denmark (wife of James VI and I), 210

Annulment of marriage, 14, 37, 38, 92 f., 103, 108, 113
Anti-Clericalism, 33, 77, 99, 100, 103
Antonio of Portugal, Don, 215
Antwerp, 15, 24, 56, 115, 117, 154, 175, 191, 200, 222, 223, 238, 239 f., 246, 248, 250, 251, 257, 258, 260 f.
Appeals, Act of, 108
Appellant Catholics, 169
Arable farming, 257
Aragon, 7, 57
Arbroath, 136
Archangel, 251
Ardres, 127
Argyll, Archibald Campbell, Earl of, 176
Armada, 4, 22, 26, 28, 66, 91, 158, 185, 207, 210, 212, 217 f., 229 f.
Arminius, 109 n.
Arran, James Hamilton, Duke of Chatelherault, 2nd Earl of (d 1575), 131, 136, 165, 176
Arran, James Hamilton, courtesy Earl of (d 1609), 165, 176
Arran, James Stuart, Earl of (d 1596), 210
Arras, Union of, 201
Arthur Tudor, Prince, 55, 63
Arundel, Henry Fitzalan, Earl of, 145
Asia, 30, 249, 251
Assertia Septem Sacramentorum, 82
Atlantic, 12, 20, 27, 63, 160
autarky, 255
Ayton, Truce of, 54, 66
Azores, 26, 215, 219, 220

Babington, Anthony, 204, 206

Bacon, Francis, 61, 232 n., 237
Bacon, Nicholas, 42
Bagenal, Henry, 212
Baltic sea, 19, 62, 160, 219, 241, 245 f., 247 f., 251, 256
Baltinglass, James Eustace, Viscount, 211
Barbarossa, 114
Barcelona, Treaty of, 98
Barnet, Battle of, 48
Baroque, 109
Barton, Elizabeth, 111
bastard feudalism, 43
Bayonne, 71
Beaton, Cardinal David, 115, 123, 125, 131 f.
Beaujeu, Anne of, Regent, 4, 9, 61 f.
Beaulieu, 116
Bergen op Zoom, 187
Bertie, Peregrine, Lord Willoughby, 22
Berwick, 65, 131, 134, 145, 177, 210
Berwick, Treaty of (1560), 177
Berwick, Treaty of (1586), 169, 210
Bible, 7, 16, 39, 138, 172
Biscay, Bay of, 230
Black, J. B., 169 n., 171 n., 203 n.
Blackfriars, 98
Blackwater (Essex), 146
Blackwater (Ulster), 156
Blois, Treaty of, 167, 183
bloody question, 205
Blount, Charles, Lord Mountjoy, 213
Boleyn, Anne, *see* Anne Boleyn
Boleyn, George, Viscount Rochford, 105
Boleyn, Mary, 95, 108
Bond of Association, 206

Index 269

Bordeaux, 19
borrowing, 260 f.
Boston, 18
Bosworth, Battle of, 49, 65
Bothwell, John Hepburn, Earl of, 179
Boulogne, 60, 61, 79, 87, 115, 128, 129, 130, 134, 135, 138, 139
Bourbon, Antony, Duke of Navarre, 181
Bourbon, Charles, Constable of France and Duke of, 86, 88
Bourbon, Henry, *see* Henry IV of France
Bourbon, Louis, Prince of Condé, 180, 181
Bourbourg, negotiations at, 228
Brabant, 190, 227
Brandon, Charles, *see* Suffolk, Duke of
brass, 257
Brazil, 20, 23
breach with Rome, 4, 21 f., 33, 91, 99, 109 f., 122, 125, 131, 135
Brest, 138, 185, 186, 232
brick-making, 256
Brill, 183, 187, 193, 223, 227
Bristol, 19 f., 28
Bristol Channel, 229, 230
Bristol, Treaty of, 243
Brittany, 50, 60 f., 72, 186, 232, 245
Bromley, J. S., 14 n.
Bruges, 85, 222
Bruges, Treaty of, 85, 86
Brussels, 53, 180, 190, 193, 222, 243
Buckingham, Edward Stafford, Duke of, 55, 67, 83
Bulls, Papal, 110, 112, 113, 115, 195, 203
bullion, 26, 29, 190, 214 f., 246, 265

Burgley, William Cecil, Lord:
home affairs, 40, 165, 166, 167, 177, 194, 195, 206, 207; economic, 225, 247, 252, 253, 257 f., 263, 265; France, 36, 167, 174, 181, 183; Ireland, 212 f.; Netherlands, 183, 192, 193, 221; Scotland, 165, 166, 176 f., 209, 210; Spain, 36, 197, 202, 218, 225, 233; also, 9, 27, 39, 42, 112, 266
Burgundian alliance, 47, 48, 188, 190
Burgundy, 8, 47 f. (see also Netherlands)
Burgundy, Charles the Bold, Duke of, 47, 48, 49 61 f.
Burgundy, County of, 151
Burgundy, Duchy of, 49, 89, 90, 127
Burgundy, Margaret of York, Duchess of, 47 f., 53, 54
Burgundy, Philip Duke of, *see* Philip, Duke of Burgundy
Butlers of Ormond, 50 f., 123, 124
Butler, Piers, 8th Earl of Ormond, 123, 124

Cabot John, 20, 63, 249, 256
Cabot Sebastian, 20, 63, 250, 251, 256
The Cacafuego, 215
Cadiz, 29, 216, 219
Calais, 28, 40, 41, 53, 55, 56, 60 f., 80, 81, 85, 87, 101, 114, 127, 129, 145, 148, 149, 155, 174, 175, 178, 181, 185, 230, 232, 238 f., 243
calamine, 257
Calshot, 116
Calvinism, 15, 160, 161
Cambrai, League of, 64

Cambrai, Treaty of, 98, 114
Campbell, Archibald, Earl of Argyll, 176
Campeggio, Cardinal, 79, 97, 98
Canary Isles, 23, 24, 216, 238
Canon Law, 55, 107
Caraffa, Cardinal, *see* Paul IV, Pope
Carberry Hill, Battle of, 179
Carew, Peter, 197
Carey, Henry, Lord Hunsdon, 194
Caribbean Sea, 13, 14, 24 f., 30, 31, 189, 215, 216
Carlisle, 225
Carlisle, Christopher, 31
Carthusians, 111
Casimir, John, 222
Castel Sant' Angelo, 96
Castile, 7, 57, 63 f., 73, 241
Cateau-Cambrésis, Treaty of, 36, 155, 173, 174, 181, 190
Cathay, 20
Catherine of Aragon, 14, 37, 55, 63 f., 73, 83 f., 90, 92 f., 101, 110, 117
Catherine Howard, 121, 125
Catherine de Medici (Regent of France), 101, 178, 181
Catholicism, 7, 12, 13, 36, 38, 149 f., 151, 161, 174, 179, 190, 194, 195, 202, 203, 204, 206, 208, 211, 227
Cecil, Robert, Earl of Salisbury, 170, 171, 208
Cecil, William, *see* Burghley, Lord
Challis, C. E., 263 n.
Chambord, Treaty of, 147
Chancellor, Richard, 251
Channel ports, 4, 26, 60, 181, 182, 185, 186, 187, 231

Chantries, Dissolution of, 139
La Charité, 168
Charles the Bold, Duke of Burgundy, 47, 48, 49, 61 f.
Charles VIII of France, 4, 53, 61 f.
Charles IX of France, 182
Charles V, Holy Roman Emperor etc., 5, 14, 23, 38, 63, 64, 67 f., 77 f., 84 f., 93 f., 112, 121 f., 127 f., 145 f., 150, 241, 250
Charles, Archduke of Styria (son of Emperor Ferdinand), 165, 177
Chatelherault, James Hamilton, 2nd Earl of Arran and Duke of (*d* 1575), 131, 136, 165, 176
Chaucer, Geoffrey, 6
Cherbourg, 60, 73
Chester, 28
China, 250, 251
Christendom, 4, 7, 15, 59, 89, 90, 105, 189, 191, 202
Church of England, 39, 109, 115, 161
Clarence, George, Duke of, 50
Claude, Princess of Valois (daughter of Louis XII), 63
Clement VII (Medici) Pope, 38, 79, 88, 93 f., 105, 110, 112, 113
Cleves, 115, 227
Cleves, Anne of, *see* Anne of Cleves
Cleves, John, Duke of, 117
cloth trade, 10, 14, 23, 24, 31, 53, 238 f., 245 f., 251, 263, 264
Clyde, 129, 138
coal-mining, 255, 256
Cockburn, John, of Ormiston, 138
Cognac, League of, 93, 95
Colet, Dean John, 78
Coligny, Admiral Gaspard de, 26, 180, 181, 182, 192

Index

colonisation, 5, 31, 216, 253
Como, Tolomeo Gallio, Cardinal of, 203
Concarneau, 61
Concordat, 105, 149
Condé, Louis Bourbon, Prince of, 180, 181
conscription, 15, 26
Constantinople, 253
Contarini, Cardinal Gasparo, 78
Convocation, 110
Conway, Agnes, 52 n.
copper, 239, 257
Cork, 52, 54
Cornwall, 15, 54
Corunna, 218, 219, 229
Counter-Reformation, 173
Courtenay, Edward, Earl of Devonshire (d 1556), 21, 152
Courtenay, Henry, Earl of Devonshire and Marquis of Exeter (d 1538), 116
Courtenay, William (d 1512), 56
Cranmer, Thomas, Archbishop of Canterbury, 21, 94, 100, 107, 109, 110, 111, 135, 143
Crépy, Treaty of, 129
Cromwell, Oliver, 174, 187 n., 215 n.
Cromwell, Thomas, Earl of Essex, 21, 23, 33 f., 39, 87, 88, 106, 107, 108, 111, 112, 114, 115, 117, 121, 122, 123, 174
Cruickshank, C. G., 224 n.
Crusades, 5, 6, 7, 69, 70, 79, 112, 113, 115, 173, 176, 194
Cumberland, 257
Curtis, E., 124 n., 155 n.
Czecho-Slovakia, 3, 8

Dacre, Lord Thomas, 86
Damascus, 253
Danzig, 246
Darcy, Lord Thomas, 69
Darien, 25, 215
Darnley, Henry Stuart, Lord, 179, 209
Dauphin Francis (d 1536; son of Francis I), 78, 81
Dauphin Francis (later Francis II), 138, 139, 173, 175, 178
Davis, C. S. L., 62 n.
Davison, William, 207
Deal, 53
debasement, 129, 241 256 257 f. 262 f.
Dee, John, 30, 251
Dendermonde, 222
Denmark, 247
Deposition, 110
Deptford, 67, 198, 215
Desmond, Gerald Fitzgerald, 15th Earl of (d 1583), 211
Desmond, James Fitzgerald, 14th Earl of (d 1558), 53
Deuteronomy, 94
Deventer, 22, 227
Devereux, Robert, see Essex, 2nd Earl of
Devereux, Walter, 1st Earl of, 212
Devonshire, Edward Courtenay, Earl of (d 1556), 21, 152
Devonshire, Henry Courtenay, Marquis of Exeter and Earl of (d 1538), 116
Dickens, A. G., 13 n., 39
Dieppe, 60, 154, 181, 185, 186
Discourse for a . . Passage to Cataia by H. Gilbert, 31

Dispensation, Papal, 55, 57, 94 f., 97, 100
Dissolution of Monasteries, 11, 138, 153, 260
Dissolution of Chantries, 139
Doesburg, 227
Donaldson, Gordon, 16 n., 122 n., 176 n.
Dorking, 257
Dorset, Thomas Grey, Marquis of, 71
Douai, 42, 161, 202
Douglas, Archibald, 5th Earl of Angus (*d* 1514), 65
Douglas, Archibald, 6th Earl of Angus (*d* 1557), L 73, 94, 131 f.
Douglas, Archibald, 8th Earl of Angus (*d* 1588), 209
Douglas, James, 4th Earl of Morton, Regent (*d* 1581), 176, 179, 180, 195, 208, 209
Dover, 116, 183, 192, 193, 228
Dover, Straits of, 60, 175
Drake, Francis, 13, 25, 26 f., 159, 193, 198, 214 f., 229, 252, 253
draperies, 243
Dublin, 50, 52, 196, 197, 211, 213
Dudley, Guildford, 40, 147
Dudley, Henry, 154
Dudley, John, Viscount Lisle, Earl of Warwick, *see* Northumberland, Duke of
Dudley, Robert, *see* Leicester, Earl of
duel, law of, 42
Dumbarton, 209
Dumfries, 138
Dungannon, Hugh O'Neill, Earl of Tyrone and Baron of, *see* Tyrone, Earl of

Dutch, *see* Netherlands
dynastic interest:
Henry VII, 6, 47 f., 55 f.;
Henry VIII, 5, 6, 7, 67 f., 82 f., 92 f., 102 f., 125 f.; Northumberland, 143 f., 147; Mary, 150 f.; Elizabeth, 162 f.

East Anglia, 14, 138, 243
East India Company, 8, 31, 253
Easterlings, 10, 11
Eastland Company, 247, 251
economic policy, 5, 10 f., 18 f., 237 f.
Edict of Union, 185
Edinburgh, 132, 134, 176, 180, 195, 209
Edinburgh, Treaty of, 178, 180
Edward I, 64
Edward III, 33
Edward IV, 18, 19, 48, 50, 56, 65, 245
Edward VI, 42, 92, 121, 125, 133, 134, 135, 136, 138, 145 f.
Effingham, Admiral Lord Charles Howard of, 28, 29, 229 f.
Egmont, Count, 190
Elbing, 247
Eleanor of the Netherlands (sister of Charles V), 57, 90
Elizabeth I:
economic, 24, 243, 246, 247, 252 f., 257 f., 261, 263, 265;
France, 4, 5, 21, 35, 160, 167 f., 173 f., 180 f., 182 f., 191, 199, 201, 204, 208, 231, 232; Ireland, 194, 196 f., 211 f.; marriage and succession, 21, 36, 40, 109, 122, 133, 134, 143, 147, 151 f., 155, 160, 162 f., 168 f., 173, 174, 178,

Index

179, 182; Mary Queen of Scots, 163 f., 173, 178, 179, 195, 201 f., 206, 207, 210; Netherlands, 4, 14, 15, 22, 36, 41, 182 f., 184 f., 190 f., 197, 199, 200 f., 214 f., 221 f., 225 f., 247; Parliament, 35, 36, 152 f., 163, 165, 169, 174, 191, 195, 196, 206, 207, 224, 231, 261; religious affairs, 36, 39, 161, 203, 207; Rome, 4, 5, 160, 189, 193, 195, 203, 208; Scotland, 4, 5, 35, 86, 160, 165, 175, 176 f., 190, 194 f., 201, 208 f., 230; Spain, 4, 5, 22, 24, 26, 28, 41, 158, 159, 160, 164, 167, 171, 173, 180, 182, 184, 185, 188 f., 190 f., 197, 198, 199, 202, 214 f.; also, 9, 27, 30, 40, 91, 112, 158, 190
Elizabeth of Valois (wife of Philip II), 146, 173, 175
Elton, G. R., 55, 108 n.
Emden, 247
Empire, the idea of, 4, 5, 59, 102 f., 189, 191
English Channel, 24, 26, 28, 62 f., 67, 71, 85, 129, 138, 139, 144, 146, 158, 188, 192, 193, 217, 221, 225, 229 f.
The 'Enterprise', 194, 209
Erasmus, Desiderius, 37, 38, 71 n., 78, 109
Erastianism, 21
Erskine, John, Earl of Mar, Regent (d 1572), 194, 195
Essex, 129, 229
Essex, Earl of, *see* Cromwell, Thomas
Essex, Robert Devereux, 2nd Earl of, 41, 170, 171, 213, 218, 219 f., 232

Essex, Walter Devereux, 1st Earl of, 212
Etaples, Treaty of, 53, 62, 73
Eustace, James Viscount Baltinglass, 211
Evelyn, George, 257
exchequer, 100
excommunication, 189, 195, 203
Exeter, Henry Courtenay, Earl of Devonshire and Marquis of (d 1538), 116
explanatio, 203

Falmouth, 219, 232
Farnese, Alexander, *see* Parma, Duke of
Fécamp, 60
Ferdinand of Aragon, 55, 63 f., 67 f., 232, 239
Ferdinand I, Holy Roman Emperor, 165
Feria, Gomez Suarez, Duke of (ambassador), 164, 174, 189
Fidei defensor, 82
Field of the Cloth of Gold, 80
Firth of Forth, 138, 175, 177
Fish, Simon, 21
Fisher, F. J., 240 n.
Fisher, John, Bishop of Rochester, 82, 108, 110, 111, 112, 113
fish-days, 258
fishing, 256
Fitzalan, Henry, Earl of Arundel, 145
Fitzgerald, Gerald, 8th Earl of Kildare (d 1513), 50 f.
Fitzgerald, Gerald, 9th Earl of Kildare (d 1534), 123
Fitzgerald, Gerald, 15th Earl of Desmond (d 1583), 211

Fitzgerald, James, 14th Earl of Desmond (*d* 1558), 53
Fitzgerald, James Fitzmaurice (*d* 1579), 196, 197, 211
Fitzgerald, 'Silken Thomas', 10th Earl of Kildare (*d* 1537), 123, 124
Fitzroy, Henry, Duke of Richmond, 90, 92, 181
Flanders, 61, 114, 158, 228, 229, 243
Flemish, 10, 14, 18, 200
Flemish shilling, 241
Flodden, Battle of, 65, 74, 94, 122
Florence, 249
Flushing, 14, 22, 29, 183, 187, 193, 223, 227, 228
The Foresight, 27
Fotheringay, 207
Fox, Edward, Bishop of Hereford, 115
Fox, Richard, Bishop of Winchester, 69, 79
France:
    Huguenot Wars, 4, 5, 15, 26, 40, 41, 144, 160, 167, 168, 177, 178, 180 f., 185, 192, 243; and Henry VII, 4, 47, 49, 50, 53, 59 f.; and Henry VIII, 4, 6, 15, 33 f., 38, 40, 71 f., 79, 84, 86 f., 93, 101, 113 f., 120 f., 126 f., 263; and Somerset, 4, 128, 129, 136 f., 147; and Northumberland, 133, 144 f.; and Mary, 42, 153 f.; and Elizabeth, 4, 21, 35, 160, 167, 168, 173 f., 176 f., 180 f., 182 f., 191, 196, 199, 201, 204, 208, 231 f.; economic relations, 18, 23, 238 f., 249, 255, 258, 263
Franche Comté, *see* Burgundy, County of

Francis I of France, 4, 75 f., 96, 98, 101, 112, 113 f., 122
Francis II of France, 138, 139, 173, 175, 178
Francis of Valois, Dauphin (*d* 1536), 78, 81
Francis of Valois, Duke of Alençon and Anjou, 167, 168, 183, 184, 222
Frith, John, 16
Frobisher, Martin, 30, 253
Fuenterrabia, 71

Gaelic traditions, 16, 51, 124, 155 f., 196, 212
Gallicanism, 149
Gaping Gulf by John Stubbe, 21, 168
Gardiner, Stephen, Bishop of Winchester, 42, 97, 111, 117, 121, 143, 151
Gascon wine, 62, 256
Gattinara, Mercurino Arborio de, 85
Gaunt, John of, 169, 249 n.
General Councils, 109, 113
Gembloux, Battle of, 201
Genoa, 87, 192, 261
Germany, 39, 102, 114, 115, 239, 241, 245, 248, 257, 263
Ghent, 214, 222, 238, 243
Ghent, Pacification of, 200
Gibraltar, 215, 220, 230
Gilbert, Humphrey, 25, 30, 183, 193, 197, 253
Giovio, Paolo, 94
Glasgow, 209
glass, 256
Glastonbury, 116
Gold Coast, 24

Index

The Golden Hind, 215, 253
Gonson, Benjamin, 24, 27
Gonson, Catherine, 24
Gordon, George, 4th Earl of Huntly (d 1562), 179
Gordon, George, 6th Earl of Huntly (d 1632), 209, 210
Gould, J. R., 233 n., 266 n.
Gourdon, Girault de Mauleon, Governor of Calais, Lord of, 185
Granvelle, Cardinal, Lord of, 193, 197, 243
Grave, 227
Gravelines, 81
Gravelines, Battle of, 230
Gray, Patrick, Master of, 210
Greater Britain, 34, 62, 64, 120, 121 f., 125 f., 131 f., 136 f., 139
Greenwich, 62
Greenwich, Treaty of, 133, 136, 146
Gregory XIII, Pope, 203, 209
Grenville, Richard, 25, 30, 216
Gresham, Thomas, 261, 265
Grey, Lady Catherine, 164
Grey, Henry, Duke of Suffolk, 147
Grey, Lady Jane, 40, 145, 147, 164
Grey, Leonard, Deputy-Lieutenant of Ireland, 124
Grey, Thomas, Marquis of Dorset, 71
Grindal, Edmund, Archbishop of Canterbury, 174
Guienne, 71, 87, 127
Guinea, 251
Guines, 155
Guise, Francis Duke of, 138, 155, 175, 176 f., 180 f.
Guise, Henry, Duke of, 168, 182, 185, 190, 195, 196, 198, 201, 202, 204, 208 f., 231

T

Guise, Mary of (Regent of Scotland), 115, 123, 132 f., 136, 138, 175, 176, 178
gun-powder, 18, 218, 224, 230, 257

Hague, The, 227
Hakluyt, Richard, 30, 31
Hale, J. R., 7 n., 42 n., 71 n.
Hall, Edward, 10
Hamburg, 115, 192, 193, 247
Hamilton, James, Duke of Chatelherault and 2nd Earl of Arran (d 1575), 131, 136, 165, 176
Hamilton, James, courtesy Earl of Arran (d 1609), 165, 176
Hampshire, 207
Hanse, 10, 11, 18 f., 62, 240, 242, 245 f., 256
Hapsburgs, 5, 7, 10, 14, 21, 29 f., 35 f., 49 f., 63 f., 77 f., 84 f., 90 f., 112, 121 f., 129, 145 f., 150, 154, 160, 164, 165, 169, 173, 175 f., 184 f., 188, 190, 195, 199 f., 209 f., 214, 217, 221, 222, 230, 232, 241, 242, 250, 252
Harfleur, 60
harvests, 15, 265
Havre, Le, 60, 129, 181, 185
Hawkins, John, 5, 13, 24 f., 189, 190, 195, 218, 219, 224, 252, 253, 259
Hawkins, "Old William" (d 1554), 20, 23, 24, 252
Hawkins, William (d 1589), 24, 25, 26, 28, 192
Henry II of England, 50
Henry V of England, 5, 33, 86
Henry VI of England, 47
Henry VII of England:
Burgundy/Netherlands, 47 f.,

53 f., 56 f., 60, 63, 260; dynastic, 6, 47 f., 55 f.; economic, 5, 10, 19 f., 237 f., 245 f., 256, 258, 260; France, 4, 47, 49, 50, 53, 59 f., 232; Ireland, 50 f.; Scotland, 50, 53 f., 59 f., 62, 64 f.; Spain, 55 f., 61, 63 f., 232; also 37, 63
Henry VIII of England: ecclesiastical, 21, 33, 39, 75, 82 f., 106 f., 111, 124, 127, 130; economic, 241, 250, 256, 262; France, 4, 6, 15, 33 f., 38, 40, 67 f., 71 f., 74, 84, 86 f., 93, 101, 113 f., 120 f., 126 f., 263; Ireland, 123, 124; marriage and succession, 14, 38, 55 f., 64, 67 f., 83 f., 87, 92 f., 110, 117, 121, 125, 126, 133, 134, 143, 162; Netherlands, 67, 69 f., 115, 127; Parliament, 33 f., 71, 77, 87, 80, 99, 100, 102 f., 106 f.; Scotland, 4, 16, 33 f., 67, 74 f., 77 f., 86, 113 f., 120 f., 125 f., 129 f., 263; Spain, 4, 5, 14, 40, 55 f., 67, 77 f., 84 f., 93 f., 112 f., 127 f.; also 5, 37, 42, 43, 136
Henry II of France, 96, 101, 136, 138, 139, 144, 145 f., 154 f., 173, 175
Henry III of France, 167, 182, 184, 185
Henry IV of France, 149, 183, 185, 186, 187, 231, 232
The Henry Grace à Dieu, 67
The Henry Imperial, 102
Henry, W., 219 n.
Hepburn, John, Earl of Bothwell, 179
Herbert (of Raglan), Charles Somerset, Lord, 72

de Herrera, Antonio, 224
Hertford, Edward Seymour, 1st Earl of, *see* Somerset, Duke of
Hertford, Edward Seymour, 2nd Earl of, 164
Hess, A. C., 199 n.
Holland, Province of, 190, 200, 222, 223, 225, 227
Holy Alliance (1496), 54
Holy League (1511), 70
Holyrood, 66
Hooker, Richard, 39, 109
Horn, Philip of Montmorency, Count of, 190
Howard, Catherine, 121, 125
Howard of Effingham, Admiral Lord Charles (d 1624), 28, 29, 229 f.
Howard, Edmund (father of Queen Catherine), 12
Howard, Admiral Sir Edward (d 1513), 67, 71
Howard, Henry, courtesy Earl of Surrey (d 1547), 135
Howard, Thomas, Earl of Surrey and 2nd Duke of Norfolk (d 1524), 65, 70, 72, 73
Howard, Thomas, Earl of Surrey and 3rd Duke of Norfolk (d 1554), 38, 86, 90, 111 f., 121, 123, 125, 128, 130, 134
Howard, Thomas, Earl of Surrey and 4th Duke of Norfolk (d 1572), 40, 177, 194, 195
Howard, Admiral Thomas, Earl of Suffolk (d 1626), 219
Huguenots, 4, 5, 15, 26 40, 41, 144, 160, 167, 168, 177, 178, 180 f., 185, 192, 243
Hull, 248

Index

humanism, 37, 38, 39, 69, 71, 78 f., 109, 115
Hunsdon, Henry Carey, Lord, 194
Huntly, George Gordon, 4th Earl of (d 1562), 179
Huntly, George Gordon, 6th Earl of (d 1632), 209, 210
Hurst castle, 116
Hurstfield, J., 170 n., 207 n.

Iceland, 20
Ijssel river, 22, 226, 227
Imperial ambassadors, 114, 115, 146, 151 f.
Imperial candidate, 80, 91
Index, 38, 109
India, 31, 216, 253
Indian ocean, 20, 160
inflation, 241, 261 f.
Inquisition, 13, 15
Intercursus Magnus, 239, 240
Intercursus Malus, 57, 240
Interdict, 111
Inverness, 208
Ireland, 15, 16, 41, 50 f., 120, 123 f., 127, 155, 190, 196 f., 201, 211 f., 220, 229
Isabella of Castile, 55, 56, 63
Isabella of Portugal, 90, 91
Isabella, Infanta of Spain, 23, 169, 170
Italy, 4, 61, 62, 64, 67, 69, 73, 75, 76, 86, 88, 93 f., 114, 138, 146, 158, 192, 200, 241, 243, 249, 263

James III of Scotland, 65, 76
James IV of Scotland, 53, 54, 65, 66, 67, 73, 94, 122
James V of Scotland, 73, 75, 113, 115, 122, 125, 130, 133 n.

James VI of Scotland and I of England, 5, 36, 164, 167, 168 f., 179, 180, 206, 208, 209 f., 261
Jane Grey, Lady, 40, 145, 147, 164
Jane Seymour, 83, 92, 110, 121
Jarnac, Battle of, 26
Jay, John, 20
Jesuits, 22, 169, 202, 204, 205, 208
Jewel, John, Bishop of Salisbury, 39
Joanna of Castile (wife of Duke Philip of Burgundy), 56, 63 f.
John of Austria, Don, 184, 200, 201, 202, 214
John, Duke of Cleves, 117
John of Gaunt, 169, 249 n.
Joinville, Treaty of, 202
Jordan, W. K., 109 n.
Julius II (Rovere), Pope, 55, 70
Justices of the Peace, 83, 106
Justin of Nassau, 229

Kent, 129, 152, 229, 232, 243
Kildare, Gerald Fitzgerald, 8th Earl of (d 1513), 50 f.
Kildare, Gerald Fitzgerald, 9th Earl of (d 1534), 123
Kildare, 'Silken Thomas' Fitzgerald, 10th Earl of (d 1537), 123, 124
Kilkenny, 52
King's County, 157
King's Lynn, 19
Kinsale, 213, 232
Knight, William, Bishop of Bath and Wells, 97
Knollys, Francis, 167
Knollys, Lettice, 167
Knox, John, 177

La Charité, 168

Lancashire, 207
Lancaster, James, 29, 31, 253
Lancastrians, 18, 47, 48, 52, 54, 124, 131, 245
Landriano, Battle of, 98
Languedoc, 89
La Rochelle, 26, 183, 192
Laslett, Peter, 109 n.
Lautrec, Odet de Foix, Viscount, 96
Lee, Rowland, Bishop of Lichfield, 123
legate a latere, 37, 79, 112
Le Havre, 60, 129, 18, 185
Leicester, Robert Dudley, Earl of, 22, 40, 41, 165, 166, 167, 169, 179, 205, 212, 224, 226 f., 231
Leinster, 124
Leith, 35, 134, 176 f.
Leix, 157
Lennox, Esmé Stuart, Earl and Duke of, 208, 209
Lennox, Matthew Stuart, 4th Earl of, 132, 179, 194
Leo X (Medici), Pope, 77, 79, 80, 82
Lepanto, Battle of, 7
Lethington, William Maitland of, 176, 180
Levant Company, 253
Leviticus, 94, 95
Leyden, 197
Lima, 214
Lincolnshire, 112
Lisbon, 211, 216, 217, 218, 219
Lisle, John Dudley, Earl of Warwick, and Viscount, *see* Northumberland, Duke of
Litany, 159
Lockyer, R., 242 n.
Lok, Michael, 253

London, 10, 11, 12, 14, 15, 18, 19, 24, 28, 29, 31, 41, 60, 152, 207, 224, 231, 232, 238, 240, 242, 248, 250, 251
London Company, 30
London, Treaty of (1516), 78
London, Treaty of (1518), 79, 80, 84, 91
Lords of the Congregation, 176
Louis XI of France, 4, 47, 48, 49
Louis XII of France, 38, 63 f., 70 f., 75
Louise, Princess (daughter of Francis I), 78
Lübeck, 115
Ludlow, Edmund, 187 n.
Luther, Martin, 104, 115, 117
Lutheranism, 82
Lutheran Princess, 39, 90, 104, 114, 115, 129, 147

Maas river, 227
Macaulay, Lord Thomas, 225
Madeira, 20
Madrid, 89
Magellan, Straits of, 30
Magnus Intercursus, 239, 240
Maitland, John, 210
Maitland, William of Lethington, 176, 180
Maldon, 146
Malus Intercursus, 57, 240
Mao Tse-tung, Chairman, 7
Mar and Moray, James Stuart, (illegitimate son of James V), Regent, Earl of (d 1570), 176, 179, 180, 194
Mar, John Erskine, Regent, Earl of (d 1572), 194, 195
Marck, William de la, 192, 193

Margaret of Anjou, 18, 47
Margaret Tudor (daughter of Henry VII), 65, 66, 73, 76, 94, 122, 131
Margaret of Valois (wife of Henry IV), 183
Margaret of York, Duchess of Burgundy, 47, 53, 54
Margate, 230
Marians of Scotland, 180, 194, 195
Marie de Medici (wife of Henry IV), 14 n.
Marignano, Battle of, 76
Marsiglio of Padua, 21
Mary of Guise (Regent of Scotland), 115, 123, 132 f., 136, 138, 175, 176, 178
The Mary Rose, 67
Mary, Queen of Scots, 5, 26, 36, 40, 66, 109, 130 f., 136, 138, 139, 146, 151, 163 f., 168, 169, 173, 175, 176 f., 188, 193, 194, 195, 196, 198, 200, 201, 202, 204, 206, 210
Mary Tudor (daughter of Henry VII), 64, 72, 73, 75, 76, 94, 134, 164
Mary I (Mary Tudor, daughter of Henry VIII): economic, 24, 242, 246, 250, 252, 258, 260, 265; France, 153 f.; Ireland, 155 f., Netherlands, 151; Parliament, 35, 36, 150, 154 f.; marriage and succession, 21, 24, 35, 36, 40, 78, 81, 83 f., 85, 86, 89, 90, 91, 92, 96, 113, 121, 122, 133, 143, 150 f.; Rome, 111, 145 f., 149 f., 159; Spain, 144, 149 f.
Maryborough, 157
masts, 245

Matilda, Queen of England, 83
Matthias, Archduke, Governor of Netherlands (later H.R.E.), 201
Mattingly, Garrett, 14 n., 22 n., 158 n., 190 n., 229 n.
Maurice of Nassau, 231, 232
Maurice of Saxony, 154
Maximilian, Archduke and H.R.E., 10, 49, 50, 54, 56, 63 f., 67 f., 232
May Day, 1517, 11, 12
Lord Mayor of London, 11, 12, 250
Medina del Camp, Treaty of, 55, 63, 249, 252
Medina Sidonia, Alfonso de Gusman, Duke of, 185, 217
Mediterranean sea, 12, 62, 114, 117, 160, 216, 249, 253, 256, 258
Medway, 229
Melancthon, Philip, 115
Mendoza, Bernardino de (ambassador), 201, 204, 253
mercenaries, 154, 222
Merchant Adventurers, 10, 19, 53, 56, 238 f., 247
Merchants of the Staple, 19, 114, 238, 243, 244
Merchant of Venice, 12, 32
Merriman, M. H., 138 n., 176 n.
Merriman, R. B., 33 n., 87 n.
metallurgy, 18, 255, 256, 257
Metz, 147
Midway Island, Battle of, 230 n.
Milan, 35, 76, 77, 85, 96, 117
Mile End, 224
militia, 112, 116, 224, 229, 257
'Mineral and Battery Works', 257
'Mines Royal', 257
Mohacz, Battle of, 95
Monasteries, Dissolution of, 114, 138, 153, 260

monastic land sales, 260
Monmouth Duke of, 223
Montague, Henry Pole, Lord, 116
Montreuil, 128
Moor House, Treaty of, 93
moors, 69
Moray, James Stuart (illegitimate son of James IV), Earl of, (d 1544), 132
Moray. James Stuart (illegitimate son of James V), Regent, Earl of Mar and (d 1570), 176, 179, 180, 194
More, Thomas, 30, 38, 39, 78, 82, 103, 107, 111, 250
Morgan, Thomas (R.C. conspirator), 206
Morgan, Thomas ('the warrior'), 22, 193, 221
Morlaix, 61
Morocco, 24, 251
Morton, James Douglas, Regent, 4th Earl of (d 1581), 176, 179, 180, 195, 208, 209
Moscow, 251
Moslems, 7
Mountjoy, Charles Blount, Lord, 213
Munster, 196, 197, 211, 213
Muscovy Company, 30, 247, 251, 252, 259
Myddelton, Thomas, 29

Nancy, Battle of, 49
Naples, 78, 96, 153, 158
Napoleon I, 4
Napoleon III, 4
Narva, 247
naval re-armament, 5, 18, 26 f., 62, 67, 115, 116, 224

Navarre, 71, 73, 78
Navarre, Antony Bourbon, Duke of, 181
Navarre, Henry of (see Henry IV of France)
Navigation Acts, 62, 256, 258
Navy, 5, 18, 26 f., 62, 67, 72, 115, 116, 138, 145, 223, 229 f., 258
Navy Board, 26 f.
Neale, J. E., 163 n., 169 n., 174 n., 175 n., 177 n., 189 n., 191 n., 203 n., 227 n.
Nef, J.U., 256
Netherlands:
  8, 18, 138, 144, 146, 158; Dutch revolt, 4, 36, 160, 190 f., 200 f., 215, 243; and Henry VII, 47 f., 53 f., 56 f., 60, 63, 260; and Henry VIII, 67, 69 f., 115, 127; and Northumberland, 243; and Mary, 150, 151, 154; and Elizabeth, 4, 14, 15, 22, 36, 41, 182 f., 184 f., 190 f., 197, 199, 200 f., 214 f., 221 f., 225 f., 247; economic relations, 10, 13 f., 18, 19, 24, 53, 63, 84, 96, 113, 114, 214 f., 238 f., 243, 247, 263
Neville, Charles, 6th Earl of Westmorland, 194
Newcastle, 134, 248
Newfound Lands, 20, 31, 249, 256
Nice, Truce of, 114
Nieuport, Siege of, 232
Nombre de Dios, 25, 193, 198
Norfolk, 15
Norfolk, Thomas Howard, 2nd Duke of (d 1524), 65, 70, 72, 73
Norfolk, Thomas Howard, 3rd Duke of (d 1554), 38, 86, 90, 111 f., 121, 123, 125, 128, 130, 134

Index

Norfolk, Thomas Howard, 4th Duke of (*d* 1572), 40, 177, 194, 195
Normandy, 127
Norris, John, 22, 201, 219, 221, 222, 223, 232
North-East passage, 30, 251, 252
Northern Earls, 15, 180, 194
Northumberland, John Dudley, Viscount Lisle, Earl of Warwick and Duke of:
  economic, 242, 246, 251, 260, 263, 264; France, 4, 128, 129, 139, 144 f.; Ireland, 157; Netherlands, 243; religion, 147; Scotland, 4, 134, 139; Spain, 4, 145 f., 147; succession, 143 f., 147; also, 30, 39, 43, 135, 139
Northumberland, Thomas Percy, 7th Earl of, 194
North-West passage, 20, 30, 31, 249, 250, 253
Norwich, 14
Noyon, Treaty of, 77, 78
Nymegen, Treaty of, 193

Obedience of a Christian man, 21, 105
Observant Franciscans, 111
Offaly, 155
O'Neill, Hugh, Baron of Dungannon, *see* Tyrone, Earl of
O'Neill, Shane, Earl of Tyrone (*d* 1567), 196
O'Neill, Turloch, Lord of Tyrone (*d* 1595), 212
Orange, William of (the Silent), 190, 193, 199, 203, 222
Orange, William of (William III), 223
Ormond, Butlers of, 50 f., 123, 124

Ormond, Black James (illegitimate son of 5th Earl of Ormond), 52
Ormond, Piers, Butler, 8th Earl of, 123, 124
Ostend, 187, 222, 232
Outhwaite, R. B., 261 n.
Overijssel, 227
Oxenham, John, 25, 26, 214, 215

Pace, Richard, 77, 80
Pacific ocean, 30, 160, 214, 250
Pacification of Ghent, 200
Paget, William, 40, 42, 150, 152
Pale of Calais, 72
Pale, The Irish, 52, 123, 124, 157, 211
Panama, 25, 214, 215
Papal candidature, 75, 82
Papacy, *see* Rome
Paris, 5, 87, 89, 127, 204, 183, 193, 195 f., 204, 208, 209, 212
Parker, Matthew, Archbishop of Canterbury, 109
Parliament:
  general, 33 f.; and Henry VIII, 33 f., 71, 77, 87, 88, 99, 100, 102, 103, 106 f.; and Mary, 35, 36, 150 f., 154; and Elizabeth, 35, 36, 152, 163 f., 165, 169, 174, 191, 195, 196, 206, 207, 224, 231, 261
Parma, Alexander Farnese, Duke of, 22, 184, 199, 201, 215, 216, 222, 223, 224, 225, 227, 228, 229, 231, 243
Parsons, Robert, 23
Paul III (Farnese), Pope, 110, 112, 114, 115
Paul IV (Caraffa), Pope, 153, 154
Paulet, Amyas, 207
Pavia, Battle of, 88
Peckham, Gorge, 31

Pendennis castle, 116
Percy, Thomas, 7th Earl of Northumberland, 194
Perpetual edict, 200
Persia, 251
personal interest, 8 f.
Peter Pomegranate, The, 67
Philip, Duke of Burgundy, 10, 49, 56, 57, 63 f., 232, 239, 240, 260
Philip II:
    and England, 7, 150 f., 160, 164, 169, 175, 188, 190 f., 195, 197, 199, 201, 204, 209, 217, 222 f.; and France, 154, 173 f., 185, 188 f., 197 f., 201, 204, 209, 232; and Ireland, 211 f., 232; and Mary Queen of Scots, 175, 195, 196; and Netherlands, 15, 190 f., 197, 199, 221 f.; and Scotland, 175, 209, 210, 230; also, 5, 21, 22, 24, 29, 35, 36, 91, 232, 242, 252
Philip III, 213, 232
Philipstown, 157
Picardy, 49, 60
Picquigny, Treaty of, 48
Piedmont, 8
Pilgrimage of Grace, 15, 112
Pinkie, Battle of, 39, 136
Pisa, 70, 249
pitch, 246
Pius V, Pope, 193, 195, 196, 203
plantations, 157
Plessis le Tour, Treaty of, 184
Plymouth, 20, 23 f., 28, 192, 215, 218, 225, 229, 230, 231, 252
Poland, 8
Polar seas, 30, 250
Pole, Edmund de la, Earl of Suffolk (*d* 1513), 55, 56, 68, 72, 240

Pole, Henry, Lord Montague, 116
Pole, Margaret Countess of Salisbury (*d* 1541), 116
Pole, Cardinal Reginald (*d* 1558), 39, 112, 113, 116, 150, 151, 152, 154
Pole, Richard de la (*d* 1525), 88
Pole, William de la, 56
'politique' policies, 40, 112, 149, 174, 182, 183, 191, 199, 201
Pollard, A. F., 37, 40 n., 74, 98 n., 99 n., 114, 120, 126
Pollard, A. W., 6 n.
poll tax, 242
Poole, 231
population, 10
Portsmouth, 62, 129, 231
Portugal, 12, 23, 29, 31, 91, 215, 216, 222, 239, 249 f., 252, 253, 263
Poynings, Edward, 53 f., 65
Power, E., 14 n.
Praemunire, Statute of, 100, 105
prayer book (1552), 147
Prescott, H. F. M., 144 n., 146 n., 147 n., 151 n.
Price-Zimmermann, T. C., 94 n.
privateering, 14, 26, 28 f., 252
prize-money, 14
Protestantism, 7, 12, 13, 14, 16, 20 f., 39, 41, 42, 145, 147, 164, 174
Provence, 87, 89
Provisors, Statute of, 100
Pyrenees, 87, 192

de la Quadra, Alvaro (ambassador), 189
Queen's County, 157
Queen's Safety, Act for the, 169

Index

Rabb, T. K., 32 n.
Radcliffe, Thomas Earl of Sussex, 4, 182
Rait, R. S., 132 n.
Raleigh, Walter, 30, 31, 197, 211, 253
Rastell, John, 30, 250
Raymond, George, 31
Read, Conyers, 9, 165, 166 n., 167 n., 168 n., 178, 189 n., 194 n., 197 n., 221 n., 258 n., 263 n.
Reading, 116
Re-armament, 224 f., 257, 260, 261
Regency Councillors, 126, 139, 145, 146
The Regent, 62, 256
regulated companies, 238
Renard, Simon (ambassador), 151 f.
Renée, Princess of Valois (daughter of Louis XII), 38, 96
Reneger, Robert, 251
reprisal, letters of, 29, 253
de Requesens, Luis, Governor of the Netherlands, 197, 199, 200, 243
The Revenge, 27, 219
Rhine river, 4, 62
Rhinelands, 138, 144, 146, 154, 239, 243
Richard III, 19, 49, 67
Richard, Duke of York (d 1483), 50
Richelieu, Armand-Jean du Plessis, Cardinal, 71
Richmond, Henry Fitzroy, Duke of, 90, 92, 181
Richmond, Treaty of, 181
Ridolfi, Roberto, 195
Riga, 246
right of discovery, 250, 253
right of effective occupation, 189, 250, 253
Rizzio, David, 179
Roanoke Island, 216
Robsart, Amy, 40, 165
Rochelle, La, 26, 183, 192
Rochford, George Boleyn, Viscount, 105
role, 7, 67, 122 f., 125 f., 135 f., 139, 143 f., 148, 158 f., 162
Rome, 4, 5, 12, 13, 21, 38, 39, 55, 70, 71, 77, 79, 80, 82, 88, 93 f., 96 f., 103 f., 108, 110, 112 f., 149 f., 153 f., 193, 195, 196, 203, 204, 208 f., 222
Roses, Wars of, 16, 47, 135
Rotterdam, 227
Rouen, 186, 232
Rowse, A. L., 109 n., 205 n., 257 n.
Russia, 247, 251
Ruthal, Thomas, Bishop of Durham, 69
Ruthven raid, 209, 210

Sagres, 216, 217
St Albans, Battle of, 18
St Andrews, 134, 136
St Asaph, 103
St Bartholomew's eve, 183, 196, 197
St Germain, Treaty of, 181
St Leger, Anthony, 124
St Malo, 185, 186, 232
St Mawes, 116
St Thomas of Canterbury, 116
Salisbury, Margaret Pole, Countess of, 116
Salisbury, Robert Cecil, Earl of, 170, 171, 208
salt-mining, 23, 237, 255

salt-petre, 224, 257
Sandwich, 84
The San Felipe, 29, 218
San Juan de Uloa, 24, 26, 189, 190
San Sebastian, 219
Sant' Angelo, Castel, 96
Santa Cruz, Alvaro de Bazan, Marquis of, 217, 221, 224
Santander, 217, 219
Sauchieburn, Battle of, 65
Saunders, Nicholas, 211
Savage Thomas, 54
Saxony, 115, 116, 117, 154
Scales, Lord, 61
Scarborough, 154
Scarisbrick, J. J., 21 n., 37, 70 n., 77 n., 256, 82 n., 85 n., 88 n., 95 n., 120, 250 n.
Scilly Isles, 219, 232
Scotland:
general, 15, 144, 176, 178 f., 194, 195, 208, 209; and Henry VII, 50, 53, 54, 59 f., 62, 64 f.; and Henry VIII, 4, 16, 33 f., 67, 74 f., 77 f., 86, 113 f., 120 f., 125 f., 129 f., 263; and Somerset, 4, 7, 16, 39, 40, 134, 136 f.; and Northumberland, 139; and Elizabeth, 4, 5, 35, 86, 160, 165, 175 f., 190, 194 f., 201, 208 f., 230
sea beggars, 14, 183, 192, 193, 243
Seine river, 232
'Seven Cities', 20
Seville, 19, 29, 30, 238
Seymour, Edward, 1st Earl of Hertford, *see* Somerset, Duke of
Seymour, Edward, 2nd Earl of Hertford, 164
Seymour, Jane, 83, 92, 110, 121
Shakespeare, William, 12, 32, 231

sheep-breeding, 242
ship-building, 18, 26 f., 62, 67, 91, 216, 224
short-cloths, 15, 240, 242, 248
Shrewsbury, George Talbot, Earl of, 72
Sidney, Philip, 168
silk, 237
de Silva, Guzman (ambassador), 189
silver, 239
silver blockade, 26, 190, 193, 198, 214 f.
Simnel, Lambert, 50
Six Articles, 121
Sixtus V, Pope, 222
Skeffington, William, 124
Skiddaw, 225
Skye, Island of, 179
slave trade, 24
Sluys, 227, 228
small-pox, 166
Smerwick, 211
soap, 237
Solway Moss, Battle of, 130, 131
Somerset, County of, 14, 257
Somerset, Edward Seymour, 1st Earl of Hertford and Duke of: economic, 242, 260; France, 128, 129, 136 f., 147; Ireland, 157; religion, 39; Scotland, 4, 7, 16, 39, 134, 136 f.
Somme towns, 49
Sound, 247
Southampton, 252
Southampton, Thomas Wriothesley, Earl of, 129, 145, 263
Southwark, 11
The Sovereign, 62, 256
Sovereignty, 102, 103, 104, 108, 109, 111 f., 123, 125

Index

Spain:
Dutch revolt, 4, 36, 160, 190 f., 200 f., 215, 243; and Henry VII, 55 f., 61, 63; and Henry VIII, 4, 5, 14, 40, 55 f., 67, 77 f., 84 f., 93 f., 112 f., 127 f.; and Northumberland, 4, 145 f., 147; and Elizabeth, 4, 5, 22, 24, 26, 28, 41, 158, 159, 164 f., 171, 173, 180, 182, 188 f., 190 f., 197 f., 204, 209 f., 214 f.; economic relations, 12 f., 18, 23 f., 28 f., 63, 189, 192, 193, 216, 238 f., 241, 249 f., 252, 253, 263
Spanish Fury, 193, 200, 221, 243
de Spes, Guerau (ambassador), 192, 193, 194, 195, 197
Speyer, Diet of, 104, 105
spice, 239, 263
Spinola, Ambrogio, Marquis of, 232
Spurs, Battle of, 72
Stade, 247
Stafford, Edward Duke of Buckingham, 55, 67, 83
Stafford, Thomas, 154
Standish, Henry Bishop of St Asaph, 103
Stanley, William, 22, 227
Staple, Merchants of the, 19, 114, 238, 243, 244
Steelyard, 10, 11, 247
Stirling castle, 76
Stoke, Battle of, 49, 50
Strongbow, Richard, 50, 51
Stuart, Alexander, Duke of Albany (d 1485), 76
Stuart, Esmé, Earl and Duke of Lennox, 208, 209
Stuart, Henry, Lord Darnley, 179, 209

Stuart, James (illegitimate son of James IV), Earl of Moray (d 1544), 132
Stuart, James (illegitimate son of James V), Earl of Mar and Moray, Regent (d 1570), 176, 179, 180, 194
Stuart, James, Earl of Arran (d 1596), 210
Stuart, John, Duke of Albany (d 1536), 76, 78, 86, 122
Stuart, Mary, see Mary, Queen of Scots
Stuart, Matthew, 4th Earl of Lennox, 132, 179, 194
Stubbe, John, 21, 168
Submission of the clergy, 107, 108
succession problem, see dynastic interest
Succession, Act of (1543), 133, 143, 147, 148, 151, 155, 164
Suffolk, Edmund de la Pole, Earl of, 55, 56, 68, 72, 240
Suffolk, Charles Brandon, Duke of, 70, 73, 75, 87, 94, 105, 121, 135
Suffolk, Henry Grey, Duke of, 147
Suffolk, Admiral Thomas Howard, Earl of (d 1626), 219
Suleiman, Sultan of Turkey, 114
sulphur, 257
Sultan of Turkey, 114, 253
Supplication against the Ordinaries, 21, 107
Supreme Head of the Church, 106, 107, 108, 124, 127, 130
surrender and re-grant, 124
Surrey, Henry Howard, courtesy Earl of (d 1547), 135

Surrey, Thomas Howard, 2nd Duke of Norfolk and Earl of, *see* Norfolk, 2nd Duke of
Sussex, 207
Sussex, Thomas Radcliffe, Earl of, 4, 182
Sutherland, N. M., 178 n.
Sweden, 247, 252
Swiss, 49, 73, 76, 77, 78

Talbot, George, Earl of Shrewsbury, 72
Taunton, 54
Tawney, R., 14 n.
Ten Articles, 108
Terra Australis Incognita, 30, 252
Tewkesbury, Battle of, 48
Thames, 62
Thérouanne, 72, 73, 127
Thomas, William, 9
Thompson, I. A. A., 224 n.
Thorne, Robert, 30, 250
Throckmorton, Francis (conspirator), 204
Throckmorton, Nicholas (ambassador), 152, 176, 178, 181
Tilbury, 231
tin, 23
Tipperary, 52
Tordessillas, Treaty of, 12, 250
Toul, 147
Toulouse woad, 62, 256
Tournai, 72, 73, 78, 85
trained bands, 224, 231
treason statutes, 153, 205
Tresham, Thomas, 205
Trevor-Roper, H., 109 n.
Tripoli, 253
Troyes, Treaty of, 181
Tunis, 114, 253

Tunstall, Cuthbert, Bishop of Durham, 89, 90, 102, 104, 106
Turkey, 9, 79, 90, 95, 199
Tyndale, William, 16, 21, 105
Tyrone, Hugh O'Neill, Baron of Dungannon and Earl of (*d* 1616), 212 f.
Tyrone, Shane O'Neill, Earl of (*d* 1567), 196
Tyrone, Turloch O'Neill, Lord of (*d* 1595), 212

Ulster, 53, 139, 196, 212 f.
undertakers, 211
undressed cloth, 240, 242, 246
unemployment, 14, 31
Union, Act of (1707), 66
Utrecht, Treaty of, 245
Utrecht, Union of, 201

Valois, Claude of (daughter of Louis XII), 63
Valois, Elizabeth, *see* Elizabeth Valois
Valois, Francis, *see* Alençon and Anjou, Duke of
Valois, Francis, Dauphin (*d* 1536), 78, 81
Valois, Henry, Dauphin after 1536, *see* Henry II
Valois, Henry, *see* Anjou, Duke of (Henry III)
Valois, Louise (daughter of Francis I), 78
Valois, Margaret, *see* Margaret of Valois
Valois, Renée of (daughter of Louis XII), 38, 96
Vaucelles, Truce of, 154
velocity of circulation of currency, 262

Index

Venetian Company, 253
Venice, 62, 64, 69, 78, 93, 241, 256
Venloo, 227
Verdun, 147
Vere, Francis de, 22, 232
Verona, 78
Vervins, Treaty of, 232
Vigo, 216
Virginia, 30
Voyages and discoveries, by R. Hakluyt, 30

Waad, Armigal, 175 n.
Walcheren Island, 191, 223
Wales, 64, 120, 123, 230
Walloon, 200
Walmer Castle, 116
Walsingham, Francis, 41, 42, 167, 183, 204, 206, 209, 221, 253
Waltham, 21
Warbeck, Perkin, 50, 52 f., 65, 239
Warham, William, Archbishop of Canterbury, 69, 70, 107
Warwick, Edward, Earl of (son of Duke of Clarence; d 1499), 50, 54
Warwick, John Dudley, Viscount Lisle and Earl of, *see* Northumberland, Duke of
Waterford, 30, 52, 53, 250
Watts, John, 29
Wellington, Duke of, 225
Wentworth, Peter, 169
Wernham, R. B., 9, 42, 61 n., 120, 144 n., 186 n., 215 n., 232 n., 237 n., 258 n.
Wervekin, Clais van, 14
West Africa, 20, 23, 24
Westminster, 131
Westmorland, Charles Neville, 6th Earl of, 194

Weymouth, 56
White sea, 247, 251
Wicklow, 211
William of Orange (the Silent), 190, 193, 199, 203, 222
William III, of Orange, 223
Williamson, J. A., 13 n., 26, 27 n., 249 n.
Willoughby, Hugh, 251
Willoughby, Peregrine Bertie, Lord, 22
Wiltshire, 14
Windsor, 83
wine, 23, 237, 249, 256
'Wineland and Markland', 20
Wisbech castle, 205
Wittenberg articles, 115
Wolsey, Cardinal Thomas: dismissal, 98; ecclesiastical, 75, 79, 82, 102, 103; economic, 14, 241, 250; France, 34, 71 f., 79, 96; marriage and succession, 83 f., 99, 102; military, 71 f., 85 f.; Netherlands, 73, 77 f.; Scotland, 34, 67, 74 f., 77 f.; Spain, 67, 74 f., 77 f., 84 f., 96; also, 5, 21, 37, 38, 42, 43, 74 f.
Wood, Benjamin, 31
wool, 19, 237 f., 249
Woolwich, 62
Wriothesley, Thomas, Earl of Southampton, 129, 145, 263
Wyatt, Thomas, 21, 152, 154
Wyndham, Thomas, 24, 252
Wynter, William, 24, 25, 27, 35, 177, 247

xenophobia, 10 f.

Yellow Ford, 212

York, 125, 130
York, Richard Duke of (*d* 1483), 50, 180
Yorke, Rowland, 22, 227
Yorkists, 18, 47, 49, 54, 55, 57, 65, 88
Yorkshire, 112, 138, 207, 240

Ypres, 222, 238

Zeeland, 177, 190, 200, 222, 223, 225
zinc, 257
Zutphen, 22, 227

ST. AUSTELL SIXTH FORM COLLEGE
LIBRARY